LUCE

BOOKS BY JOHN KOBLER

LUCE: HIS TIME, LIFE, AND FORTUNE
THE RELUCTANT SURGEON
AFTERNOON IN THE ATTIC
THE TRIAL OF RUTH SNYDER AND JUDD GRAY
SOME LIKE IT GORY

⁓ LUCE ⁓

HIS TIME, LIFE, AND FORTUNE

by John Kobler

DOUBLEDAY & COMPANY, INC., GARDEN CITY, NEW YORK

1968

Letter from Harold W. Ross on pages 73–78
© 1936 The New Yorker Magazine, Inc.

LIBRARY OF CONGRESS CATALOG CARD NUMBER 68–11033
COPYRIGHT © 1965, 1968 BY JOHN KOBLER
ALL RIGHTS RESERVED
PRINTED IN THE UNITED STATES OF AMERICA
FIRST EDITION

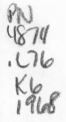

For Evelyn

A NOTE OF ACKNOWLEDGMENT

Portions of this biography appeared originally in *The Saturday Evening Post.* My greatest debt is to William A. Emerson, Jr., the editor, and Otto Friedrich, the managing editor, who encouraged my efforts and bore with me through many months of research and writing.

Published material about Henry R. Luce is scanty. There exists no full-length biography and few biographical sketches. Luce had no liking for personal publicity. He felt, however, that as editor-in-chief of periodicals dependent on people's willingness to be interviewed it ill-behooved him to shut his door against reporters. Among the major sources of this biography were a reluctant Luce, who nevertheless spared me a good deal of time, and members of his family, including his wife, Clare Boothe

Luce, his brother, Sheldon Luce, his sisters, Mrs. Leslie Severinghaus and Mrs. Maurice T. Moore, his son, Henry R. Luce III. To all of them I am deeply indebted.

I wish also to thank members of the Luce organization past and present as well as numerous friends, associates, admirers, and critics outside of it, who generously pro-vided information, specifically:

George Abell, Roy Alexander, Gerald Astor, James At-water, Honor Balfour, Lincoln Barnett, Luigi Barzini, Edward Behr, Felix Belair, Jr., Lester Bernstein, Howard Black, Margaret Boeth, George Bookman, Robert Boyd, John Brooks, Joe David Brown, Helena Burke, Alexander Campbell, Randolph Churchill, Robert Coughlan, Hedley Donovan, John Dowd, Robert Elsom, Clay Felker, Judith Friedberg, Otto Fuerbringer, B. A. Garside, Jay Gold, Fritz Goodwin, Walter Graebner, James Greenfield, Thomas Griffith, Allen Grover, William Harlan Hale, Philippe Halsman, Rev. Erdman Harris, Overton Harris, Ernest Havemann, Andrew Heiskell, Serrell Hillman, John Hersey, Laura Z. Hobson, Raimon von Hofmanns-thal, Edward Hughes, Eileen Hughes, Emmet Hughes, George Hunt, Thomas Hyland, Ralph Ingersoll, C. D. Jackson, Sidney James, Robert Jennings, Oliver Jensen, John K. Jessup, William Johnson, Robert Kaiser, Stanley Karnow, Andre Laguerre, Steven Laird, Roy E. Larsen, James A. Linen, Ray Macklin, Mrs. Edward L. Mac-withey, Frank McCulloch, St. Clair McKelway, Robert Manning, Dwight Martin, John Stuart Martin, Thomas S. Matthews, Charles Mohr, Charles J. V. Murphy, Father John Courtney Murray, Robert Neville, Nedville Nordness, Russell Olsen, John Osborne, James Parton,

William and Beverly Pepper, Curtis Prendergast, Tom Prideaux, Edward Rees, Louis and Richard de Rochemont, William Rospigliosi, Duchessa Lante della Rovere, Nicholas Samstag, Winthrop Sargeant, Don Schanche, William Schlamm, Robert Sherrod, Charles Stillman, Edward K. Thompson, Joseph Thorndike, Corinne Thrasher, Henry Walker, Lael Wertenbaker, Frank White, Theodore H. White, Dwight Whitney.

LUCE

❧ *one* ❧

A television interviewer once asked Henry Robinson Luce if he didn't think he had too much power for one man.

"It seems to me that's a very abstract question," said Luce.

"No, I think it's a very practical question."

"How can you measure power? You can't weigh it."

"You surely have great power, do you not?"

"Well, I wouldn't even say power."

"You wouldn't say this is power?"

"Influence perhaps and upper responsibility. I associate power more clearly and semantically with public office."

"Yes," said the interviewer, "but your magazines certainly influence public office."

"Well, if you like the word," Luce conceded.

It was a modest concession. One yardstick of a man's

power is how many minds he can reach, and by that yardstick few private citizens ever wielded greater power than the cofounder, principal stockholder and editor-in-chief of Time Inc. From a seventy-million-dollar Manhattan skyscraper, of which the corporation owned 45 per cent, in a chastely elegant thirty-fourth-floor office, dominated by a wall-size map of the world, Luce controlled access to millions of minds. *Time the Weekly Newsmagazine*, keystone of the Lucean arch, had a circulation of 2,900,000.* His other periodicals included *Life* (7,000,000), *Sports Illustrated* (1,005,000), *Fortune* (400,000), *Architectural Forum* (62,000), and *House & Home* (140,000). International editions of *Time* and *Life*, distributed in some two hundred countries, brought the total to about 13,000,000.

Comparing the influence on the American character of Luce with that of the University of Chicago, Robert M. Hutchins, the university's former chancellor, concluded, "Mr. Luce has from two to twenty-five times as much influence. . . . I might even say that Mr. Luce and his magazines have more effect on the American character than the whole education system put together."

Luce had a further distinction as a capitalist. He was among the few Americans of his generation to have built up so vast a personal fortune from scratch. He owned 16.61 per cent of the corporation's eighteen million outstanding shares or about $43,000,000 worth, yielding him an annual dividend income of more than $1,250,000.

In addition to periodicals, Time Inc. owned a mail-order

* *Unless otherwise specified, all corporate statistics refer to the year 1964.*

book division which, in 1964, sold 8,000,000 books at home and 1,000,000 abroad; a textbook subsidiary (6,000,-000 sales); a book club, The Time Reading Program, with close to 100,000 subscribers; five radio and six television stations, reaching 2,500,000 homes; paper mills; timberland; oil fields; and assorted real estate. The 1964 *Fortune Directory of the 500 Largest U.S. Industrial Corporations* listed Time Inc. 157th, ahead of such titans as Georgia Pacific, Phelps Dodge, and Kaiser Industries. That year, the most profitable since its inception, Time Inc. netted $14,204,000.

But neither profit nor personal glory motivated Luce as deeply as a missionary urge to improve his countrymen, and he exercised his power in the sincere, if not unanimously shared belief that he knew what was good for them. A rock-ribbed Republican and devout Presbyterian, the son of a missionary, intense, blunt, literal, humorless, and sometimes self-deluded, he was dedicated to what he conceived to be America's high destiny. Speaking of his boyhood in China to an audience of Time Inc. executives, he said, "First of all I probably gained a too romantic, too idealistic view of America. This was not simply because America looked better at a distance. And it had nothing whatever to do with America being an El Dorado. Indeed, I was brought up to think that if anything was wrong in America it was that too many people were too rich and rich people were apt to be more sinful than other people. My ancestors in America for three hundred years had been solvent, sometimes distinguished, but never rich. The idealistic view of America came from the fact that the

Americans I grew up with—all of them—were good people.

"Take then the idea that most Americans (except for a few necessary villains like robber barons and Tammany politicians) are good Christian people. Put along with that the idea that America was a wonderful country, with opportunity and freedom and justice for all, and you get not only an idealistic, but a romantic view—a false romantic view. Such a view implies that *inherently* there is no problem of Evil; that it is possible, even natural, for men to be all at the same time good, well-to-do if not rich, educated, energetic, ambitious, practical, spiritual, and happy. I do not speak here of disillusionment with America. The fact is . . . I never went through any special period of disillusionment. I was never disillusioned with or by America, but I was, from my earliest manhood, dissatisfied with America. America was not being as great and as good as I knew she could be, as I believe she was intended to be."

Luce, who seldom missed Sunday church or went to bed without praying on his knees, worried over what he considered America's shortcomings as a Christian nation. He respected anybody who took a traditional religion seriously, whether a Presbyterian, Roman Catholic, or Orthodox Jew, and deplored Unitarians, lapsed Catholics, and Reformed Jews. In his writings and speeches he often referred to God, Scripture, and "the American proposition." The last he defined as the product of two mainstreams flowing together—"eighteenth-century French libertarianism and revealed religion."

In an address at Union Theological Seminary, three

4

years after the Second World War, he declared the American proposition to be essentially a spiritual and moral one, even though "America is far from being a Christian country." He insisted, contrary to the prevailing intellectual climate, that "the American capacity for successful cooperation is directly related to our country's constitutional dependency on God." It was his feeling, he went on, that "no nation in history, except ancient Israel, was so obviously designed for some special phase of God's eternal purpose." (The Republican party, he intimated on other occasions, was a medium for the execution of that purpose.)

Not long after, at the opening of Southern Methodist University's new Legal Center, he called on lawyers to "reverse" Oliver Wendell Holmes because of such Holmesian pronouncements as, "I see no reason for attributing to man a significance different in kind from that which belongs to a baboon or a grain of sand. . . . Truth is the majority vote of that nation which can lick all the others." Appalled, Luce denounced the great jurist for his philosophy of "materialism, militarism, relativism, agnosticism and, in the most charming and civilized sense of the word, cynicism."

Luce was a battleground of paradoxes and incompatible values—his individual ethics vs. group ethics, his ownership vs. concern for his neighbor, his puritanism vs. his pride and self-esteem, his Calvinist Christianity vs. the realities of business success. Of his early struggles as a publisher he said ruefully, "The bitch goddess sat in the outer office."

Few heads of state ever took their responsibilities or

themselves more seriously. He acted as if Time Inc. were an extension of the U. S. State Department, or vice versa. His parting words, in 1940, to the first correspondent he assigned to Berlin were, "When you get there, remember you're second only to the American ambassador." A member of his board of directors carried this notion still further: "After the President and Congress, Time Inc. is the most important institution in the United States."

When crises were mounting for South Vietnam's despotic Diem oligarchy, which both *Time* and the State Department favored to crush the Viet Cong, Luce ran into an Assistant Secretary of State who formerly worked for him. "I see," he said, "we're both in trouble in Vietnam."

Operating in the area of national and foreign affairs like a state within a state, *Time* was seldom content to print news as its correspondents filed it from the scene. Such stories had to be pondered at New York headquarters in the light of Lucean policy decisions. There would be weighty conferences and staff luncheons resembling a convocation of the National Security Council by the President of the United States. Frequently, editors and executives would take quick fact-finding trips like congressmen. While many of these top-echelon figures were intelligent, perceptive men, some were ignoramuses whose intervention sowed confusion. During a visit home in 1963 *Time*'s Hong Kong correspondent, Stanley Karnow, was repeatedly asked by the big brass, "What's the alternative to Diem?" They seemed to feel that they ought not to criticize the beleaguered ruler unless they could propose a successor. *Time* should confine itself to reporting the war, said Karnow, instead of trying to make policy. He cut no ice.

In a memorandum to an editor, following a visit to Indonesia in 1953, Luce wrote, "I shall begin by stating bluntly what I think our policy should be with regard to this big new country: do not force anything on them, either money or ideas. The Indonesians are very touchy about white men, suspicious, sophomorically arrogant, etc. Therefore, our attitude should be: we want nothing from them and need nothing; if they want anything from us, let them ask.

"Naturally we should maintain expert diplomatic and other relations with them, being in all things very polite and discreetly relaxed. There are ways we could show interest in the peoples of Indonesia, in the culture, but we should have nothing but strictly business-like relations with the Government or the political parties.

"Some may ask: can we afford not to interest ourselves actively in Indonesia? Don't we have to continue there as elsewhere the conflict against Communism, and our efforts to allay the dissatisfactions which open the way to Communism? My answer is that we must hold the line Manila-Saigon-Singapore—and hold it vigorously and oppressively—against Communism. If we do that, we can take a chance on local trouble in Indonesia."

And in a 1963 memorandum, he wrote, "I hope you will be able to follow-through on a purposeful study of our South American policy and personalities. By 'our' I mean both Uncle Sam and TIME INC."

In 1961 Luce committed Time Inc. to the "dominant aim and purpose" of defeating Communism throughout

7

the world. "Is that a declaration of private war?" he asked at an executives' dinner. "And if so, may it not be unlawful and probably mad? Perhaps so, but there are some mighty fine precedents for the declaration of private war." He cited Sir Francis Drake, who waged his own naval war against the king of Spain long before the Armada. "Now, of course, we of Time Inc. do not have the means to wage war as Francis Drake did. [Some listeners discerned a note of regret.] He was able to wangle a few fighting ships—usually as a matter of private enterprise, with Queen Elizabeth taking the biggest cut. We have no ships, no guns, no bombs. Furthermore, this is not an age of piracy. However, unlike the sixteenth century, ours *is* an age of journalism—and at least on that battleground, we can do some service. Private war? No—the term is out of date in this organization age. But even the organization man doesn't have to wait for the government to do everything. Every individual and every organization in the land can strike a blow for Liberty and against Communism—now."

In advanced age Luce had the remote and chilly dignity of a Pilgrim Father sculptured in marble. Tall and lean, his jaw firm, his mouth thin, he peered at people intently but impersonally out of small, pale-blue eyes set under shaggy brows. His hands were long and shapely, the backs covered with hair. The top of his head was denuded and the white strands at the sides of what had been reddish hair, sparse. His normal facial expression was one of granitic inscrutability. Though hard of hearing, he refused to wear a hearing aid until the last years of his life. "You ought to make up your mind to it," a fellow sufferer told him. "It takes a lot of time and patience to get used to." Patience Luce lacked. He brushed aside the advice, claiming, "If ten people are talking around me, I can understand seven of them and the other three probably don't matter." But this was an illusion. During staff conferences he was apt to lash out at Editor A for some unacceptable comment uttered by Editor B. Once he caught only the last word when a Time Inc. executive, opposed to another executive's proposal, said, "The idea is insane." "I'm not insane," said Luce.

His busy mind outraced his tongue, resulting in a conversational style hard to follow. The idea might be complete and cogent at its origin, but it tended to tumble out in elliptical fragments. He would leap forward from sentence to choppy sentence, backtrack, repeat, lapse into enigmatic silence, pick up a new thread. He had a disconcerting habit, when somebody produced an unfamiliar or surprising fact, of barking, "What's that? What's that?" In his youth he stuttered, and when excited or angry—he had a hot temper—his tongue would trip. Luce discoursed rather than conversed and until he finished he left his listeners no openings for the word edgewise. He disdained small talk. While capable of an occasional dry witticism, he seldom attempted a joke. When he did, it was likely to fall flat, whereupon he would repeat it and laboriously explain the point. Having embarked on a topic, he didn't know how to let go of it quickly after it became boring both to himself and his listener. At lunch one day with the Duke of Windsor the conversation somehow strayed to the art of cooking fish, a subject neither man could have cared about less. A *Life* editor who was present recalled,

"The ghastly dialogue stumbled on all through the first course." Luce's occasional self-conscious efforts to be "one of the boys" at company festivities, such as the annual baseball game between the editorial and business departments, were piteous to behold. As a catcher he would try to "talk it up" with all the conviction of a teetotaler trying to ingratiate himself at a beer-drinking orgy.

For a man accustomed to rank and wealth, a world-traveled acquaintance of the great, educated at Hotchkiss School, Yale, and Oxford, Luce exhibited astonishing social deficiencies. Whether host or guest, he was a clock-watcher and a foot-tapper. Easily distracted when the conversation lost altitude, he would not hesitate to get up from the dinner table while others were still at coffee. He would forget to pass the salt and pepper, to see if everybody's glass was full. He fancied old-fashioneds himself, but drank no more than two or three an evening ("I may as well be drunk as Luce," was one of his stock sallies) and normally none during the day. A chain smoker, unable to swear off despite a persistent cough, he would absently pre-empt any matches and cigarettes in sight. He once broke up a party an American diplomat gave for him in Hong Kong by glancing at his watch and announcing, "Time to go." "De big boss done spoke," said the diplomat, and everybody went.

The gourmets among Luce's employees endured excruciating torments because of his indifference, if not positive antagonism, to the pleasures of the table. They ascribed it partly to his intense preoccupation, partly to the Calvinist tradition of asceticism in which he was reared. One day Luce summoned the managing editor of *Life*,

John Shaw Billings, and a staff writer, Lincoln Barnett, to lunch at the Waldorf. "I was scared of Billings," Barnett recalled, "and Billings was scared of Luce." Did they want a cocktail? the waiter asked. Luce didn't. So Billings and Barnett, longing for several, declined. They were ravenous and the menu listed an abundance of delectable dishes. Luce ordered frankfurters and beans, Billings and Barnett likewise. Luce sliced off a bit of sausage, raised it to his mouth, put it down again. "Now about that series . . ." Billings and Barnett had to stop eating to listen and react. So it went throughout the meal. They managed about two mouthfuls each. When they got back to the office, Barnett thanked Luce for his hospitality, then ducked across the street to a cafeteria.

Another time, wanting to discuss an article at lunch with a *Life* editor, Oliver Jensen, Luce sent him ahead to the Cafe Louis XIV nearby to order for them both. After careful deliberation, Jensen chose extra-dry Martinis and *filet de sole Marguery*. Luce arrived half an hour later, gulped down his drink, wolfed his food. "I hope you liked what I ordered," said Jensen. "Just fuel," said Luce, "fuel, fuel."

A group from the Paris bureau took him to the celebrated seafood restaurant, Méditerranée, having ordered bouillabaisse beforehand. As the proud patron set the fragrant tureen on the table, Luce sniffed and said, "Fish soup. Don't want it. Take it away." The owner looked fit to burst into tears. Luce's hosts explained that the dish had been specially prepared for him. "Okay," he said, "give me some. What the hell." In another great Paris restaurant he asked the maître d'hôtel, "Anything good to eat here?" "Well, monsieur," replied the offended dignitary, "our *canard à l'orange* is highly thought of." "That's duck with orange, isn't it? Fine. Only give it to me with applesauce."

Luce's office was a good deal less ornate than those of some of his executives. Few fripperies relieved its functional severity. There was a bronze bust of Luce by Jo Davidson, which Mrs. Luce commissioned. There was a bucolic painting by Winston Churchill which Luce acquired while a guest at Chartwell, the Prime Minister's country seat. (Churchill offered him a choice of any painting in his studio. Luce said he would like one of Chartwell. "With or without sheep?" Churchill asked. "With," said Luce. But the artist found he had none with. So he painted in a flock.) There was a lacquered panel, a gift from President Diem, depicting the branches of a bamboo tree, which, according to the inscription, "in the art and literature of Viet Nam signifies righteous." And there was a drawing of a Buddhist temple in Tengchow, Luce's birthplace. Beside his desk stood a photograph of Mrs. Luce—"for my darling Harry from his Clare."

As befitted a Calvinist, Luce imposed upon himself a frugality and simplicity in his personal habits which to others seemed exaggerated. For a brief period, to save time, he had Joe, the head barber from the subterranean level of the office building, shave him in his office. Then he resumed his custom of going to the barbershop. "Greater contact with humanity," he explained. *Time's* Chicago bureau once reserved a suite for him at the Blackstone Hotel so that he could change into a dinner jacket for a political banquet, though he planned to leave the city immediately after. When he learned that the suite cost fifty-four dollars, he complained, "For God's sake, why couldn't I change in the men's room?"

It irked him when riding an elevator to his office to have to interrupt his train of thought in order to exchange amenities with his employees, and for some years an unwritten law prevailed whereby nobody entered an elevator carrying Luce. Early one morning a young employee unfamiliar with Luce's aversion crossed the lobby to find him waiting by the elevator bank, impatiently swinging his briefcase, shoulders hunched, hat shoved low over his forehead. "Good morning, Mr. Luce," said the employee, adding, "Serrell Hillman." Luce, who clearly didn't remember the name, nodded. "Oh, yes, Serrell." An elevator door opened. Luce stepped in with Hillman following hard behind. "Twenty-fourth floor," Hillman said to the elevator operator. Luce shot him a stern glance. "We're going all the way, but you can ride with me." Then, abruptly, "What are you working on this week?" Hillman was still explaining when the elevator reached the executive floor and Luce stalked out. "Good-bye, Mr. Luce," he called after him weakly. "Nice to have seen you."

On the way down the elevator operator folded his arms, leaned back against the door, and shook his head pityingly. "Brother," he said, "you're through. Might as well pick up your pay check." "What do you mean?" said Hillman. "Didn't anybody ever tell you when that guy gets into an elevator you're supposed to turn around and blow?"

Hillman confessed his *faux pas* to his immediate superior, James Shepley. "I can top it," Shepley told him. He and

13

his researcher had left together for dinner one evening to discuss a story. In the corridor Shepley discovered he had forgotten his papers and asked her to hold the elevator while he dashed back to his office. When he returned, he found her with her foot in the elevator door, and inside, Luce snapping his fingers and demanding, "Why don't we go? Why don't we go?"

"You know what I did?" Shepley told Hillman. "I just kept walking. For all I know, the girl is still there." He eventually became publisher of *Time*, and Hillman, head of its Toronto bureau. Luce, meanwhile, had long since overcome his reluctance to share an elevator, it having occurred to him that this was undemocratic.

What leisure hours Luce and his wife had the time and the capacity to enjoy they enjoyed most at 43 Biltmore Estates, their winter retreat in Phoenix, Arizona. It was one of many homes they had shared since their marriage in 1935. The first was a seven-thousand-acre plantation in Mepkin, South Carolina, which they donated to the Trappist order after the Trappist writer, Father Thomas Merton, remarked to them what an ideal setting it would make for a monastery. (The Trappists' reading matter is rigidly restricted and Our Lady of Mepkin became probably the only chapter to receive *Time* and *Life* regularly.) The Luces divided the early years of their marriage between a suite on the forty-first floor of the Waldorf Towers and a rented house in Stamford, Connecticut. Later there was a Manhattan apartment in River House, at 435 East 52nd Street; a house in Ridgefield, Connecticut; an apartment at 993 Fifth Avenue; the Phoenix retreat; a beachside pleasance in Hawaii.

For a multimillionaire's properties they were not exceptionally opulent. What rare, costly objects adorned them reflected mainly Mrs. Luce's taste. Except for paintings, of which Luce was a moderately discerning collector (he sat on the board of directors of the Metropolitan Museum of Art), he took only a casual interest in his physical surroundings. He had no lust for acquisitions. If anything, the trappings of wealth and power embarrassed him. According to the Calvinist doctrine of predestination, material success does not endanger the soul of the "elect." It is evidence of God's will. On the other hand, success is not given for the elect to enjoy or exult in. It confers no approval upon his individual efforts. It merely betokens his election.

The Phoenix property encompassed a long, one-story house, an aviary, a cactus garden, and a heated swimming pool. The patio bordered the Hotel Arizona Biltmore golf course, which made it easy for Luce to obey his doctor's orders and exercise. He played at least nine holes a day, a mediocre game, seldom shooting lower than the middle forties. Too impatient to walk the course, he drove a golf cart. Mrs. Luce applied herself to writing or one of her various artistic avocations, including mosaic murals. Before lunch husband and wife would meet at the heated pool. Both wearing bathing caps, they would enter at the shallow end and slowly side-stroke up and down, conversing gravely as they swam.

Bridge with their affluent neighbors was an occasional after-dinner recreation. The professional expert, Charles Goren, a contributor to *Sports Illustrated*, was a favorite house guest. Luce himself came to the game late in life and then only at the instigation of Mrs. Luce. She thrust Goren's book into his hands one day with the announcement, "We have to play bridge tomorrow. Read it tonight." He never mastered the game. His mind was too prone to wander to weightier matters and he took forever to play a card. Disapproving of gambling, he limited the stakes to a quarter of a cent. When an opponent even richer than he groused over the loss of ten dollars, Luce said, "Where can you get a better meal for that?"

In Phoenix as elsewhere, traveling or giving speeches, Luce worked far harder than he played. He kept his desk in his bedroom and maintained daily communications with New York by telephone or memoranda.

Luce's most conspicuous natural endowments were his curiosity, an instinctive sense of timing, and prescience. The combination enabled his magazines to keep far enough ahead of the reader to flatter his intelligence, but not so far ahead as to confuse or elude him. He mistrusted the reader surveys that so many publications relied on. In 1945 he called together his editors to discuss the policy they should pursue toward the prospective United Nations. William Schlamm, an Austrian-born intellectual on his staff, argued against supporting it on the grounds that it was doomed to failure if it included Russia because Russia must oppose its quintessential principle. Luce asked for a show of hands. Schlamm was in a minority of one. Luce told him privately, "You realize, Willy, I have to put you on ice. For all I know you may be right. Ten years may prove you so. But an editor's job is to stay ahead of his readers by three weeks, not ten years."

Yet Schlamm did not find this position cynical. "Not

when a man believes, as a good Calvinist should, that success is a divine confirmation of the elect," he said later. "You accept everything as a given fact, the will of God, including the necessity to be a good editor and keep in tune with your readers."

To people who identified Luce, with reason, as a standard-bearer of the Right, his policies were sometimes perplexing. While conservatism was his natural ideological climate, he had an independence of mind which now and again led him into atypical positions. In 1928 he deviated so far from the expected as to support Al Smith for the presidency against Herbert Hoover because he considered Smith genuinely progressive and approved his anti-prohibition stand.

Before World War II the American power elite was predominantly isolationist. But Luce recognized at an early stage the evils of Hitler and the inevitability of America's involvement in a Europe threatened by him. In the glow of optimism following VE-day Russia did not seem so menacing to most Americans. But Luce perceived the nature of the Communist threat and was denounced by liberals for the alarm he sounded, virtually accused, in fact, of treason. A few years later he recognized danger of another kind from the extreme Right as exemplified by Senator Joseph McCarthy. In Luce's view internal Communism was no longer a serious threat and McCarthy's fulminations only weakened the fight against the real peril of international Communism. In a memo to *Life*'s editorial writer, John K. Jessup, dated September 10, 1951, he wrote, "*McCarthyism*. It's about time now to hit this hard. But our aim must be accurate. The general proposition is that 'Communism' has been the explanation scape-goat of everything that's wrong with us. The fact is that Communism is no longer a real issue, even indirectly, in America. Shame and scallions that it ever was as indeed it was, in the era of Franklin Roosevelt. But it no longer is. . . . From 1945–1950, Anti-communism served many good purposes, including the posing of the serious questions of Religion. Anti-communism has now outlived its usefulness. In the U.S., it is a phony, good only for journalistic and other demagogues." And the Luce magazines hit McCarthy hard.

Luce fought in the liberal camp on many issues of civil rights, notably segregation. No other course, he felt, was consistent with Christianity. In 1946 the General Motors plant in Detroit was struck. Luce sympathized with the management. Yet he signed a petition circulated by a committee to aid the strikers' families and gave money to its relief fund. "I don't believe hunger should be used as a weapon," he said. He showed no antagonism when the New York Newspaper Guild organized a *Time* unit, but laughingly asked, "Can I join too?"

In a shrewd analysis of "the American Establishment" the political writer Richard H. Rovere pondered what rank he could assign to Luce and *Time* only to conclude that they didn't belong to it at all. "It [*Time*] goes too far in attacking Establishment positions and it has treated many Establishment members with extreme discourtesy and at times vulgarity. The Establishment fears *Time*, of course, and it now and then shows cravenness in its attempts to appease it by putting Henry Luce on some commission or other . . . or by giving his wife some political job. But the Luce publications must generally be considered as outside the Establishment."

Though neither profoundly erudite nor profoundly responsive to aesthetic experience, Luce had an almost infallible intuition for what novel intellectual and artistic ideas would prove exciting, significant, influential. He was a taste-maker. He anticipated America's cultural expansion as a result of increased leisure and his magazines ventured deeper into the arts and sciences. The teacher-preacher in Luce longed to elevate the American mind, taste, and ethics. "America's intellectual health" was a phrase frequently on his tongue.

Brusque and flinty though Luce often was, with a seeming insensitivity that sometimes verged on cruelty, scores of his employees, including many who quit in fury, professed affection for him. By and large, it was not the kind of affection that personal warmth or charm inspires, but rather the response of craftsmen to a master of their craft. "If you loved magazine writing, you had to love Luce," said Theodore H. White, once a *Time* correspondent in China, who broke with Luce over the latter's pro–Chiang Kai-shek policy, but in later years, reconciled, wrote articles for *Life*. "He was brilliant, brave and opinionated, a good, rugged fighter. He fought to win. If you were on his side, he had the utmost generosity, but he was a devastating enemy. He was a prisoner of his own virtues. Any man as positively domineering as Luce had to be a skull-basher. Only a man that positive could have had such a tremendous effect on journalism. He revolutionized the thinking of American readers. He was a major American."

∾ *two* ∾

In an uncommon mood of wistfulness and self-revelation Luce once told his executives, "You could never guess what I have most missed in my life. It is the fact that I have never had—and cannot have—a hometown, an American hometown. 'Where do you come from? Where were you born and raised?' These are basic questions. Few learned anthropologists have pointed out the deep and special significance of those questions to and in America. The other day Vice-President Barkley got himself off the hook for not being a teetotaler by saying that he came from Kentucky. You see, an American always explains himself satisfactorily by citing where he comes from—be it the sidewalks of New York or the farm lands of Illinois, or Houston, Texas. 'Where do you come from?' I would give anything if I could say simply and casually, 'Oskaloosa, Iowa.'"

But he could only say, "Tengchow, China." His parents were Presbyterian missionaries from Scranton, Pennsylvania, poor but socially well-connected. The Reverend Dr. Henry Winters Luce (Yale '92) traced his ancestry to the early seventeenth-century settlers of Martha's Vineyard, Massachusetts. Elizabeth Root Luce, a YWCA worker before her marriage, counted among her forebears English landowners, soldiers, clergymen, and civil servants. In Tengchow, an ancient port of the promontory of Shantung Province that juts into the Yellow Sea, Dr. Luce taught physics at a burgeoning Christian college. An eloquent fund-raiser, he persuaded rich American Presbyterians to finance two universities in China, and by his efforts to revise Chinese education according to Christian democratic standards he played an important part in the country's rebirth as a modern nation. Dr. Luce was a Bull Moose Republican and, though trained in the hard-shelled Calvinism of his generation, a theological liberal. Orthodoxy concerned him less than practical good works. He believed that the conflicting doctrines of Christianity should be reconciled. He recognized values in Buddhism and Oriental philosophies. He typified a new missionary trend that stressed education as a means of conversion.

Henry Robinson (after the Reverend Charles E. Robinson, pastor of Scranton's Second Presbyterian Church) Luce was born on April 3, 1898, the first of four children, behind the mud-brick walls of a mission compound. A missionary named Calvin Mateer baptized him. By custom foreigners received Chinese names phonetically similar to the original. Dr. Luce's name had been transliterated into three characters pronounced *Lu Ssu-i*, the last two meaning "one who seeks righteousness." Henry R. Luce, who learned Chinese from an opium-smoking amah before he spoke English, became *Lu Shao-i*—"Small Boy Luce."

Spartan austerity governed his formative years. Writing home from the Tengchow compound, his mother described the family's daily schedule:

6:00 A.M.	Rise, cold bath, dress.
6:30–7:00	Bible study.
7:00	Breakfast.
7:40–8:20	A little more study.
8:30–11:30	Chinese lessons.
12:00 Noon	Lunch.
12:40–1:20	Nap.
1:30–4:30	Chinese lessons.
4:40–5:30	Walk.
6:00	Supper.
Evenings	General reading and more Chinese study.

In June, 1900, China's long-smoldering hatred of the "foreign devils," who were exploiting her resources, erupted in the Boxer Rebellion. Terrorists calling themselves "Righteous Harmony Fists" ("Boxers" in loose translation) murdered scores of foreigners, among them several missionaries. The Luces, now increased by a daughter, Emmavail, fled. A Chinese gunboat, the *Hai Chai*, commanded by a friend of the missionaries, Captain Sah Cheng-ping, rode at anchor in the sampan-choked harbor and he took them aboard. Meanwhile, from Chefoo, further east along the peninsula, the U. S. consul had sent a steamer to evacuate American nationals. It entered the harbor during the night of June 30 and at dawn Captain Sah transferred the Luces to it, handing the two infants from sampan to sampan.

The Luces stayed for some weeks in a refugee camp at Chefoo, tormented by withering heat, overcrowding, and hunger. At length they found a haven among missionaries across the water in Seoul, Korea. They sailed back to Tengchow the following autumn after European troops had quelled the uprising. Three years later, with the addition of a second daughter, Elizabeth, they moved inland to another missionary compound near Weihsien. Their fourth child, Sheldon—*Shao-ling* ("Little Bell")—was born there nine years later.

In 1906 the Luces returned to America on their first furlough. Mother and children waited in San Francisco while Dr. Luce went east to raise money for a Chinese college. In Chicago he called on a prospective donor, to whom he had a letter of introduction, Mrs. Cyrus H. McCormick, whose late husband invented the reaping machine and founded the International Harvester Co. It was a meeting of profound consequence for the Luces in which Mrs. Luce sensed "the unseen Hand . . . part and parcel of the divine Will working."

When Dr. Luce entered the McCormick mansion on Rush Street he was exhausted and suffering from the early symptoms of multiple disorders. Mrs. McCormick, a regal woman, still bearing the traces of her girlhood beauty, when she attended Abraham Lincoln's inaugural ball, received the missionary in her library. "Harry was never clear about their first conversation," Mrs. Luce later wrote to a friend. "But ever after he recalled her unequalled presence—her face, lighted by an inner glow; the fine eyes, all fire and spirit and intelligence; above all, the kindly look which seemed to lift his loneliness and all his unspoken problems from his own heart and lay them upon her own."

After a few minutes' talk, Mrs. McCormick broke in, "You are very tired. Come with me." She led him across a hall to a suite of rooms. "These are my son's rooms, but he is not here now. I want you to use them as your own, and I want you to go right to bed. I will send to your hotel for your bags. Later in the evening I want you, if you will, to tell me all about your work in China."

Not long after, Mrs. Luce brought the children east. At the hotel where her husband met them, flowers and an invitation to dinner from Mrs. McCormick awaited them. Mrs. Luce fretted over her wardrobe, shabby and outmoded after eight years in remote Chinese mission compounds. Dr. Luce tried to soothe her. "Just wait," he promised, "you'll see." She scrubbed the children and brushed their clothes and, quaking inwardly, started for Rush Street.

In the drawing room, waiting for Mrs. McCormick, Henry, aged eight, stood by the window, gazing with awe at the elegant passing carriages. The two girls sat stiffly on a sofa, their legs too short to touch the floor. None of them ever forgot that evening. "She came to us in her lovely way," wrote Mrs. Luce. "Moving into the room, her arms outstretched, she seemed to gather us all into her great heart of love and that was our true homecoming. . . . But what stands in my mind, forever beyond the reach of years, is the grandeur of a woman's soul. For all that is true and lovely and good is bound by love into the structure of an immortal spirit. And the things of the spirit can neither be lost nor destroyed."

During their furlough of fifteen months they saw Mrs. McCormick often. She wanted Henry to live with her as her adopted son, but after praying together for guidance, his parents felt they must take him back to China. To the end of her life, sixteen years later, Mrs. McCormick remained their benefactress, contributing not only to their missionary work, but to the education of their children.

Of Small Boy Luce his mother wrote in 1911, "He is the queerest child! He pores over a new 'Yale Bulletin' and has been trying to find out what the 'Entrance Exams' will be for the year 1915, when he hopes to enter! Some specimen Exams are given & yesterday I found him working over a French Exam-paper—isn't it funny! As he was 13 in April, I tell him he'd best 'bide a wee' and let future Exams alone for the present."

Signs of precocity in her first-born had amused Mrs. Luce since his infancy. At the age of four, having been exposed to the thundering Sunday sermons of the mission elders, he began dictating to her sermons of his own composition. The cadences of Holy Writ charmed the tot's ear. He excelled at a family parlor game, "Clumps," a variant of "Twenty Questions" based on the Scriptures. The Christmas boxes shipped to the Luces by their Scranton supporters contained, at his request, an American Revised Standard Bible, sets of Shakespeare and the Victorian novelists, tin soldiers, a chess set. Though no chess prodigy, he brought to the game a ferocious concentration that sometimes vanquished better players. (During his prep school days, when traveling to and from home, he carried a folding set; in later life he once played a game lasting twenty hours to a draw.) At the age of eight he underwent a tonsillectomy. The anesthesia wore off before the operation was over. To that trauma, his mother always ascribed the stutter which he developed soon after.

Except for tennis, he showed little interest in sports. A military history buff, he would reconstruct famous battles on the nursery floor with the tin soldiers and building blocks, obliging his sisters, Emmavail (whose Chinese sobriquet was "Plum Blossom") and Elizabeth ("Peach Blossom"), to tread cautiously for days on end lest they disturb the gun emplacements of Valley Forge or Waterloo. The plain surrounding the compound, dense with sorghum and millet growing taller than a man, and studded with Buddhist burial mounds, offered choice terrain for more active combat games. The mission boys, totaling about a dozen, formed two armies—"the Bloody Triangle," consisting of the three oldest, biggest boys, and "the Howling Caterwaulers," consisting of all the others, whose strategy was mapped by Small Boy Luce.

Insatiably curious about his environment, fascinated by the tumult of Chinese street life, he collected hundreds of picture postcards illustrating native trades, dress, types of vehicles. He was a devotee of the boys' magazine, *St. Nicholas,* to which he wrote at the age of ten,

"My Dear St. Nicholas:

"I am a boy in China. I live in the country near Wei Skein (Way Shen) city, in an inclosed compound or big yard about two blocks long. There are eight dwelling-houses, a boys' and girls' school, a college, a big church, and two hospitals.

"A new house is being built (the house we are to live in) by Chinese carpenters and masons.

"It will take about eight months to build it. What a long time! The Chinese have no sawmills, but every log has to be cut and sawed by hand.

"I think you are fine.

"Your true friend and reader,

"Henry R. Luce."

If he was serious-minded beyond his years, life at Weihsien scarcely inspired frivolity. Around the compound, which sheltered about fifty Westerners and two hundred Chinese students, ran a stone wall twelve feet high, its only gate barred and guarded at night against marauders. Bandits or skirmishing war lords made it hazardous to venture far outside. By the gate stood rough shelters where the itinerant evangelists, returning from disease-infested villages, would be quarantined, sometimes for weeks. Bubonic plague periodically ravaged the province. Typhus, cholera, and tuberculosis were rampant. Black smallpox killed one mission child. To the Chinese, hunger was a specter so familiar that they traditionally greeted each other, not with a "good morning," but with the question, "Have you eaten rice yet?" Luce never forgot the purpose served by certain stone towers he passed during cross-country hikes. On top of them destitute families would abandon the babies they couldn't feed.

"I loved China, but I was immunized against illusions about her. What the rich tourists and the great intellectuals like John Dewey and Bertrand Russell never understood was that Chinese civilization had fallen into terrible decay. They saw only the outward forms of a graceful old culture. But the dynamism was gone. 'We must have a new China!'—that was the cry of the revolutionists under Sun Yat-sen, and of Chiang Kai-shek after him, and of the Chinese Communists. . . ."

The Luces' house at Weihsien, the first they ever owned, they owed to the bounty of Mrs. McCormick. It was no bower of luxury. Constructed of gray, kiln-baked bricks and containing eight small, dark rooms, it lacked gas, electricity, and adequate plumbing. The Luces read by candlelight or kerosene lamps and bathed in portable tubs filled from the kitchen tap. A capricious hot air furnace gave meager protection against the winter winds. The summers were blistering. Sandstorms silted up the rooms.

In their isolation and penury the missionaries had to contrive their own diversions. The compound became a force bed for creative endeavor. Everybody with talent devoted it to the entertainment or enlightenment of the community. There were theatricals and musicales. Dr. Luce played the violin, accompanied on the piano by his wife. He edited the first synopsis of the Bible in Chinese. His son launched his maiden journalistic venture—a handwritten boys' newspaper, the hand being entirely his own.

An indelible influence in Luce's boyhood was the ubiquity of British might. British ships tied up, as the saying went, at "the No. 1 buoy" in the Whangpoo River. British merchant princes dominated Chinese trade; and an American, especially an American of no wealth, held second-class status. Luce both resented and admired these cocks o' the walk.

His ambivalence was intensified at the British-run boarding school in Chefoo to which his father sent him when he was ten. Headmaster McCarthy, a martinet known by the nickname of "Ires" (Wraths), strove to emulate Eton and Harrow. If he failed to equal them academically, he surpassed them in the severity of his discipline. The iron-clad rules he imposed bounded the students' every waking hour. As both a health and moral safeguard, he forbade all contact with the native Chinese. Infractions were noted in a registry. For the first few entries the offender was "quadded," that is, confined to the grounds during the next holiday. Additional entries cost him a thrashing with a bamboo cane over the knuckles or buttocks. One of Luce's classmates had the pluck to challenge a master's statement of fact. "If I tell you the moon is made of green cheese," said the master, "I expect you to agree." "But, sir, I couldn't do that," said the boy. He got a hundred strokes.

By diligence Luce managed to stay second or third from the top of his class, broke few rules, and so endured only occasional canings. He found it hard, however, to stomach the food. John Hersey, who worked ten years for *Time*, chanced to be traveling on a coastal steamer that put in at Chefoo just after World War II. The school was still there and he asked an aged master if he remembered a boy named Harry Luce. "He wouldn't eat his porridge," said the master.

Yet Luce's scorn for progressive schools, which *Time*'s

education section sometimes mirrored, stemmed from his experience at the unprogressive Chefoo school. "I hated it and loved it. I was terribly homesick. When I didn't have a bloody nose or a skinned knee, my face and hands were swollen with chilblains. The school was very religious and very rough and tough. It had never heard of any of the pedagogical ideas taught at Columbia. Yet, after Chefoo, I found the getting of A's at Hotchkiss and Yale was for me a relatively easy matter. If scholarship in America had not been so soft, I might be an educated man today.

"But in the story of an American the Chefoo school is important because it was British. About one-fifth of the 120 or 130 boys were American. We were a strong, conspicuous, successful minority. The British code—flogging and fagging and toadying—violated every American instinct. No wonder that hardly an hour passed, in classroom or on football field, that the American didn't have to run up the flag. For example, a master insists that Ohio is pronounced O-hee-ho. What are you going to do? Will you agree? The American can't agree; it would betray every other American. So first your knuckles are rapped, then you get your face slapped—by the master—for insubordination.

"My Anglo-Americanism is deeper than any words. Indeed, it is written in the blood of that shameful, futile, endless two hours one Saturday afternoon when I rolled around the unspeakably dirty floor of the main schoolroom with a British boy who had insulted my country. You see, I know the British intimately. I knew them long before I went to Oxford. I can recite the list of English kings. I have read much of their poetry. The best they have—a very great best—is bred into me as much as anything can be bred in me. I love the beauty of Britain and the power and the strength, the grace of ritual on cricket field or Aldershot tattoo. I would be utterly not-me without it. But I know the British. They are not me; they are not American."

During the hottest weeks of the summer the Luces would retreat to a breeze-cooled point at Tsingtao where they had built a little cottage. Tsingtao was a German colony, full of German soldiers. "We could sit on our porch and see way out in the ocean white moving targets and the splashing foam of high-explosive shells as they hit short or long. The shells came right over our cottage from gun emplacements in the hills behind.

"Then early in the morning while we dozed, we could hear from across a little valley, behind us, the heavy tramp of German soldiers and the songs they sang, the German lieder, as they marched from barracks to maneuvers. '*O Wanderer, Wanderer meiner lust.*' It was all, to be sure, a little militaristic, but also very remote from our real lives as missionaries or as young Americans.

"We liked the German town—the clean streets, the good music and bands, even the beer which my mother shockingly insisted was no sin for her to drink. But we learned about the Germans. We learned about Germans in relation to Chinese rickshaw coolies. This is how it was—a universal law. Germans beat rickshaw coolies. They beat them over the bare back with their sticks. Britishers on the other hand never beat coolies; Britishers were simply high-handed; after a long pull they would give the coolies only a minimum fare or less and walk haughtily away. The Americans didn't beat coolies; they always overpaid. If an American did lose his temper, that was a lucky break for the coolie—because it meant he got twice as big a tip."

The moral of this reminiscence, as Luce drew it for the benefit of his executives many years later, was political. "When Secretary Acheson—or Owen Lattimore—says that the United States cannot intervene strongly in Asia for fear of being 'imperialistic' he is not, in my view, making sense. You remember when Wendell Willkie came back from his world tour and spoke of the vast reservoir of American good will in Asia, which he said was leaking. There was still plenty of that good will in 1945 when I revisited Tsingtao. If American policy had fully co-operated with that good will, China would not now be Communist."

Luce saw England for the first time in his fourteenth year. His father had heard of a grammar school at St. Albans, whose headmaster supposedly knew how to cure stutterers. But when Luce left a few months later, he still stuttered. He had meanwhile won a scholarship at Hotchkiss. Before he sailed for America his parents allowed him to take a three-week tour by himself of France, Switzerland, and Italy. It hardly strained their budget. So frugal and resourceful was their son that the total expense came to only sixty-three dollars.

At the Chefoo school Luce had belonged to a minority of about twenty. At Hotchkiss he was a minority of one. Two gaps in his knowledge made him feel particularly un-American—he understood neither baseball nor shooting craps. In a welcoming speech to the new boys, the Reverend Dr. Huber Gray Buehler announced that Hotchkiss had only one rule: it expected them to be gentlemen. This struck Luce, accustomed to the restraints of Chefoo, as overcasual; he preferred to know where he stood. Dr. Buehler later summoned him to his study and lectured him about his nonconformist attitude. "I thought they shouldn't fuss so much about my attitude," Luce remembered. The ideal of the good fellow, he felt, which translates into Rotarianism and clubbability, lay beyond his reach.

His schoolmates nicknamed him "Chink" and chaffed him for being the only boy at Hotchkiss who, as they mistakenly imagined, could never become President of the United States because he was born abroad. He hastened to disabuse them. His birth, he informed them, had been registered at a U.S. consulate and therefore he stood as good a chance of election as any of them. The scholarship students, of whom there were six in a class of sixty-four, had to clean the classrooms and wait on table. "I detested it, but I wasn't humiliated. I felt no sense of injustice. I was happy to be there on those terms."

He maintained high grades, better ones than his brother Sheldon, who followed him at Hotchkiss. "I flunked my Algebra and passed my Latin," Sheldon wrote to his father. ". . . To sum up all this nastiness, I can put it in a few words. The family is not pleased with me, and I don't think I'm so hot. In other words, out of four children, the batting average is 75%. Not bad!"

"My dear lad [Dr. Luce replied]: . . . There is just

one battle field for you, just only one. That battle field is your own *will*. No Luce has ever fallen down for lack of determination or will power. They may have lacked ability, or tact, or other things, but never in the 'will-to-do.'

". . . No, we do not have a batting average of seventy-five per cent. The other three have not scored a hundred by any means, and both they and your parents know that you have some excellent qualities which the other three do not have at all. There is only one problem for you, and that is how to apply your native Luce-power to your studies. . . ."

"Chink" Luce, aloof, proud, and industrious, his reddish eyebrows already beetling, commanded more respect than popularity. He avoided athletics as a waste of time better devoted to intellectual pursuits. Throughout his Hotchkiss career his scholastic record read "Honor Roll, Leader of Class." On his college board Greek exams he scored the highest marks in the country, a feat which moved Dr. Buehler to declare a school holiday. Luce controlled his stutter enough to captain a debating team and win oratorical contests. Smoking and drinking he considered foolish drains upon health and pocketbook. Prudish about sex, he appeared to disdain girls. Also, he couldn't afford to entertain them. He spoke with contempt of divorce. If he ever married, he swore, it would be forever.

He spent his most gratifying hours outside the classroom as editor-in-chief of the *Hotchkiss Literary Monthly*. By wheedling articles out of prominent Americans, reporting school activities critically, and introducing picture layouts, he made it one of the country's liveliest school magazines.

His own contributions were mostly poetic, with Oriental or religious overtones. A poem entitled *Egotist* ran,

> My heart's desire my idol is;
> My creed, that he who aims and
>   struggles high
> Shall see all things subservient to his,
> Until they pass from him, when he
>   shall die
>   And fall away.
>
> My idol is my heart's desire;
> It shall I serve, and know no god;
> It shall I see, and with the fire
> Of energy consume it on the road
>   Of life, of day.
>
> No Oriental superstition shall I fear,
> Chasing through fever avenues of my
>   life,
> Not for one sentimental cause shed
>   one small tear;
> But, taking things as take I may,
>   Shall win the strife.
>
> Thus happiness, obtainable, obtained
>   by me,
> Shall mark the path of Fortune for
>   the mind.
> Triumphant in myself, nor shall I
>   flee
> When all around, beneath, before,
>   behind,
> Cries: "Enter Death!"

Luce was also assistant managing editor of the weekly school newspaper, the *Record*. The managing editor was Briton Hadden. They made an incongruous pair. Born to prosperous New Yorkers in the fashionable Brooklyn Heights section, Hadden was cocky, gregarious, volatile and raucous. A baseball fanatic and a master of the mucker pose, he affected the mannerisms of the dugout, chewing gum and talking tough out of the corner of his mouth. In the breezy *Record*, which he intended to outshine the high-flown *Lit.*, he twitted Luce's poetic flights. Luce retaliated by billing the *Lit.* as "First in the Prep School World." The rivalry extended to other fields. At the annual literary contest Hadden won the declamations award with a fiery rendition of *Casey at the Bat*. Luce, pale and tense, won the extemporaneous-speeches award. His topic: "Things Learned Outside the Classroom." He wrote the lyrics for the class song, "Hotchkiss, Thy Blue and White," splitting the fifty dollars prize money with the composer. Hadden never approached Luce's scholastic achievements. But he shone in the Dramatics Association and the Music Art Club, and he delivered the class oration. Luce was the class poet.

No intimate friendship ever flowered between them. But in their common passion for journalism and their conviction that it could be vastly bettered they became steadfast allies.

When the graduating class cast its votes for the "Mosts," "Chink" Luce placed

Brightest, third.
Most absent-minded, fourth.

Most pious, sixth.
Most versatile, sixth.
Worst woman-hater, ninth.
Most eccentric, twelfth.
Most energetic, twelfth.

Neither Luce nor Hadden drew a single vote for "most likely to succeed."

They both went to Yale where they found wider scope for collaboration as well as competition. Luce's father paid five hundred dollars toward his initial expenses. The rest Luce earned, fifteen hundred dollars the first three years at such spare-time jobs as manager of student eating-houses and commission agent for a tailor. His grave demeanor, growing graver with the increasing weight of his thoughts, moved Hadden, who loved baiting him, to hilarity. "Look out, Harry," he once quipped as Luce passed him on the campus with the air of a cabinet minister pondering a national crisis, "you'll drop the college."

The most prestige-laden extracurricular office, and the most lucrative, was chairman of the board of the Yale *Daily News*. Competitors for any position on the paper—"heelers," they were called—were judged according to the quantity and quality of copy they got into print and the number of ads they sold. Hadden achieved an all-time record, with Luce a close second. From among the winning heelers the board established the succeeding staff by vote. Normally, elections took place in the junior year. But with America's entry in World War I most older classmen left for army camps. Thus, in their sophomore year Hadden became chairman and Luce editor.

In 1918, now campus grandees, they too interrupted their rise to take officers' training at Camp Jackson, South Carolina. Ever since Hotchkiss they had agreed that too many Americans were abysmally ignorant about the state of the world, and at Camp Jackson they determined someday to publish a periodical that would spread enlightenment. They were due to sail overseas when the war ended.

Returning to Yale and the management of the *News*, they proceeded to make collegiate journalistic history. They expanded the coverage of world events, fomented controversy over such issues as longer hours of student military training (they were for it) and whether the Yale song should be adapted to a tune more appropriate than "Die Wacht am Rhein" (they argued against a change, braving the displeasure of alumni, faculty, and city authorities). Occasionally Luce ventured too far to suit Hadden. "During my absence," the chairman complained in a letter to his parents, following a student riot for which the local press lambasted the university, "Chink Luce wrote a very bombastic editorial about 'small-town journalists.' . . ."

To Dr. Amos Wilder, the father of Luce's classmate and friend, Thornton Wilder, journalism was no pursuit for a Christian gentleman, and he pleaded with him, "Harry, don't go into journalism. It will turn you into a cynic and corrupt and corrode you. It will turn your wine into vinegar. You will lose your soul." (Recalling Dr. Wilder's warning, Luce said in later years, "To the extent that I have become corrupted and corroded I can't blame it on journalism. Partly because I had good luck and had no reason to become sour and cynical about my profession, and partly because the climate of journalism changed."

Luce and Hadden, the collaborating rivals, graduated with the class of '20 in a blaze of glory. Luce, who had won a Phi Beta Kappa key, was voted "most brilliant," Hadden "most likely to succeed." Both had been tapped for Skull & Bones, Yale's oldest, lordliest senior secret society. It carried secrecy to such lengths that, according to legend, it conferred honorary membership upon the architect who designed its headquarters in the style of an Egyptian tomb so that he would be bound by oath never to describe the interior. The doors were always locked against the profane. Though the members convened at least once a week and curious outsiders kept watch, few ever saw anybody enter or exit. An exception was a freshman, spying from an adjacent roof, who surprised some initiates sunning themselves. Detecting his presence, they scurried inside, but by what ingress he never discovered. The by-laws supposedly obliged Bones men to leave the room if anybody so much as breathed the society's name. Thirty-five years after Luce and Hadden graduated, *Time* scheduled a story about New York's Governor Averell Harriman (Yale '13). The writer disclosed Harriman's membership in Skull & Bones. Back came the typescript from Luce with the forbidden words deleted.

Legend further says that Bones men undertake to lend each other a helping hand through life. If true, fraternal bonds must have undergone some strain thirty-two years later when Robert A. Taft (Bones, class of '10) ran against Dwight D. Eisenhower for the Republican presidential nomination. Though Luce preferred Taft's kind of intellect, he decided the party could not win with him. Here is how *Time*'s word colorists pictured Eisenhower before the convention in Chicago:

"Ike's trip across the country . . . had been something of a triumph. At station after station, thousands of people gathered to catch a glimpse of him, hear him denounce Taft's steamroller methods. For a while, after his arrival, Eisenhower forgot politics and attended the annual reunion of the veterans of the 82nd Airborne Division. Amid flickering candles and muffled drums for the dead, Eisenhower wept. He recalled how he had visited the 82nd on the eve of its drop into Normandy, how the men had smiled and told him in effect: 'Don't worry.' Now, at Chicago, the men of the 82nd cheered his words and, again, smiled."

And here *in toto* is how *Time* described Taft's arrival:

"That night, Taft arrived on the battlefield, welcomed by brass bands and crowds of loyal supporters. Television covered his entry, and the resulting fuss annoyed Bob Taft. 'That,' snapped he, 'is a good example of why we don't have TV at national committee meetings.' But Eisenhower seemed to enjoy Taft's arrival on TV."

Luce and Hadden separated after graduation. Hadden, having chosen the New York *World* as a medium to develop his talents, barged unannounced into the office of its editor, Herbert Bayard Swope, in whose presence, it was said, "one did not swope until swopen to," and demanded a job as a reporter. Ordered to leave, he declared, "Mr. Swope, you are interfering with my destiny." The editor relented and hired Hadden at twenty-five dollars a week.

Luce, with four thousand dollars saved out of his earnings on the Yale *News* plus one thousand dollars from Mrs. McCormick, determined to enlarge his intellectual equipment at Oxford. He proposed to study modern European history, but settled for the eighteenth century after the tutor he consulted informed him, "We consider modern history to have ended with the Reformation. After that everything is hearsay."

Luce squandered the rest of his savings during winter and spring vacations on Continental jaunts. "I thought it was my last opportunity to have a good time." He visited the Balkans. He toured Hungary and Germany by bicycle. At an American Academy dance in Rome he met a Miss Lila Ross Hotz of Chicago, of whom he retained tender memories. He got back to the U.S. in 1921 with two Savile Row suits, a mustache, and twenty cents.

It was to Miss Hotz's city that Luce went in search of work. His benefactress, Mrs. McCormick, had hoped he would follow in his father's footsteps into the ministry, but since he showed no such inclination she favored big business as the next best career for him. Her grandson Harold headed the board of International Harvester and so Luce had expectations of a job there. He wanted only a temporary one, however; his heart wasn't in it. He would make a quick fortune, he promised himself, then buy a newspaper. But he got no further than a talk with the general manager, Alexander Legge. The country was in the grip of a postwar depression and Legge told him, "Sure, we can find an opening for you. We'll just have to fire somebody." Luce applied instead to the Chicago *Daily News*, which took him on at sixteen dollars a week and assigned him as a legman to Ben Hecht, who was then writing his popular column, *One Thousand and One Nights in Chicago*.

Shortly, a Yale classmate, Walter Millis (later the author of the pacifist book *The Road to War*, which Luce deplored) lured him east again. Millis was writing editorials for the Baltimore *News* and he notified Luce that a forty-dollar-a-week reporter's job could be his for the asking. He sent a similar letter to Hadden on the *World*, who forwarded it to Luce with the notation, "If we're ever going to start that paper, this looks like our chance."

In Baltimore, the two Hotchkiss-Yale alumni resumed their rivalry and reaffirmed their alliance. As reporters they vied with each other in the number of stories they could land on the front page (Hadden maintained a slight lead). During their free hours they hatched plans for a weekly news magazine to be called *Facts*. The name they finally chose was Luce's inspiration. Riding a Manhattan subway late one night, he noticed an advertising slogan, TIME TO RETIRE or TIME FOR A CHANGE. He forgot the exact wording, but "time" stuck in his mind. Next morning he proposed it to Hadden, who instantly agreed.

∾ *three* ∾

The prospectus which they eventually circulated under the title *Time the Weekly News-Magazine* (they dropped the hyphen in the fifth year of publication) remains one of the most quoted, argued about, and germinal documents in the annals of journalism. Brashly challenging the prevailing tenets of the craft, the twenty-four-year-old upstarts set forth:

"Although daily journalism has been more highly developed in the United States than in any other country in the world.

"Although foreigners marvel at the excellence of our periodicals, *World's Work, Century, Literary Digest, Outlook*, and the rest.

"People in America are, for the most part, poorly informed.

"This is not the fault of the daily newspapers; they print all the news.

"It is not the fault of the weekly 'reviews'; they adequately develop and comment on the news.

"To say with the facile cynic that it is the fault of the people themselves is to beg the question.

"People are uninformed BECAUSE NO PUBLICATION HAS ADAPTED ITSELF TO THE TIME WHICH BUSY MEN ARE ABLE TO SPEND ON SIMPLY KEEPING INFORMED.

"TIME is a weekly news-magazine, aimed to serve the modern necessity of keeping people informed, created on a new principle of COMPLETE ORGANIZATION.

"TIME is interested—not in how much it includes between its cover—but in HOW MUCH IT GETS OFF ITS PAGES INTO THE MINDS OF ITS READERS."

After outlining the process (in about one hundred short articles all important information, culled from the press of the world, would be reduced to its essence) and the arrangement of material (under fixed department headings much as Foreign News, The Arts, Sports), the prospectus explained how *Time* would differ from other periodicals.

"TIME, like all weeklies, differs from the daily papers in what it omits.

"It differs from other weeklies in that it deals *briefly* with EVERY HAPPENING OF IMPORTANCE and presents these happenings as NEWS (fact) rather than as 'comment.' It further differs in that it is from three to fifteen days more up-to-date than they.

"TIME is not like *The Literary Digest* and is in no way modelled after it.

"*The Literary Digest* treats at great length with a few subjects selected more or less arbitrarily from week to week. TIME gives *all* the week's news in a brief, organized manner.

"*The Digest* makes its statements through its time-honored formula of editorial excerpts. TIME simply states.

"*The Digest,* in giving both sides of a question, gives little or no hint as to which side it considers to be right. TIME gives both sides, but clearly indicates which side it believes to have the stronger position.

"EDITORIAL BIAS

"There will be no editorial page in TIME.

"No article will be written to prove any special case.

"But the editors recognize that complete neutrality on public questions and important news is probably as undesirable as it is impossible, and are therefore ready to acknowledge certain prejudices which may in varying measure predetermine their opinions on the news.

"A catalogue of these prejudices would include such phrases as:—

1. A belief that the world is round and an admiration of the statesman's 'view of all the world.'
2. A general distrust of the present tendency toward increasing interference by government.
3. A prejudice against the rising cost of government.
4. Faith in the things which money cannot buy.
5. A respect for the old, particularly in manners.
6. An interest in the new, particularly in ideas.

"But this magazine is not founded to promulgate prejudices, liberal or conservative. 'To keep men well-informed'—that, first and last, is the only axe this magazine has to grind. The magazine is one of news, not argument, and verges on the controversial only where it is necessary to point out what the news *means*."

Luce later observed, "The *New Yorker* says it's not for the lady from Dubuque. Well, we do write for the lady from Dubuque—and for the President of the United States."

In February, 1922, Luce and Hadden left Baltimore for New York. For fifty-five dollars a month, which came out of Hadden's pocket, Luce's being empty, they rented as an office one room on the second floor of a dilapidated two-story brownstone at 141 East 17th Street. It was barely large enough to contain them and the brass washtub they installed to receive their cigarette butts. They nevertheless squeezed in a third partner, a Yale classmate named Culbreth Sudler, because he supposedly understood something about advertising, having the previous summer sold space in Chicago buses. Sudler borrowed $548.88 to contribute to the partnership. He loved eating crackers. Two pretty, emancipated young women, who read Havelock Ellis, occupied a back room of the brownstone, and he would indulge his appetite in their company.

Luce and Hadden spent the next eight months seeking professional advice and capital. They found no scarcity of the former. Most of it could be summed up in the three words of Charles Lanier, who owned *Review of Reviews*, "Don't to it." They had anticipated no trouble raising the $100,000 they figured they needed to get started. Surely, they told each other, they knew at least ten rich Yale men willing to risk ten thousand dollars in the new company's shares. This was gross over-optimism.

In their naïveté the partners failed to realize that the rich are just as reluctant to look foolish as anybody else.

A few Yale alumni, including five Skull & Bones members, agreed to help, but the average investment fell far below ten thousand dollars. The first investor, Harry P. Davison (Yale '20), the son of a Morgan partner, risked four thousand dollars. Another classmate, Seymour Knox, pledged his support before the partners had barely begun to describe their project. They could sign him up for five thousand dollars, he said casually, and how about a drink? Hadden was incensed. He refused to accept a penny until Knox understood the nature and purpose of the magazine.

The most unexpected supporter was the Morgan banker, Dwight Morrow. They went to him with an uneasy conscience for advice, not money. The older brother of a Yale classmate, John Wesley Hanes, an investment banker (later Under Secretary of the Treasury under Roosevelt), had drawn up their capital structure plan. It called for an issue of four thousand shares of preferred stock at twenty-five dollars a share. Subscribers who bought two shares would receive as a bonus one share of class A common stock, of which two thousand in all were to be issued. Finally, eight thousand shares of class B common were to be reserved for management, namely Luce and Hadden. They wondered whether this was not perhaps excessive. Upon reading their prospectus, Morrow didn't think so. Without their exertions, he assured them, the stock would be worthless and so they were entitled to the eight thousand shares. Morrow was the first to express enthusiasm for the idea of a news magazine and he himself bought one thousand dollars' worth of stock.

(It is beguiling to contemplate the evolution of those original Time Inc. shares. A single unit, that is, two preferred and one common, costing $50, was worth, forty years later, $22,000 and had yielded dividends totaling $11,000.)

From Yale alumnus Samuel Meek of the J. Walter Thompson advertising agency the partners learned something about promotional techniques. Meek, moreover, introduced them to William Eaton, the mail-order specialist for the publishers Doubleday, Page & Co., who explained to them the tricks of his trade. Cleverly phrased, he pointed out, mail-order circulars could serve not only to raise money, but to pretest the kind of response the law of averages might confer on an unpublished magazine. Better still, Eaton slipped them the list of subscribers to *The World's Work*, a Doubleday periodical. For $218 they had 7000 circulars printed. Eaton felt they should draw a response of between 3 per cent and 6.5 per cent. But only 250 of those circularized showed any interest.

The total capital raised stood at thirty-five thousand dollars when Hadden's cousin, John Stuart Martin, joined the venture as a writer. A Princeton athlete, he had lost his left arm in a hunting mishap. This did not prevent him from shooting tournament-caliber golf. At Martin's suggestion they struck out across the land, using their social connections to get into country clubs where they might meet potential investors in relaxed, receptive moods. In Cleveland the former Secretary of War, Newton D. Baker, turned Hadden down because he refused to commit himself as to where *Time* would stand on the League of Nations. (As Baker hoped, the magazine supported it.) In Cleveland too they found a concentration of gold-plated friends at the wedding of a rich Skull & Bones man, but they considered it gauche to exploit the opportunity.

The cross-country expedition left them barely halfway toward their goal. It was the Harkness family of New York who brought them closer to it. William Hale Harkness (Yale '22), his sister Louise, and his father's cousin, Edward, each pledged five thousand dollars. In addition, young Harkness arranged for the stock salesmen to call on his philanthropic mother. An elderly widow, almost stone deaf, Mrs. Harkness heard little of their sales talk, understood less, and sat silent as the Sphinx. Then, after half an hour, she said, "That will do, boys. Put me down for twenty thousand dollars."

With eighty-six thousand dollars from seventy-two investors, the partners ran out of prospects. They decided to plunge ahead anyway. Moving to a drafty loft in the Printing Trades Building at 461 8th Avenue, they incorporated the firm on November 28, 1922. Their operating expenses for the first six months totaled $1646.66. Culbreth Sudler, meanwhile, had pulled out. They refunded all but $72.81 of his investment, a shortage partly accounted for by his consumption of crackers.

By the fall of 1922 Luce and Hadden had also acquired the nucleus of a staff. As circulation manager they hired a Harvard alumnus, Roy E. Larsen, who carried the distinction of having managed the Harvard *Advocate* profitably for the first time in its history. But just as Yale predominated among *Time*'s original backers, so did they predominate on its original staff. The first editorial employee, later managing editor, Manfred Gottfried, was a Yale man. So were eleven of the eighteen people listed on the first masthead. They included Stephen Vincent Benét and Archibald MacLeish.

Both Luce and Hadden thought of themselves primarily as editors. Yet one of them, they realized, would have to manage the business side. They agreed to swap posts every year. But who would edit first? They tossed a coin. Luce lost and he became so entangled in business problems that three years passed before he could shift to the editorial desk. To his dying day he felt that had he won the toss, the magazine would have evolved differently. Three years sufficed for Hadden to stamp it with his personality. Though Luce would rank above everybody in the corporation—president, chairmen, publishers—the title he preferred in the mastheads of all the magazines was the one that implied his supreme concern—editor-in-chief.

Luce's family, all but his sister Emmavail, who had stayed behind to teach at the Pekin YMCA, were on home leave in New York during the prepublication months, a stroke of luck for him, since they provided free board and lodging. He also got free labor from his eleven-year-old brother Sheldon. At night, with dummies of the magazine spread over the dining-room table, Sheldon would sharpen pencils and run errands. "I was *Time*'s first office boy," he recalled. When he graduated from Yale, he worked in its advertising department, then as its personnel manager. But the publishing world never suited him and he moved to Palo Alto, California, where he became a rancher.

Luce's sister Elizabeth, a Wellesley graduate, wrote some of the trial copy. Later, during the early years of her marriage to Maurice T. Moore, a corporation lawyer and Time Inc. director, she wrote book reviews for the magazine. "I learned a lot about journalism from Harry," she said. "He had a knack of focusing your attention on the essential. He could show you how to cut through a mass of material to the heart of it. 'I think the point is this,' he would tell you, 'but I don't want more than a hundred words.'"

On December 22, 1923, in Old Greenwich, Connecticut, Luce married Lila Hotz. She bore him two sons, Henry III and Peter Paul. It was a marriage of extreme opposites. The husband was precise, deadly serious, unsocial; the wife, lighthearted, gregarious, and incurably unpunctual. "Where the hell is Lila?" Luce would be fuming when they had an appointment. Disliking small talk, he would come home from work to find a bevy of her friends still chattering over the tea table. He took to sneaking in the back way.

Hadden remained a bachelor.

four

It was "the Jazz Age," "the Era of Wonderful Nonsense," the lull between World War I and the rise of Hitler. Calvin Coolidge occupied the White House, dedicating himself to the proposition that "the business of America is business." Niagaras of bathtub gin flowed in defiance of the Volstead Act. "Scarface Al" Capone became a folk hero. Sinclair Lewis created Babbitt as the archetype of complacent, Main Street philistinism. H. L. Mencken flailed the "booboisie." Women's skirts and hair were short, lipsticks vivid. Superpatriots stalked the land, drumming up the Red Scare. A popular pastime of leisured matrons was mah-jong; of the young, petting parties. Millions repeated after Émile Coué, "Day by day, in every way, I am getting better and better." Theda Bara, Norma Talmadge, Douglas Fairbanks, Charlie Chaplin reigned in Hollywood. At the

Ziegfeld Follies Gilda Gray introduced the "shimmy." Freud was fashionable. Woodrow Wilson, his dream of American membership in the League of Nations fled, died, a lonely, broken man. Out of diametrically opposite views of life arose two of the most successful magazines in publishing history—the DeWitt Wallaces' *Reader's Digest* and Harold Ross's *The New Yorker*.

Vol. I, No. 1, of *Time the Weekly News-Magazine* carried the date March 3, 1923. It sold for fifteen cents. The cover framed a black-and-white lithograph drawing, by an artist named Oberholtzer, of Republican Speaker Joseph Gurney ("Uncle Joe") Cannon. The pictures inside the magazine looked to the humorist Robert Benchley "as if they had been engraved on pieces of bread." The week's news, divided into twenty-two departments (the same number as today and, with a few exceptions, under the same headings), had been lifted almost entirely from *The New York Times* and recast. The magazine could afford no wire service, let alone its own reporters and correspondents—only agile rewriters. Its reference library consisted of files of *The New York Times* going back twenty years, but lacking index volumes and therefore useless, an obsolete encyclopedia, *Who's Who*, and *Roget's Thesaurus*. The legality of appropriating material from newspapers had been decided in 1918 by the U. S. Supreme Court (International News Service vs. Associated Press) in favor of the appropriators. News twenty-four hours old, the court ruled, belonged in the public domain.

Responding to Larsen's circulars, twenty-five thousand people had agreed to look at three issues and, if pleased, to pay fifteen dollars for a year's subscription. Among the first subscribers were Herbert Bayard Swope, H. L. Mencken, and New York's Governor Franklin Roosevelt, who wrote a letter of appreciation. How many copies of the first issue reached their intended destinations nobody will ever know, because Larsen recruited a covey of debutantes to address the three sets of wrappers and the pretty creatures mixed them up, so that some people received three copies of the first issue and others no copy of any issue. Perhaps nine thousand saw the first issue, Larsen guessed. He also sent five thousand to the newsstand distributor, of which three thousand were unsold.

To accommodate Earl Crowe, the cantankerous head of an advertising agency, E. R. Crowe & Co., whom Luce and Hadden persuaded to sell ads in *Time*, they moved into the same building at 9 East 40th Street, Crowe having complained that he couldn't conveniently handle their business with them many blocks away. Luce's new office was so cramped that his secretary, Katherine Abrams, had to get up to let him pass whenever he went to or from his desk. Relations with Crowe proved stormy. The expenses he charged to *Time* included his own secretary's salary of thirty-five dollars a week. Miss Abrams was getting only twenty dollars. When Luce protested that he couldn't afford the charge, Crowe advised him not to meddle in such matters. The final breach occurred over Vol. I, No. 4. The choicest advertising space in any magazine is the rear cover and a publisher so hapless as not to sell it would at least use it to promote the magazine itself. But in their innocence Luce and Hadden had left the back of their fourth issue bare. This struck Crowe as so silly that he refused to have anything more to do with them.

Circulation climbed to 110,000 the third year and advertising revenue to $283,000. But not until 1927 did *Time* show any net profit. It amounted to $3860. The turning point came the following year with a net of $126,000, and thereafter profits began to soar.

What hooked the attention of a mass audience was the bag of stylistic tricks that Hadden encouraged his writers to develop. They revolted purists, maddened many of the people *Time* portrayed, tickled the irreverent, and gave rise to a host of imitators. Two basic ingredients of early *Time* style, the double epithet and the inverted sentence, Hadden adapted from the *Iliad* and the *Odyssey*. But whereas the Homeric epithets are poetic ("rosy-fingered Aurora, Zeus, the cloud-gatherer, fleet-footed Achilles"), *Time*'s were abrasive ("snaggle-toothed, hog-fat, purse-potent, moose-tall, weed-whiskered, kinky-bearded, bald-domed, beady-eyed"). The Homeric line sings ("Then to the city, terrible and strong,/With high and haughty steps he tower'd along"), *Time*'s inversions were merely acrobatic ("Ghostly was His Eminence's mission").

Under Editor Hadden's prodding, and later Editor Luce's, the repertory of attention-getters grew to include:

The tantalizing picture caption. "Perfumer Francois Coty and his divorced wife. For her smell work, $5,200,-000." *Time* once carried a story about the artificial insemination of cows solely in order to be able to caption the picture of a prize seed bull "Cuckolded by a capsule."

Compound words. "Cinemactor (Lon Chaney was the first, and Gloria Swanson the first "cinemactress"), "cinemaddict," "cinemalefactor," and so on *ad nauseam;* "Broadwayfarer," "detectifiction," "nudancer," "sexational." One of the few to enter common usage was "socialite." Webster lists it.

Archaisms like "moppet" and "tosspot"; neologisms like ecdysiast (coined by H. L. Mencken for "stripteaser," but popularized by *Time*); slang like "oldster"; exotic courtesy titles like "tycoon" (from the Japanese *taikun,* meaning prince), "pundit" (from the Hindu *pandit,* meaning sage), "mameluke," and "shogun"; euphemisms that skirted libel like "great & good friend" for mistress; the repetition of phrases until they became *Time* trademarks like "As it must to all men, death came last week to . . ." and "in time's nick."

Avoidance of "he said." In *Time* people snapped, snapped back, burbled, gruffed, croaked, chuckled, gushed, sneered, guffawed. Nor did they simply walk. They strode, stalked, popped out, bounced, leaped, shot ahead. They didn't just get into vehicles either. They "climbed in" or "piled in."

Hadden kept close at hand a translation of the *Iliad* and a small, black, loose-leaf notebook. In the *Iliad* he underscored the epithets and covered the margins and end papers with pseudo-Homeric coinages. He filled the notebook with words and phrases which he considered compelling and he would urge "neophytes," one of his pet archaisms, to study them.*

The author served a brief tenure as a "contributing editor" in 1939. Like most of the neophytes, in struggling to achieve the requisite style, I produced travesty. Among the grossest examples I recall was an adjective I coined to describe the gloomy and acidulous Dean Inge of London's St. Paul's Cathedral—"lemon-

Hadden built up an armory of sly weapons for ridiculing people he deemed ridiculous, pinpricking swollen egos, and reducing the high and mighty to ordinary dimensions. He discovered that, for reasons hard to analyze, giving the full name of people who customarily used middle initials could be deflating. Somehow Ivy L. Lee, the Rockefellers' public relations counsel, Harry M. Daugherty, the malfeasant attorney general under Warren Harding, Cyrus H. K. Curtis, ruler of the Curtis publishing empire, sounded faintly absurd when exposed as Ivy Ledbetter Lee, Harry Micajah Daugherty, and Cyrus Hermann Kotzschmar Curtis.

Hadden further discovered the mischief that could be wrought with informal snapshots, and unless no other was available, he seldom illustrated a story with the kind of posed, studio portrait most subjects would have preferred. *Time* pictured Mussolini, hands on hips, wearing a baggy bathing suit that looked like underwear; Secretary of Agriculture Henry Wallace grinning foolishly as he milked a cow; Senator Robert M. La Follette's daughter Fola munching a banana. For victims who protested Hadden had a stock defense, "The camera can't lie."

Hadden extended his racy touch even to the Letters department. To enliven it, he had his staff invent cor-

---

choly." A tear sheet came to my desk with the word circled by Luce himself and the comment "Good!" I also, to my shame, referred to Hitler as "führious." While this too reached print, it prompted a memo from one senior editor to another, asking, "Isn't this sherry Kobler too rich?" I was fired soon after with the explanation by Manfred Gottfried, "You're just not the Grade A Time type."

respondents eccentric, irascible, outrageous or comical. "The noun 'virgin,'" wrote a fictitious spinster, "Mary Elizabeth Robin," who had thus been characterized by another spurious letter-writer, "is not one which gentlemen or ladies employ, in any other than a religious connection. I shall enquire from my attorneys whether its use in the letters to which I refer is or is not libelous. You may rest assured that my married or unmarried state, as the case may be, is not a subject upon which I shall stoop to satisfy curious vulgarians."

One of the longest fake correspondences, to which almost every staff member contributed, began in the issue of August 8, 1927.

> "Sirs:
> "They all lay down sooner or later!
> "First Ford, now Lewis!
> "Henry Ford tried to twist the Jews' noses, but he won't try that again.
> "Now I see in TIME [Aug. 1] that Sinclair Lewis sat down and blubbered over some foreigners.
> "Then he gets up & writes about 'romance' and other typical Main Street guff.
> "I tell you, TIME, they all lay down sooner or later.
> > "Morris ('Al') Epstein Jr.
> > "Brooklyn, N.Y."

Hadden fabricated a correspondent to upbraid "Epstein" for his grammar. There was no need, however. Many genuine readers attacked the offender. Unchastened, Epstein went on,

"Now here's where TIME lay down last week: in the Sports department were only bowling for old ladies and two little stories about GOLF. That's another of those old maid's games, golf, where you go around after a little ball and only give it a hit about every five minutes.*

"Where TIME lay down was in not printing some of the real sport news of the week.

"Why not tell how Babe Ruth socked his 37th, 38th and 39th and 40th homers? . . .

"*An error. Average time for an 18-hole round of golf is 150 minutes. Even should a player take so few as 67 strokes, as did Golfer Robert Tyre Jones Jr. in the national amateur qualifying round last week, his strokes would come out at an average of less than three minutes apart.—ED."

The name of Epstein cropped up for the last time in the issue of September 27, 1927, when ED. announced, "One or more of his letters has reached TIME every week for ten weeks. But TIME has ceased to publish the letters of Morris ('Al') Epstein."

Luce and Hadden received so many more entertaining letters, authentic or fabricated by their staff, than they could find space for, that they decided to publish a separate periodical. The overflow, however, was not abundant enough and after trying to pad out *Letters* with trumped-up correspondence and miscellaneous curiosa, they dropped it.

With the sources of their stories limited to the daily press and their store of personal knowledge, *Time* writers drew heavily on their imaginations. They developed a wondrous facility for inflating a paragraph from *The New York Times* into a column of semifiction. It devolved upon the researchers (then as later, female) to square fantasy with fact. Luce and Hadden had devised a fact-checking system, requiring them to pencil a dot over each word, signifying that they had checked its accuracy, an impossible task in many instances. Bitter bickering disturbed the peace as researchers accused writers of violating truth and writers accused them of stifling creativity. To bear the brunt of *Time*'s transgressions, the cofounders concocted an editor, "Peter Mathews," and when a reader wrote a justifiably angry letter, the Letters editor would shunt the blame to his shadowy colleague. "Peter Mathews" was fired in 1938, rehired, then fired for good.

Time's treatment of minorities was exemplary throughout most of its history. But in their youth the cofounders did not fully appreciate the obligations of a democratic society. *Time* then tended to reflect the social attitudes of well-born Yale men and the Long Island country-club set. Its favorite epithets for delinquent Negroes were "blackamoor" and "blackamoron." It began a story about a Negro organization (August 11, 1924), "One cannot deny that the Negro race has imagination. Its gestures may be futile, but as a race it is a master of gesture." At times the magazine would go to the opposite extreme of referring to Negroes as "Mr." and to whites by their last names only. They would report every lynching. But this was mainly because it amused Hadden to rile Southern white supremacists.

In stories involving Jews the prewar *Time* would identify them, often sneeringly, by race ("Fannie Hurst, Smart, Semite Novelist" . . . "Smart Jew David Lilienthal"), a practice it dropped with the rise of Hitler. Neither Hadden nor Luce restrained their Foreign News editor, Laird Goldsborough, from tainting his copy with pro-Fascist, anti-Semitic sentiments. Perched on a huge, black swivel chair chuckling to himself as he pecked out the words on his typewriter, he would describe the French statesman Léon Blum as "lean, spidery . . . Socialist and Jew" and "Jew Blum." ("Before Hitler," Luce explained many years later, "it was not considered pejorative to label a man a Jew. In 1933 we adopted a policy against such labeling. Hitler knocked out our casual enjoyment of Yiddish humor.") Long autonomous in his department, Goldsborough eventually lost his prestige and left *Time* to free-lance. He rented an office in the same building. One day in 1950, he jumped, or fell, out of the window, gripping a cane and wearing a bowler hat.

As *Time* prospered, the flamboyant Hadden and the sobersided Luce grew temperamentally further apart. Work wholly absorbed Luce. Hadden found leisure for play. He loved bizarre parlor games—of which he invented several—noisy card games like slapjack, baseball, collecting China dogs, live alley cats, and carousing. At night he would preside over a coterie of kindred spirits in a Third Avenue Hungarian tavern. He cut a dashing figure, handsome, with greenish eyes and dark-brown hair, nervous, taut, his body rarely in repose. A hearty drinker, he composed a drinking quatrain:

> His is not drunk who from the floor
> Can rise again to drink some more.
> But drunk he is who prostrate lies
> And who can neither drink nor rise.

Luce worked with grim-lipped intensity, fists clamped to his temples, a tableau *vivant* of Thought. Hadden, for whom journalism was partly a game to be played with brio, was all raucous motion. Arriving at the office building, if the elevator didn't respond instantly to his ring, he would bang the door with his cane. In his headlong sprint through the corridors he would knock aside any furniture blocking his path. He once kicked viciously at a suitcase. It was full of books and he almost broke his ankle. When editing, he plied enormous red pencils made to his design (*Time* editors used the same kind for years after), nervously crunching the ends between his teeth, bellowed his delight over neat turns of phrase, snarled at clumsy ones, scribbled terse directives on memos attached to news clippings—"Let's blat this guy," "Flay!" "Makes sense."

In both his game-playing and his professional activities Hadden made a fetish of questionnaires. He was constantly devising new ones to test the intellect of job-seekers. Even prospective office boys would be asked, "Who's Andy Gump? Where's City Hall? What's the capital of Wisconsin? Name five brands of chewing gum." Hadden would confront girls applying for a research job with a questionnaire based on *Alice in Wonderland*.

His obsession led to *Time*'s first radio program, billed at the outset, in 1924, as *The Time Questionnaire,* then as *The Pop Question Game*. Hadden and Larsen devised it together. Hadden was the announcer and Larsen the timekeeper. Broadcasting from Aeolian Hall over WJZ every Thursday at 8:30 P.M., Hadden would proclaim, "A pop question game, invented by *Time the Weekly News-Magazine,* will now be played. Eleven questions, based on the news of the week [as reported in the last issue, naturally] will be asked. After each question will come an interval of ten seconds. After each interval will come the correct answer. The object of the game is for you to shout out the correct answer before I do. If you shout it out first, you score one point plus. If I shout it out first, you score one point minus. You win the game in the event that you shout out a majority of correct answers before I do. The ten-second interval will be counted off on the chimes like this." Here Larsen would strike a set of chimes. "Are you ready? Then play the game." And he would pop the first of a series of current-events questions.

The program drew applause from the daily press. The New York *Herald Tribune* pronounced it the most popular on the air, one which "tickled the vanity of the intellectual and awakened the interest and pride of the less quick-witted."

After the rupture with E. R. Crowe *Time* moved to the third floor of a former brewery at 236 East 39th Street. There were no lavatories and the new tenants installed some at considerable expense. They neglected to furnish toilet paper, however, with the result that the newspapers used by the staff clogged the plumbing, causing four hundred dollars' worth of damage.

From the brewery every Monday around 5 P.M. Luce and Hadden would set out with the next issue's copy for the printer far downtown on Vesey Street. One by one the rest of the staff would follow, an office boy lugging a suitcase containing *Time*'s reference library, now augmented by *The World Almanac*, the *Almanach de Gotha*, a set of social registers, and *Bartlett's Quotations*. In a dark, malodorous cubicle, throbbing with the rhythm of the nearby presses, Hadden and Luce would correct proofs, bickering noisily over punctuation, shades of meaning, facts. Toward midnight they would dash out for the early editions of the morning newspapers. Haring across the street, oblivious to traffic, Luce would snatch the *Times*, still damp, from the delivery truck. Then, over a snack in an all-night diner, the cofounders would whisk through the papers, eyes peeled for last-minute news to rewrite. If changes or updating were indicated, they would phone the printers and dictate them. The researchers and other underlings, meanwhile, would be eating sandwiches and drinking coffee brewed over the lead melter on the linotype machine. Usually, the sun had risen before Luce and Hadden administered the final touches to the proofs.

In 1924 a combination of collegiate loyalties and respect for lofty literary endeavor moved them to undertake a somewhat quixotic venture. The "Literary Review," a supplement of the New York *Evening Post*, had foundered, chiefly, so they believed, because the publisher had replaced the editor, Henry Seidel Canby, with an incompetent dilettante. Canby was a former Yale professor. He had, moreover, encouraged Luce and Hadden during the darkest hours of their journalistic nonage. And so, despite their own shortage of money and readers, they decided to revive the fallen "Literary Review" as an independent publication to be called *The Saturday Review of Literature*. Larsen launched a promotional campaign. Office space was found for the review cheek-by-jowl with *Time* in the ex-brewery. Though published by Time Inc., Canby and his fellow editors, Christopher Morley and William Rose Benét, exercised absolute editorial control. The association lasted until 1927 after *Time* had shifted its base of operations to Cleveland. By then the new magazine was established as the first national literary review in America.

Economics dictated the move to Cleveland. It distressed Hadden, a passionate New Yorker, but he had acceded to it upon learning that the corporation could save some twenty thousand dollars a year in printing bills, overhead, and distribution costs. *Time* then had a dozen young girls handling subscriptions and it lost them all because their families objected to their living so far from home without chaperonage. In their place Larsen hired native labor. Within a few months he was inundated with letters from subscribers complaining that they had sent their five-dollar bill, but received no magazine. An investigation disclosed that some of the local subscription girls were graduates of a reform school.

Luce and Hadden quarreled a good deal, especially after Hadden reluctantly took his turn as business manager, but they would close ranks if anybody tried to step between them. Hadden found little in *Time* under Luce's editorship that fully satisfied him. Itching to edit again, he started a new magazine, *Tide*, devoted to the advertising business. Its heckling, Haddenesque tone toward its subjects, including some of *Time*'s best customers, made life uncomfortable for *Time*'s ad salesmen. Typically, ". . . occasionally advertising appears to miseducate. Its advice is sometimes unsound, its teaching brings no lesson. Wrong answers are learned in advertising's little red schoolhouse. Teacher turns up with a cloven hoof. Observe, for instance, a current advt. for no less a reputable product than Phillips Milk of Magnesia . . . 'over-indulgence is no crime, and it is folly to suffer for every little indiscretion.' . . . Thus the Phillips' message—eat, drink and be merry. . . . No high regard for safety in motor cars is shown by advertising for the Reo Flying Cloud. . . . Copy whispers speed—speed—speed. . . . So, with cloven hoof, urges the Speed Demon. . . . So numerous and so palpably misleading are advertisements which concern themselves with extraordinary bargains in men's clothing that few people bother to read them." Though Luce's name appeared in the masthead as editor, he detested the whole idea and in 1930 *Tide* was sold to an advertising agency for ten thousand dollars.

Cleveland bored Hadden. "I've been here forty-four weeks and I've made thirty-three trips to New York," he complained. Not many members of the staff liked Cleveland either; they too missed the big city and they began defecting. A factor greater than homesickness was that the New York newspapers, particularly the *Times*, on which *Time* relied so heavily, could not be obtained fast enough. Luce agreed with Hadden that they should retrace their steps and in 1927 they returned to Manhattan and a sixth change of address, just off Fifth Avenue, at 25 West 46th Street.

～ *five* ～

It was Hadden's stated ambition to make a million dollars by the age of thirty. He made slightly more than that, but he did not enjoy it long. In February, 1929, he contracted a streptococcus infection. In Brooklyn Hospital on the twenty-seventh, nine days after his thirty-first birthday, and six years to the hour after the first issue of *Time* went to press, he died.

Decades from now journalists may still be arguing over which founder deserved the greater credit for *Time*'s success. It is a fruitless debate. Their contributions were indivisible. If Hadden, as the first editor, gave the magazine its first distinctive characteristics, Luce, in his turn, imparted others equally distinctive. Luce, moreover, went on to create a chain of successful publications. If Hadden introduced a novel approach to news, Luce broadened it and led it on to firm ground. As a competitor expressed it, "Maybe Hadden devised the creed, but Luce built the cathedral." Luce himself said of Hadden, "Brit was what the French call an *original*. He was close to a genius." Toward the end, Luce felt, as did others, that Hadden was beginning to get bored.

Luce donated half the money, and various friends the rest, to build new quarters for the Yale *Daily News*. It was named the Hadden Memorial Building. A bronze plaque bore the inscription, "His genius created a new form of journalism."

❧ six ❧

Of *Time*'s notorious bygone style, Luce admitted, "We went too far. Writers began burlesquing themselves. The original reason for the jolting language was to get the story off the page into the reader's head, as we said in our prospectus. But you can destroy the importance of a story by overemphasizing physical traits. It may be more important to show what's inside a man's mind than the size of his nose."

Reform was slow, however, and not until the late thirties had *Time* shed its more obnoxious mannerisms. A chastening influence was the parody in *Time* style that Wolcott Gibbs wrote for *The New Yorker* in 1936. The immediate provocation was a *Fortune* article about *The New Yorker* by Ralph McAllister Ingersoll, its former managing editor and now a Luce lieutenant. Ingersoll estimated the salaries, for the most part inaccurately, of his old associates. *The New Yorker* retaliated with one sentence, "Gossip note: The Editor of *Fortune* gets $30 a week and carfare." But this failed to placate the injured. *The New Yorker* essayist, E. B. White, thought *Fortune* should be chastised at length. The founding editor, Harold Ross, disagreed. "Who reads *Fortune?*" he said. "Dentists." *Time*, he insisted, was the natural target and Gibbs the humorist to fire the missiles.

With Gibbs's reputation as a demolition expert, Ross reckoned, he would not be able to get near his victim. So, keeping him under cover, he assigned the research to two writers not known primarily as humorists, St. Clair McKelway and Alva Johnston. They misled Luce into believing that they planned a study in depth of him and all his works, and thus obtained his full cooperation.

It was *Fortune* practice to submit to the subject preliminary proofs of the article purposely crammed with rumors, distorted facts, and imaginary statistics in the expectation that as he angrily corrected them he would let slip information not otherwise available. This was decidedly not *New Yorker* practice, but as part of the parody, Ross made an exception.

In the issue of November 28, 1936, the victim read: ". . . ambitious, gimlet-eyed Baby Tycoon Henry Robinson Luce . . .

"Under eyes too beetling for a baby, young Luce grew up inside the compound, played with his two sisters, lisped first Chinese, dreamed much of the Occident . . .

"*Time*'s books, according to Chicago Statisticians Gerwig and Gerwig, show total assets of $6,755,451. Liabilities, $3,101,584. These figures, conventionally allowing $1 for name, prestige of *Time*, come far from reflecting actual prosperity of Luce, his enterprises. Sitting pretty are the boys . . .

"Grand total Timemployees on God's earth, 782. Average weekly recompense for informing fellowman, $45.67802 . . .

". . . Littered his desk with pills, unguents, Kleenex, Socialite Ingersoll is *Time*'s No. 1 hypochondriac. . . .

"Serious, ambitious Yale standards are still reflected in much of his [Luce's] conduct; in indiscriminate admiration for bustling success, in strong regard for conventional morality. . . .

". . . it has been hinted that an official connection with the House of Morgan is not impossible. Vehemently denies this Luce, denies any personal political ambition, admits only that he would like eventually to own a daily newspaper in New York.

"Most persistent, most fantastic rumor, however, declares that Yaleman Luce already has a wistful eye on the White House. . . ."

Gibbs spared no *Time* idiosyncrasy. Two lines remain among the most oft-quoted of any ever penned by a parodist: "Backward ran sentences until reeled the mind," and the profile concluded, "Where it all will end, knows God!"

When Ingersoll had read it too, nearly hysterical with rage, he phoned McKelway. "Hearst tactics!" he bellowed. "Sure," McKelway blithely agreed. "You out-Hearst Hearst every week in *Time*." Luce, calmer but hurt, spoke to Ross. That night, at Ingersoll's insistence, the four men met in Ross's penthouse. Luce walked straight up to McKelway. "Gibbs says I have no sense of humor. He's wrong. I do so have a sense of humor." "Your saying that," McKelway replied, "proves Gibbs is right."

With the proofs on the table before them, the tussle lasted all night. Ross broke out a bottle of Scotch. He took none himself. Luce nursed one drink. But McKelway and Ingersoll did not stint themselves. At one point, in their cups, they started for the street to settle matters with their fists. "I'll take Ralph home," Luce said to Ross. "You hold Mac." But the belligerents subsided.

Ross accepted a few corrections of fact, but refused to soften the bite. At the end Luce complained, "There's not a single kind word about me in the whole profile." "That," said Ross, "is what you get for being a baby tycoon."

Shortly before the profile appeared, Ross wrote Luce a letter justifying it:

"Dear Luce (Personal)
"I assume it is up to me to make certain explanations; at any rate I do so, to clear my conscience, with which I always struggle to keep current. I enclose a rough copy of the next issue with the parody. I have just been over this, reading the piece for what I pray to God is the last time and making notes of a few points I want to explain.

"The staff here wanted to be fair and McKelway and I put all of the important matters of opinion (as Ingersoll called a great many of the points raised in the *Fortune* piece on *The New Yorker*) which you raised to a sort of committee, consisting of Mr. and Mrs. White (founders of dynasty, *Fortune*, August, 1934), Gibbs, McKelway and myself. We considered these matters with a full sense of responsibility, rather solemnly. Our office differs from yours in that our contents are signed and the writer of an article has the final say on changes, if it comes right down to it. In this instance, however, Gibbs abided by the group decision in every instance. To the special points:

"You complained that there wasn't a single favorable word in the piece about you. It was generally felt that the total effect of the article and its being in existence at all was enormously favorable, and that our listing of your remarkable growth, the figures themselves, were complimentary in the highest degree, present you, in fact, as practically heroic. As Gibbs pointed out subsequently in a memo to me: 'Having chosen this parody form (and I think it's the only way we could possibly write about another magazine) the piece was bound to sound like *Time*, and you will go through a hell of a lot of copies of *Time* without finding anybody described in a way that would please his mother.' I was astonished to realize the other night that you are apparently unconscious of the notorious reputation *Time* and *Fortune* have for crassness in description, for cruelty and scandal mongering and insult. I say, frankly, but really in a not unfriendly spirit, that you are in a hell of a position to ask anything . . .

"We decided that our estimates as to some of the figures were as good for our purpose as yours would have been, since the article was a parody and some errors would only contribute to the general effect; the *New Yorker* figures in the *Fortune* piece were amusingly wide of the fact in certain instances. (Your passion for accuracy is in no wise doubted; your ability to attain it in many instances is questioned, naturally, by practical journalists.) We felt that the figure on average pay could not possibly be taken as anything other than a parody figure, since it went to five decimal points. (The figures are just out of Gibbs' head as he happened to hit the typewriter keys.)

"I was confronted with an ample mass of evidence to substantiate the statements that the writers put 'jokers' or 'slithering insults' in their copy. Remember that there has been a considerable duplication of writing talent by *Fortune* and the *New Yorker* and that writers talk much. . . .

"The paragraph on *Fortune*'s methods of getting facts was allowed to stand as being justified beyond doubt. Not only did we have the *New Yorker* as evidence on this point, but ample reports on several others. For instance, we were informed that your original piece on the Astor

Estate contained one hundred and thirty-eight misstatements or errors which had to be painstakingly worked out. . . .

"I didn't get anywhere on your argument about the inaccuracy of 'Indiscriminate admiration of business success.' This held to be amply justified on superficial evidence of publications itself, and on strength of various reports—'Indiscriminate' used loosely perhaps, but justifiably. . . .

"Ingersoll's hypochondria was adjudged to be still existent. Not only did we have the advice of one of the greatest psychiatrists in the city on this (he told us, once a hypochondriac, always a hypochondriac; on occasion it may be latent or nearly so but such periods are only temporary and that the patient should be watched carefully during them) but from direct testimony. Besides it's no slur to call a man a hypochondriac. Most New Yorkers are. . . .

"You were adjudged to be by tradition a Tory, and no doubt whatever. Ministers of the Gospel are the very spearheads of Toryism; then Hotchkiss and Yale, both conventional, Tory.

"Retention of the paragraph on presidential ambitions was also a unanimous decision. It was regarded as exactly the kind of thing *Time* is doing constantly; denying the weird, and, as we called it, 'fantastic' rumor after starting it, thereby getting the full news value out of it. Moreover, *Time* enterprises are always speculating on people's ambitions. This seemed the perfect item for parody purposes. . . .

". . . I would like to quote a couple of paragraphs from Gibbs' note to me, and do:

"'Any criticism of the policy, style, etc. is as Ingersoll said, of certain statements in the *Fortune* piece about us, purely a matter of opinion. I think *Time* has gratuitously invaded the privacy of a great many people; I think it draws conclusions unwarranted by the facts, distorts quotes, reprints rumors it knows have little foundation, uses a selective editing in getting together a story from the newspapers that throws it altogether out of focus, and that *Time*'s style is an offense to the ear. I said that Mr. Luce was humorless because I could find nothing in the source or in the reports of people who have talked to him that indicated anything else. Also I doubt very much if a humorist would last a week as President of Time Inc. I'm not even sure that 'humorless' is a disparaging term. In any case all statements and editorial conclusions in the piece are matters of honest opinion with me, usually made after reading the evidence of a great many people. Don't know if Ingersoll and Luce realize just how much source material went into this thing, and from what widely divergent people it came. In almost every case I've tried to follow the same temperamental estimate, throwing out a lot of stuff that would have made the boys' hair stand up. . . .'

"A little more from me. After our talk the other night I asked at least ten people about *Time*, and to my amazement, found them bitter, in varying degree, in their attitude. You are generally regarded as being mean as Hell and frequently scurrilous. Two Jewish gentlemen were at dinner with me last night and, upon mention of *Time*, one of them charged that you are anti-Semitic, and asked the other if he didn't think so too. The other fellow said he's read *Time* a lot and he didn't think you were anti-Semitic, especially—you were just anti-everything, he said: 'anti-Semitic, anti-Italian, anti-Scandinavian, anti-black widow spider.' 'It's just their pose,' he said. . . .

"Sincerely yours,

"Harold Wallace Ross

"Small man . . . furious . . . mad . . . no taste"

The parody had a salubrious effect. Thereafter *Time* writers found it hard to write "Timestyle" with a straight face and the magazine gradually progressed toward respectable English. The Luce publications, however, remained a favorite butt of *New Yorker* cartoonists. (Wife to socially rebellious husband: "But, Lester, is it *enough* just being against everything that 'Time' magazine is for?" One postman to another, as they sag under the weight of mailbags bursting with copies of *Life:* "If their circulation keeps going up, Joe, I swear I can't go on." Space science instructor explaining a chalkboard diagram

78

to a group of airmen: "This is where the lucky astronaut will sit—to the left of the meteorological equipment, to the right of the communications setup, and directly behind the photographer from 'Life.'")

⌁ *seven* ⌁

Fortune, the second major Time Inc. enterprise, and a daring one since the corporation had not yet earned any sizable profits, was founded in 1929. It was Luce's brainchild alone. Hadden, who died during the planning stage, could muster no enthusiasm for it. What prompted Luce was the abundance of stories *Time*'s business section had to discard every week for lack of space. Beyond that was his admiration for American businessmen. "Business," he declared in the *Fortune* prospectus, "is obviously the greatest single common denominator of interest among the active leading citizens of the U.S.A. . . . Our best men are in business." The paean linked statecraft, science, law, education, and the arts with business, "the distinctive expression of the American genius."

Nobody had ever published a quality periodical devoted exclusively to business. The *Wall Street Journal* then provided little more than a catalogue of corporate changes, staff promotions, earnings, and dividends. In other periodicals the usual treatment was either a puff or muckraking. Luce proposed to create a "business literature." The average citizen tended to think of big business as sinister and predatory. Luce wanted a magazine of luxurious format, superlative art, and writing that would give business status in the public's mind as well as in its own.

He set up an experimental department at *Time* and for two years worked with a group of its editors to develop a formula. As a name for the magazine he hesitated between *Power* and *Fortune*, settling on the latter when his wife Lila told him she liked it better. To head the editorial staff he chose *Time*'s twenty-five-year-old business editor, Parker Lloyd-Smith, a Princetonian who, like Luce, had gone on to Oxford. Luce considered him one of the most brilliant men he had ever known, with a vast erudition, a prodigious capacity for assimilating new knowledge, and an intuitive understanding of the mystiques of wealth and power. Lloyd-Smith nursed *Fortune* through its infancy, until September 1931, when he threw himself out of a hotel window, nobody knew why.

In October, 1929, three months before *Fortune*'s birth, the stock market crashed, ending a decade of prosperity. American business, to whose achievements *Fortune* was dedicated, lay flat on its face. Could the magazine still be justified? More than ever, Luce concluded, for now the range of interest was far wider. What caused the catastrophe? Who were the guilty? *Fortune*'s role would be to investigate the methods of business, its sins and its virtues.

The presses rolled with an initial print order of thirty thousand copies. Vol. I, No. 1, priced at one dollar, numbered 184 pages, more than half of them carrying ads, weighed nearly two and a half pounds, and contained lavishly illustrated reports on the meat-packing and glass industries, branch banking, New York's Biltmore Hotel, millionaire-owned islands, and Arthur Curtis James, one of the richest men in the world.

At first the general tenor was descriptive rather than critical. A respectful article about Texaco in the second issue gave rise to the canard that the oil company had paid for it. Similar slanders persisted for years. When Luce heard that one industrialist was trying to find out what it would cost to plant a story in *Fortune*, he said, "Three million dollars and he gets the magazine too."

During the first six months of 1930 the American economy seemed to recover. Then it relapsed into a depression that lasted three years, through most of Roosevelt's first term. As the depression deepened, *Fortune*'s approach to its subject changed. Luce, who from his new office in the Chrysler Building could see the Bowery Savings Bank below besieged by depositors anxious to get their money out, recognized the urgency for basic economic reforms. He began to challenge the tradition that a corporation's business was nobody else's business. Most "tycoons," as *Time* still termed them, were highly secretive. Informative annual reports were rare. J. P. Morgan considered his banking operations, despite their enormous effect on the nation's economy, to be strictly his private concern. "I plead guilty," said Luce, "to promoting the radical idea that the public has the right to know how business works. You don't need much socialism if you have proper exposure to the capitalist process."

It is a bemusing paradox that in the process of furnishing such exposure *Fortune*, the magazine of business, cast doubt upon the efficiency of the free enterprise system and even took on a faint socialist tinge. It was a mark of Luce's superb sense of timing, and of his pragmatism, that *Fortune* turned irreverent and sharply critical when it did. The public was ready to listen. The leaders of the business community had somehow fouled the machinery. People wanted to know why and how.

Some of the magazine's brightest editors and contributors, such as Archibald MacLeish, who composed prose poems ("The stair smelled as it had always smelled of hemp and people and politeness—of the decent bourgeois dust," he began a story about the embezzling Swedish match king, Ivar Kreuger), Alfred Kazin, Dwight Macdonald, John Kenneth Galbraith, stood well to the Left, but Luce realized that he needed iconoclasts to shake up businessmen and compel them to notice *Fortune*. By the mid-thirties the glossy monthly had become a scourge. With unprecedented candor it lifted the lid from the inner workings of the A&P, the United Fruit Co., U. S. Steel, the multifarious Du Ponts. It was the exposé of Europe's munitions makers by Eric Hodgins in the March, 1934, issue that probably prompted the U. S. Senate investigation, a few months later, of "merchants of death" in America.

In its efforts to penetrate corporate secrecy *Fortune* took extreme measures. Among the most enigmatic corporations to arouse its curiosity was Allied Chemical and Dye. Except for its lucrative production of heavy chemicals, even the stockholders knew little about its operations. How it invested its huge capital surplus, its annual statements never revealed. The president was Orlando F. Webber, an organizational prodigy, born in Milwaukee of German parentage. No reporter could get past his secretary. Luce himself failed. But the president's parents still lived in Milwaukee and a reporter was dispatched to interview them. By extravagantly praising their son's accomplishments the rogue won their confidence. Reminiscing about Orlando's adolescence, they produced a photograph of him winning a bicycle race at a country fair. In youth as in maturity Orlando, viewed from the rear, presented a curious configuration. He was so ample of buttock that he couldn't sit a bicycle saddle without overhanging. The reporter borrowed the snapshot. Luce sent an enlargement to President Webber with a note explaining that since *Fortune* lacked details of his adult career, it would confine itself to his youthful triumphs. Webber telephoned Luce the same day. He would, he said, be pleased to grant an interview concerning the affairs of Allied Chemical.

Fortune went so far as to support those bugbears of big business, Roosevelt and the New Deal. "I didn't vote for F.D.R.," recounted Luce, later a flaming Roosevelt-hater, "but it was all right with me that he won. He got the country part way out of trouble and he accomplished a lot of necessary reform."

Both the Right and the Left execrated *Fortune*. When it attacked business, it was a tool of Moscow. When it praised it, the bankers were the corrupting force. But Luce's intuition had not failed him. In Wall Street *Fortune* was obligatory reading. Advertisers threatened to cancel their contracts—to no avail, and none of any consequence ever did. By the end of the depression *Fortune* was earning a modest profit. In 1937 it netted close to $500,000. It subsequently topped that figure and its circulation exceeded 460,000—possibly a record for a monthly magazine that raised its price to $1.50.

As business climbed back out of the wreckage, *Fortune*'s attitude toward it changed. The shock of the fall had sobered and civilized the marketplace. *Fortune* grew more sympathetic, more confident in the resilience and creativity of the capitalist system and less tolerant of government interference. Luce repudiated Roosevelt. The President, he charged in a 1938 address to the Ohio Bankers Association, continued to treat the country as an invalid, keeping it in a state of hypochondria. He blamed the President because the gross national product had not risen above its 1930 level. "The smallness of our national production today is a national disgrace, a wicked disobedience of the ancient injunction to increase and multiply, a miserable failure to function as the intelligent creative animals we pride ourselves in being. . . . Franklin Roosevelt has made most businessmen feel that he does not like business. . . . The dangerous fact is this: while basing all his policies on the assumption that private enterprise will work, he has based his political popularity on the implication that business is antisocial, unpatriotic, vulgar and corruptive."

He concluded with a rousing exhortation: "Make money; be proud of it; make more money, be prouder of it. School yourself for the long battle of freedom in this century."

Luce used the term "the Great Society" when Lyndon Johnson was still an obscure congressman. "For centuries," he wrote in the April, 1939, *Fortune*, "the Europeans, and notably the admirable British, kept business in its place. They called it 'trade'—snobbishly and profitably. But *business* is an American word—and the business of business is no longer to provide a 5%–6% interest for the aristocracy, whether in London or Newport or Hyde Park. The business of business is to take part in the creation of the Great Society."

For a time, under the managing editorship of Russell Davenport, a progressive Republican, *Fortune* appeared to favor a mixed economy. It was Davenport who discerned presidential qualities in Wendell Willkie and persuaded Luce to back him against Roosevelt in the 1940 elections. (Luce did not start the Willkie boom, however. Mrs. Ogden Reid's *Herald Tribune* had already urged the Republican party to draft him. When she announced her intention at a dinner, Charles Douglas Jackson, future publisher of *Life*, whispered to another Time Incer, "What's the old girl doing that silly thing for?")

With America facing war and the need to produce the mightiest armament in her history, *Fortune* and Willkie, whom Davenport helped to write articles for the magazine as well as campaign speeches, took up the cry, "Give business the order and let it go!" The time for chivvying "economic royalists" was past. "When Roosevelt asked for fifty thousand planes and got them," Luce would always maintain, "that finished the New Deal."

Fortune's politico-economic policies during Luce's later years ranged a narrow spectrum centering on moderate conservatism. There were no iconoclasts among its editors. Some, indeed, held views less liberal than Luce's. The managing editor, John Davenport, Russell's younger brother, tended toward the laissez-faire economic philosophy of the nineteenth century. But Luce sensed, pragmatically, that just as the catastrophe of 1930 called for a critical, leftish editorial stance so, in the abundant sixties, a right-wing, supportive one was indicated. Psychologically, too, he had doubtless been influenced by his involvement with the country's financial mandarins, not to mention his own epic success as a businessman.

Fortune remained as visually resplendent as ever, its text as deeply researched and forcefully written. Its Business Roundup became the most respected forecast in the field. The magazine could still sting, but the full force of its strike was usually reserved for those who had let the System down, such patent malefactors as the General Electric price-fixers (1961) or such blunderers as the General Dynamics executives whose program to build jet planes lost the corporation about $500,000,000 (1962). *Fortune* implacably dissected General Dynamics, even though its president, Frank Pace, was a Time Inc. director and an intimate of Time Inc. President James A. Linen.

With the System itself, however, *Fortune* no longer quarreled. It mirrored rather than goaded business. It was like a court painter. Junior executives on the way up found it an invaluable textbook. "In the old days," an industrial public relations veteran remarked, "you prayed that *Fortune* wouldn't write about your client. Now you pray it will."

~ *eight* ~

Had Luce no other asset than his ability to mobilize brilliant business brains, Time Inc. would probably still have flourished. In James A. Linen, the eventual president of the company, Roy E. Larsen, chairman of the executive committee, and Charles L. Stillman, chairman of the finance committee—to name only three spectacular examples among a score—he found prodigies of, respectively, advertising salesmanship, promotion, and investment. Linen came to know, on a first-name-calling basis, a majority of the country's leading magnates, an acquaintanceship partly built up through his skill as a country-club golfer and as a perennial committeeman on philanthropic boards. With Linen, a plump, beaming Williams man via Hotchkiss, the Luce family had old ties. It was

Linen's grandparents in Scranton, Pennsylvania, who subsidized Dr. Luce's early missionary years in China.

Through Roy Larsen the corporation branched out into radio, then movies. It started in 1928 with a promotional scheme. To radio stations across the country Larsen distributed gratis a program called "Newscasting," assembled from *Time* stories. The stations broadcast it so extensively that Larsen pressed for a full-fledged network program. As originally planned, *The March of Time* was to run only six months. Successively sponsored by Time Inc., Columbia Broadcasting System, and various advertisers, it ran fifteen years. While it netted no substantial profits, it made millions aware of *Time the Weekly Newsmagazine*. No one who heard it was ever likely to forget the portentous voice of announcer Westbrook Van Voorhis as he intoned, "Time marches on!"

Under Larsen's supervision a series of *March of Time* movies, produced by Louis de Rochemont, began in 1935, and the next year won an Oscar for revolutionizing newsreels. It rejoiced Larsen's heart that theater owners were willing to pay money to show films promoting *Time*. De Rochemont produced 257 MOT's all together, among them *Huey Long, Men of the FBI, Child Labor, The Lunatic Fringe*. His adventures getting footage were sometimes as dramatic as the finished product. His camera crew infiltrated Father Divine's "Heavens," the German-American Bund, Gerald L. K. Smith's Fascist rallies.

One day in 1939 Ulrich von Gienanth, the first secretary of the German Embassy in Washington, called on de Rochemont with some stunning reels the Nazis had shot of the Polish blitz. *The March of Time* could use them exclusively, he said, providing his government controlled the narration. Without committing himself, de Rochemont asked to view them. On the way to the projection room, he whispered instructions to the operator. Accordingly, as each reel ended, it was rushed to the lab and duplicated. Then, handing back the originals to von Gienanth, de Rochemont told him he could not accept his conditions.

To use the duplicates would have violated international copyright law. De Rochemont consulted a friend in the Department of Justice, who showed him how the law could be circumvented. England was at war with Germany. Following the Justice man's instructions, an MOT employee left by train for Canada, taking along the reels. De Rochemont phoned Canadian customs. In Drawing Room A of *The Montrealer*, he notified them, they would find a passenger transporting German property. Perhaps Canada's Alien Property Custodian would wish to seize it. He did indeed. De Rochemont had learned that a bill of sale issued by a sovereign government confers clear title even to stolen goods. The Alien Property Custodian let him have the duplicates back for one dollar. They formed the climax of MOT's *Inside Nazi Germany*.

De Rochemont could not forgo the pleasure of inviting von Gienanth to a private preview. The German turned pale. "If Hitler sees this, I am a ruined man," he said. "De Rochemont, you will pay for this."

"Glorious, exciting days," de Rochemont recalled years later when he was making full-length features on his own. The MOT series ended in 1953, killed by competition from a plethora of documentaries and television.

The financial coups that Stillman brought off for Time

Inc. had an epical sweep. At first blush his manner and appearance belied it. A short, slight man, sparing of speech and powder-dry, clenching a cigarette tightly between his teeth, he would, in conversation, lapse into reflective pauses so prolonged and stony that people sometimes got the impression that he was no longer thinking of the subject at hand. But if they waited patiently, the sequel would come as precise and on target as a perfect pistol shot. According to a corporation legend, Stillman solved the problem of finding a taxi during rush hours by buying one, driver and all. What actually happened was that a loquacious taxi man, conveying him to work one morning, mentioned how he longed to drive his own taxi if only he could borrow the price of the required medallion, then sixty-five hundred dollars. Stillman offered to endorse a bank loan. In return the taxi was supposed to wait for him before the Time & Life Building at the end of every working day. Such an accommodation proved impossible in New York traffic. The driver did, however, repay the loan.

Stillman called his Fairfield, Connecticut, home "Baldwin Lodge," a memorial to the killing he made for his own account in Baldwin Locomotive stock. Perhaps his greatest exploit for Time Inc. was a sequence of complex maneuvers in Texas. What initiated it was the launching, in 1936, of *Life,* for which the corporation urgently needed new sources of quality paper. The advent of newsprint production in the South and, secondarily, the comparative cheapness of southern pine, set Stillman to wondering whether quality paper could not also be produced there. He decided it could. The Champion Paper & Fiber Co.

operated a pulp mill near Houston, but had no paper mill. So at Stillman's prompting Time Inc. helped it build one by buying one million dollars' worth of its preferred stock. The mill was designed specifically to supply *Life*.

The gas contractor who furnished the mill's fuel was a subsidiary of the Houston Oil Co. That connection led Stillman to investigate the parent company's assets. It owned, he discovered, all the timber rights and half the mineral rights to 660,000 acres in east Texas. The timber was what chiefly interested Stillman as insurance against future pulp and paper needs. Time Inc. began buying Houston Oil shares, eventually accumulating almost 10 per cent of the company. To do so, it sold its Champion stock. "We didn't profess to go into oil," Stillman said later, "but we found ourselves involved nevertheless." It proved to be a happy involvement. For many years the company had been only a moderately successful independent producer of oil, though it owned an important Texas pipeline system. Drilling on the outskirts of the fabulous Katy gas field, however, leased from the Humble Oil Co., it made some rich strikes. The field was extended, with the result that Houston Oil obtained a 6 per cent interest in the entire field, thereby greatly increasing its reserves. Not long after, the president of Houston Oil, George W. Hill, died, and the new management decided to build a pulp and paper mill, an enterprise Hill had always opposed. To protect its position, Time Inc. became an equal partner with Houston Oil in forming the East Texas Pulp & Paper Co. Operations began in 1954. Two years later, in response to competitive bidding, Houston Oil sold its assets. Time Inc. acquired the entire mill (later renamed Eastex) as well as the timberlands. The transaction further yielded Time Inc. a net capital gain after taxes of fifteen million dollars.

Under Stillman's guidance the corporation had also bought three other paper mills, expanded their production capacity, sold them for a stock interest in the St. Regis Paper Co., sold that at a thumping profit, synthesized the newest printing, ink-drying, and color-processing techniques for the production of its magazines, amassed vast real-estate holdings, radio and television stations. Stillman's triumphs moved one of his associates to remark, "If we'd just quit publishing magazines and let Charlie invest all the capital, we'd make really big money."

✨ *nine* ✨

In its issue of August, 1930, Condé Nast's modish monthly magazine *Vanity Fair* nominated Luce for its "Hall of Fame." The assistant managing editor who wrote the encomium accompanying his photograph was a brainy, ambitious, blue-eyed, blond beauty of twenty-seven named Clare Boothe Brokaw. A French admirer once said of her, "It is a beautiful façade, well constructed but without central heating." Cecil Beaton, the fashion photographer, found her "drenchingly beautiful."

From modest origins as the daughter of a vaudeville fiddler and an ex-chorine she had risen to become the bride of George Tuttle Brokaw, one of the richest bachelors in the New York Social Register. He was twenty-three years older and an alcoholic. The marriage lasted six years. Mrs. Brokaw won custody of their daughter, Anne Clare, and a settlement of $425,000. No woman to languish in uncreative idleness, she turned to journalism.

Her Hall of Fame caption nominated Luce because he ". . . originated the News-magazine idea; because at the age of thirty-two he is the successful editor and publisher of *Time* and *Fortune*; because he was born in China; because he was once a humble newspaper reporter on the Chicago *Daily News*; and lastly because he claims he has no other interests outside of his work, and this work fills his waking hours."

As she wrote, she thought what a dull fellow this Luce must be. She met him three years later at a dinner given by Thayer Hobson, a Yale man, and his wife Laura (who later wrote promotional copy for the Luce publications as well as the best-selling novel *Gentlemen's Agreement*). By then Mrs. Brokaw was herself a minor celebrity, having advanced to the managing editorship of *Vanity Fair*, established rapport with eminent figures in the arts and politics, and campaigned for Franklin Roosevelt's first election. ("I was the kitchen maid of the New Deal cabinet," she recalled with pride even long after she had veered to the far right.) Luce, however, appeared monumentally unimpressed. Like many people meeting him for the first time, she found him not only dull, but boorish. Early in the evening he whipped out a pocket watch, a habit of his that frequently chilled social gatherings, mumbled, "Well, got to go," and went.

Their next encounter, in the home of Countess Rosie von Waldeck, an ornament of international society, left Mrs. Brokaw breathless with indignation.

"Why don't you start a picture magazine?" she suggested.

The suggestion was hardly original—innumerable publishers, including Luce, had been considering it—and he brusquely told her so. "Problem is how to do it," he said. "For instance, the Mikado's death, how would you handle it?"

"With pictures, of course, but I wouldn't rely on the picture agencies alone. I'd have photographers under contract whom I could send anywhere in the world."

"That's not very original either."

As she opened her mouth to retaliate, out came his watch and he was gone. Smoldering, she swore revenge.

An opportunity came the following year. The scene was the Starlight Roof of the Waldorf-Astoria; the occasion, a ball staged by that incessant international hostess, Elsa Maxwell. Mrs. Brokaw, luminous as a star herself, glimpsed Luce crossing the ballroom with two *coupes* of champagne. Intercepting him, she archly asked, "Could one of those be for me by any chance, Mr. Luce?" He was, as it happened, carrying them to his wife's table. But the lights dimmed for the floor show, and he had no choice but to sit where he was.

It had been the lady's intent to belittle whatever he said, then drop him cold. Luce, however, could be powerfully stimulating, not so much by any conversational brilliance, but by his flair for drawing out others, and in spite of herself she lingered, talking earnestly through the entire floor show.

As the band struck up again, Luce, who couldn't dance a step, proposed a walk around the lobby. It was about three A.M. when, without preamble, he hurled the question at her, "How's it feel to know you're the only woman in a man's life?"

"Whose life?" she asked, stunned.

"Mine."

He asked where she lived and she told him the Sherry-Netherland Hotel. Could he drop by some afternoon? She agreed somewhat uneasily.

"Next Thursday, five-thirty," said Luce.

She started to demur, but, glancing at his watch, he cut her off in mid-sentence with a curt good night.

A more urbane suitor, and a less self-confident one, might have phoned in advance. But Mrs. Brokaw heard not a word. She was inclined to phone him and forestall the threatened visit. Better still, she would simply not be there. Curiosity prevailed, however, and she was on hand when he showed up punctually. With scant effort to ingratiate himself, he announced that he intended to marry her.

As he pressed his suit during the next week, romantic feelings began to stir in the assistant managing editor's breast. She fled to Havana to weigh the prospect in solitude. He followed her there. Still dubious, she insisted they separate for six months before she gave an answer, and she went abroad. Luce did not await her return, to ask his wife to divorce him. The settlement included a big block of Time Inc. stock.

For all his decisiveness Luce's Calvinist conscience troubled him. Divorce was unheard-of in his family. Since boyhood he had held idealistic views of marriage. It was one of the few times in his life that passion ruled him and he never entirely shook his sense of guilt.

Although *Time* did not mention the divorce, which became final in October, 1935, it reported a month later in its Milestones section, "Married. Henry R. Luce, editor and publisher of TIME, the MARCH OF TIME, FORTUNE, the ARCHITECTURAL FORUM, LETTERS: and Clare Boothe Brokaw, 32, playwright (see p. 68), one-time managing editor of *Vanity Fair;* at Old Greenwich, Conn."

The page number referred to *Time*'s review of a melodrama Mrs. Luce had written, her first invasion of Broadway, entitled *Abide with Me*. A cliché-strewn pastiche about an alcoholic sadist, it opened two days before the nuptials and closed twenty-eight days after. The critics not only demolished it, but the *Herald Tribune*'s Richard Watts ridiculed the author for taking unwarranted curtain calls. To the *Time* critic fell the prickly task of combining tact with truth. After half a dozen agonizing attempts, he appealed to Luce, who sent for his bride. Gallantly, she dashed off a review herself, describing her brainchild as "stinking" and "lousy." "No play is that bad," said the adoring husband. Between the three of them they finally composed a bland mixture of censure and faint praise.

Theatrical disaster was not the only cloud on Clare Luce's horizon during the early months of the marriage. The advent of *Life* magazine in 1936 produced another. She had reason to hope for a dominant voice in its affairs. She had, after all, been advocating pictorial journalism ever since she met Luce, and he had told her, "I don't really want more magazines, but if it pleases you, we'll go ahead." On their yachting honeymoon through the

Caribbean they had taken along for study sheaves of pictures clipped from European publications. It gratified Mrs. Luce to remind her husband of a memorandum she had addressed to Condé Nast three years earlier:

"There is a rumour that LIFE [the famous, but declining old humorous weekly] is now for sale. I do not know what the figure is, but I presume that it is fairly cheap, as LIFE has been slowly dying for some years.

"Of course, I know that it is probably a presumptuous suggestion on my part, and, in these depressed times, it is apt to seem an absurd one, but if the Condé Nast Publications were to consider buying LIFE, I can suggest a new editorial formula for it which I dare to believe would make the magazine a success.

"I should like to pattern an American magazine—and one bearing the title LIFE is admirably adapted to its contents—after the Parisian *Vu*. It would be a weekly, and would contain some of the editorial elements of *Time*, *Fortune*, and even *Vanity Fair*, plus its own special angle, which would be reporting, not *all* the news nor, necessarily the most *important* news, but the most interesting and exciting news, in photographs, and interpreting it editorially through accompanying articles by capable writers and journalists. . . .

"The editorial point of view should be light but not frivolous, satirical but not bitter. It should, in other words, treat sober facts soberly and absurd ones in a humorous manner. This would, of course, distinguish it from any comparison with Sunday magazine sections (which treat everything drearily) and bring it more into the field of *Time*.

"I can think of several departments which might become well known in the manner of Hall of Fame, Oblivion, etc. I also think *Vu*'s editorial policy of devoting almost an entire issue to one prominent event which is temporarily absorbing the public, is a very clever one. I should like to go into this theory of editing, sometime, at greater length.

"I really believe that a magazine of this type would have a universal appeal. It would interest Myron Taylor as much as Cobina May Wright; and Theodore Dreiser as much as the reader of the *Daily Mirror*. Of course, all this is without any practical consideration of the difficulty involved in starting a new publication, securing advertisements, etc., etc. It is merely a thought, and idea, which might in other times be feasible."

At that time the old magazine could have been bought for twenty thousand dollars. To acquire the rights to the name, Luce paid eighty-five thousand dollars.

The boss's wife as a boss was not a prospect that enchanted the Time Inc. hierarchy. How they felt about her she learned one evening months before *Life* first went to press. After dinner in the Luces' Manhattan apartment Ralph Ingersoll complained to her, "Harry used to work until midnight. Now he goes home at five. He can't edit with one hand tied behind your back."

Her eyes flashed fire. "He can edit a better magazine than you with both hands and legs tied." She darted into her bedroom and wept. When her tears dried, she told Luce she would never take part in any of his publications, and except for contributing occasional articles, notably as a *Life* war correspondent, she never did.

Her energies, however, found no dearth of outlets. Following her renunciation of Time Inc., she dashed off another play, *The Women*, in three days. Despite poor reviews, it achieved world-wide success and enriched her by some $200,000. Her next two plays, *Kiss the Boys Goodbye* and *Margin for Error*, likewise failed to captivate the critics and likewise were hits. In addition she wrote movie scripts, books, syndicated columns.

Physically as well as intellectually venturesome, she piloted planes; rode to hounds; hunted; skin-dived; dabbled in acting, painting, and sculpture; explored psychoanalysis, mysticism, and hallucinogenic drugs. The last experience Luce shared with her in a spirit of scientific inquiry. Gerald Heard, the English-born California mystic, who had sampled various drugs, as he said, "to investigate the possibility of a better order in one's living," and Dr. Sidney Cohen, perhaps the country's leading authority on the subject, interested them in LSD while guests at their Phoenix house. The Luces took their first "trip" under Cohen's guidance, found it rewarding, and repeated the adventure half a dozen times through the years. Mrs. Luce, who was painting at the time of her first trip, reported a heightened appreciation of color values. Luce, who was tone deaf, said he heard marvelous music and, wandering out into the cactus garden, he conducted an imaginary orchestra.*

*During the many talks I had with him he showed anger only once. That was when I told him I had written an article about LSD, though I never took any. "How dare you write about it without trying it!" he stormed at me. I replied that I had also written articles about narcotics without feeling any obligation to take heroin, an argument he contemptuously dismissed.

~ *ten* ~

The stupendous success of *Life*, whose first issue was dated November 23, 1936, transformed the corporation, in Luce's words, "from a big little business to a little big business." But recalling the gloomy portents, he marveled that he could have run the risk, for he had nothing to guide him except a hunch that the enterprise would somehow succeed. Secondarily, he knew picture magazines were bound to come and he wished to be the first to publish them. "It was a very improper publishing decision," he said. None of the prospective budgets indicated how such a magazine, which, as Larsen and the other top executives concurred, had to be printed on quality paper, yet sell for no more than ten cents, could turn a profit. Hardly anybody imagined a colossal circulation. The most optimistic estimates did not exceed a million and advertising rates were based on a quarter of that. When Luce's experimental department finally arrived at a formula for pictorial journalism that satisfied him, he announced, "We have earmarked a million dollars to see *Life* to success or an honorable grave." The figure proved to be five million too little.

A tentative prospectus drafted by C. D. Jackson promised that it would show readers the man-of-the-week, "his body clothed and, if possible, nude," reveal "the loves, scandals, and personal affairs of the plain and fancy citizen." This gave an approximate foretaste of the *sauce piquante* with which *Life* would vary its heavier fare. Early issues featured bathing beauties, Gypsy Rose Lee, glimpses of the Duke of Windsor's private life, a pictorial guide on "How to Undress before Your Husband," a midget twenty-two inches high, pictured full-size for no other reason than that he exactly fitted into a double-page spread. When a *Life* editor heard that the wife of a Washington dignitary and an Assistant Secretary of State Adolf Berle thought him such a wit she had two tubs installed in their bathroom so they could converse while bathing, he wired the Washington bureau to get a picture. His instructions ended: "Rear view will do." The bureau chief, Felix Belair, Jr., disgusted by the tasteless request, protested to Luce, "We shouldn't have to put up with this. Only some silly kid would send such a wire to the nation's capital." Luce solemnly explained, "What prompts this kind of request is that if they could get only thirty per cent of the impossible, what a thing it would be."

The Jackson prospectus failed to convey the high purpose that exemplified Luce's missionary aspirations and he wrote the final version himself:

"To see life; to see the world, to eyewitness great events; to watch the faces of the poor and the gestures of the proud; to see strange things—machines, armies, multitudes, shadows in the jungle and on the moon; to see man's work—his paintings, towers and discoveries, to see things thousands of miles away, things hidden behind walls and within rooms, things dangerous to come to; the women that men love and many children; to see and to take pleasure in seeing; to see and be amazed; to see and be instructed.

"Thus to see, and to be shown, is now the will and new expectancy of half mankind.

"To see, and to show, is the mission now undertaken by LIFE."

The first run was 466,000 copies. Instant popularity nearly killed the magazine. Within a year circulation shot past a million. But because advertising rates had been set on the basis of 250,000 the advertisers got a free ride. Every page they had bought meant a loss to *Life*. In April, 1937, at a convention of the American Association of Advertising Agencies, in White Sulphur Springs, West Virginia, Luce issued an extraordinary appeal:

"I stand before you not for any of the reasons which customarily cause a speaker to face an audience. I am here because you are the only court in the land to whom I am accountable for the sum total of my acts as an editor and a publisher.

"There are other courts and law-enforcement agencies standing guard over my behavior both as an individual and as the head of a profit-seeking corporation. But as an editor and publisher, as the senior partner of a group of editors and publishers, I operate in a world so free that its only explicit law is that there shall be no law. Ours is the only business in America whose behavior the Senate of the United States would not yet dare to investigate. This is the great freedom which remains. This is the freedom of the press.

"But irresponsible as it may be in law, and objectionable as it may be, this lawless Fourth Estate is still not mere anarchy. Then what unwritten laws does it obey? The answer presumably is that the press obeys but one law, the law of nineteenth century democratic laissez-faire economic determinism,—or, more simply that the Press shall give the public what the public wants. . . .

"The first and principal danger of the Press-which-gives-the-people-what-they-want is the obvious danger that there is no significant restraint on vulgarity, sensationalism and even incitement to criminality. The second danger, which is more characteristic and perhaps even more insidiously deleterious to public taste and morals is the fact that there is in this situation an enormous financial incentive to publish twaddle—yards and yards of mediocrity, acres of bad fiction and triviality, square miles of journalistic tripe. . . .

"But there is another and a greater danger: the danger that such a press will not give the people what they must have—what they will perish without. . . .

"The reason why the modern dictatorships are unspeakable is that they corrupt the mind from within. They suppress the truth. They lead men by lies and fraud to desire and acquiesce in their own enslavement. And how is this corruption brought about? *By the destruction of journalism.* In more than half of Europe, journalism has been destroyed; in the other half it is mostly venal or emasculated. Here in America the press is free—economically free to engage all the talent in the world, free to commit moral and intellectual suicide, free to pander to the people and by pandering to seduce them into their own enslavement.

"This is the true poison of our time. And its only antidote is truth. And not only truth in a laboratory, but truth in the ears of our people. Unless the facts, the significant facts, the difficult, complicated facts of industry and finance and politics are put before the people, the people cannot govern themselves in an industrial society. And if they cannot govern themselves, the inevitable consequence will be dictatorship and slavery.

"In so far as the Press-that-gives-the-people-what-they-want is a press which does not give the people their political daily bread—their essential and necessary information—it is an unsuccessful press.

"And you and I must share the responsibility. . . .

"Should we publish LIFE? And this is not a question only for my partners to decide. We have decided. . . . But it is also for you to decide. It is a question for each and every one of you to decide in your heart and in your mind because each of you is deciding it in the pocketbook of your client. I said that I stand before you as before a court. Your court is also the Appropriations Committee of the American Press: you are the Commissars, you exist as an alternative to the People's Commissariat of Public

Enlightment. Here today I make application not for a few incidental pennies; I ask that you shall appropriate over the next ten critical years no less than one hundred million dollars for the publication of a magazine called LIFE. You cannot escape a reply to this question. We will not let you. We will keep hammering persistently on your doors, asking for the money week after week. You will either give it to us, or you will not. If you do, there will be LIFE. If you do not, there will be no LIFE."

There was *Life*. With a circulation guarantee of 1,600,-000, the magazine raised its rates fourfold the following year to $5700 per black and white page. Many advertisers balked. Also, a severe recession beset American business. *Life* lost millions more. But by 1939, having reached a circulation above two million, it turned the corner. From then on it raced ahead, eventually outdistancing the whole field of American magazines in both circulation and advertising. In 1948, 19 per cent of every magazine advertising dollar spent in the country went to *Life*, while its readership was 21 per cent of the entire population over ten years old.

❧ *eleven* ❧

The craft of pictorial journalism didn't come as naturally to Luce as that of text editing, especially after the mid-forties when the operation became so technically complicated. He still occasionally presided over the closing of a *Life* issue, however, to the distraction of the staff. As they milled about him, paced, stared out windows, he would sit at a picture-laden table in a lithic attitude of cerebration compared to which Rodin's Thinker seemed flighty. Tearing layouts apart, calling for an ever wider choice of pictures, he would prolong the closing long past the normal hour. When hunger intruded, he would mutter what sounded like "bmewich," meaning, "Bring me a sandwich." Nobody bothered to ask what kind, a matter of total indifference to Luce. He once silenced an editor, who reminded him, as the hour got later and later, of the mounting overtime cost, "I'll take that responsibility." But when the issue finally went to press, the picture spreads showed no marked improvement over what John Shaw Billings, the managing editor, had planned to begin with.

Luce's greatest value to *Life* was of a different order. Nobody who ever worked for him equaled his ability to churn out fresh ideas, one right after the other, not only for *Life* but *Time, Fortune,* and the rest. When his age and the increasing complexities of the organization forced him into a less active role, the magazines were still run effectively by delegates who knew how to promote and sell. Ideas didn't have to be smashing, merely adequate, for the machinery to put them over. But the Lucean touch was missing. With his missionary drive to extend the reader's intellectual and spiritual horizons, he set the tone for, though he did not necessarily originate, such series in sumptuous color photography and glittering text as The Epic of Man, The Human Body, The Miracle of Greece, The World We Live In, American Arts and Skills. Let sophisticates scoff at the lurid, de Millesque depictions of prehistoric man or the science fiction-like freaks personifying bodily functions. Luce never shrank from showmanship to lure people into the lecture hall. The cultural ripples spread wider and wider as the Time-Life Books division added new titles to its World Library, Nature Library, Science Library, and History of the United States, and the Time Reading Program reprinted serious literature in paperbacks.

Luce provided a forum for thinkers of the caliber of Arnold Toynbee, Jacques Barzun, Julian Huxley. He knew personally many of the world's leading religious scholars (one of his rare few intimate friends was the brilliant Jesuit, Father John Courtney Murray), and his readers got liberal helpings of theology. *Time*'s religion section dated from its first issue. In the early days Luce himself would write it at home on Sundays. *Time* and *Life* introduced the theories of Reinhold Niebuhr of Union Theological Seminary, Paul Tillich of Harvard Divinity School, Father Pierre Teilhard de Chardin, among others, to the largest audiences ever made available to them. Though he always took pride in having recognized such luminaries as intellectually newsworthy, he eventually grew disenchanted with some of them. He found Tillich's views too full of ambiguities. Of Toynbee he complained in 1957, "They're saying [he] has done some very great work, but his conclusions aren't necessarily correct. . . . I think poorly of his current output . . . in his Rise and Fall of Civilizations, he speaks of America . . . as a peripheral civilization. I believe it's rather more than that. I have tried to suggest that a new civilization has been developing here—and don't forget this was seven or eight years ago, under the long reign of the Democrats—a new civilization, hardly a peripheral one."

Of Niebuhr, once in the front rank of Luce's intellectual heroes: "He has had a tremendous influence on all of Protestantism. As a layman I'm indebted to him. Our magazines did the job of presenting him to the American people. But now I venture to question, if not to disagree with him . . . I disagree with the role he gives to America in his philosophy of history. He doesn't assign America an important enough role in the scheme of things. . . .

". . . if you want to do good, you have to have confidence in what you're doing. No matter what you do, Niebuhr says, it's sinful. His Christian pessimism leads to futility, to what's the sense of doing anything? And, of course, there's the big paradox of Niebuhr: he's a hell of an activist himself. . . . I simply feel that man is an affirmative creature and Niebuhr's focus on sinfulness keeps anything from getting done."

Niebuhr returned the compliment, "It would be impossible to analyze Luce's theology. He has very vague ideas about it that I'm not sure he understands. But politically he seems to be a combination of American liberal Protestantism with American Republicanism—the latter more so as he has gotten wealthier and wealthier."

Niebuhr also disclosed, "I once got a note from a *Time* editor saying, 'Could you please do something to keep our boss from getting more pious and conservative?' "

It pained and puzzled Luce that his magazines met frequent rebuff where he most wanted them to be taken seriously—in the intellectual community. He was stunned to discover during a luncheon he gave in London for a group of Oxford dons that few of them ever read *Time* or *Life* and the exceptions only leafed through them for amusement. The caustic ex-*Fortune* editor, Dwight Macdonald, relegated *Life* to what he termed "Masscult, a parody of High Culture. . . ." The literary critic, Edmund Wilson, pronounced one of the severest judgments in 1943:

". . . The kind of reports that you find in *Time*, factual, lucid and terse, give you something that you cannot get from the newspapers or the liberal weeklies; and they compensate by compactness and relative perspective for the shredding and dilution of the radio. But the competence of presentation tends to mask the ineptitude and the cynicism of the mentality behind the report; and the effect on the public consciousness may be almost as demoralizing in its more non-committal way as the tirades of the old Yellow Press. For you cannot have a presentation of facts without implying also an attitude; and the attitude of the Luce publications has been infectious though it is mainly negative. The occasional statements of policy signed by Mr. Luce and others which appear in these magazines are on the level of Sixth Form orations or themes: they confirm the impression one gets from the rest of a complete absence of serious interpretation on the part of the editorial director; and the various points of view of the men who put *Time* together, appear to have been mashed down and to figure in what they print only as blurred streaks of coloration that blot the machine-finished surface. Their picture of the world gives us sometimes simply the effect of schoolboy mentalities in a position to avail themselves of a gigantic research equipment; but it is almost always tinged with a peculiar kind of jeering rancor. There is a tendency to exhibit the persons whose activities are chronicled, not as more or less able or noble or amusing or intelligent human beings, who have various ways of being right or wrong, but—because they are presented by writers who are allowed no points of view themselves—as manikins, sometimes cocky, sometimes busy, sometimes zealous, sometimes silly, sometimes gruesome, but in most cases quite infra-human, who make speeches before guinea-pig parliaments, issue commands and move armies of beetles back and forth on bas-relief battle-maps, indulge themselves maniacally in queer little games of sport, science, art, beer-bottle-top collecting or what-not, squeak absurd little boasts and complaints, and pop up their absurd little faces in front of the lenses of Luce photographers, and add up to a general impression that the pursuits, past and present, of the human race are rather an absurd little scandal about which you might find out some even nastier details if you met the editors of *Time* over cocktails. This habit of mind must have been prompted in the beginning by a natural reaction from the habit of the period just before, when Charley Schwab, Charley Mitchell and Herbert Hoover had all been celebrated as great public figures; but it turned into purely gratuitous caricature—that is, caricature without a purpose. The journalism of the age of Voltaire was a journalism which aims merely at facts, with no political or moral intent, ends by dispensing with even the conviction that the human race ought to go on, and so cannot help making it hateful. Who would drive a plane or man a ship or write a sentence or perform an experiment, or even build a factory or organize a business, to perpetuate the race shown in *Time?* It is part of an educated man—and the employes of Henry Luce are far from the old-fashioned, illiterate reporters—to try to give life some value and point; but these papers which were started on the assumption, to quote an early statement of Luce's, 'that most people are not well-informed, and that something ought to be done,' have ended by having nothing to tell them that appears to be worth the telling. . . ."

Thomas S. Matthews, another defector from the Luce

ranks, after long service as *Time*'s managing editor, wrote in his bitter memoirs, *Name and Address:*

"In moods of depression I thought of most *Time* writers as Yahoos, or of myself as the aged Ulysses condemned to rockbound Ithaca, where I must 'mete and dole unequal laws unto a savage race'—or as a governess who has taken on the hopeless task of improving the guttersnipe accent and incorrigible rudeness of a spoiled, rich, foul-mouthed brat. One change in *Time* I was determined to make, and it is sufficient evidence of my general failure that I couldn't or didn't make it: to root out *Time*'s notorious technique of innuendo—often ineptly and even clumsily done, but poisonously intended:

> *'Damn with faint praise, assent with civil leer,*
> *And without sneering, teach the rest to sneer;*
> *Willing to wound, and yet afraid to strike,*
> *Just hint a fault, and hesitate dislike . . .'"*

Pope's lines are too good for *Time*, but they apply. "And how can I exonerate myself from membership in this son-of-bitch club? I can't; in fact for six years I was the chairman and must take the responsibility (under Jove) for everything that appeared in *Time* in those six years. That record is incontrovertible and perhaps damning. The only scrap of indirect testimony I can cite in my own defense is a scene in my office, when one of my infuriated lieutenants shouted at me: 'The trouble with *Time* is, it's too f—— fair, and you're the one who does it!' Being angry, he exaggerated, of course; *Time* was no more f—— fair in those days than it is now."

(But as a colleague of Matthews remarked, "If he was a vegetarian, what was he doing working for Swift & Co.?")

In a *Time*-financed survey of eight hundred scientists the majority voted the magazine their favorite. A sociology instructor at the University of Maryland, however, polled seven hundred members of the Federation of American Scientists as to which publications' editorial policies they found congenial. None mentioned any Luce publication.

What Luce regarded as his most important statement on foreign affairs, a 1941 *Life* editorial in which he proclaimed that "the 20th Century must be to a significant degree the American Century," *The Nation*'s editor, Freda Kirchwey, called "pompous poppycock." ". . . his whole cult of American superiority is no whit less revolting and no less unjustified than the Nordic myth that provides moral sanctions for Hitler's brutal aggression . . . I maintain that such talk is both nonsensical and against the interests of the nations arrayed against Hitler. The unconcealed contempt for Europe which pervades Mr. Luce's article is not only ignorant and crude; it is exactly the attitude best calculated to create resentment among anti-Axis elements here and in the conquered countries across the Atlantic."

～ *twelve* ～

Hitler invaded Poland on September 1, 1939. In its next issue *Time* introduced a new section headed "World War" with the words, "World War II began last week"—a reality not many Americans were ready to accept. The new section, which it retained for the duration, carried some of the best combat reporting any journal ever printed.

Within six months Mrs. Luce was roving Europe as a correspondent accredited to *Life*, a venture she later recounted in a book, *Europe in the Spring*, dedicated to "H.R.L. who understood why I wanted to go." As the Germans overran Denmark and Norway, she cabled Luce, THE CURTAIN IS GOING UP, and urged him to join her in Paris. On May 10, after high-level talks in London and The Hague, they arrived together in Brussels as guests of

American Ambassador John Cudahy. Though the Germans had swept through Luxembourg and were approaching the Dutch frontier, Cudahy assured them before they retired for the night, "The scare is over."

At 5 A.M. an embassy maid shook Luce awake, shrieking, "*Les Allemands reviennent!*" He roused his wife. "The show's started," he said. "Get up." The dawn sky was cloudless and rosy. As he contemplated it through the bedroom windows, the first bombs hit the park opposite, hurling him backward. Mrs. Luce calmed the embassy servants by setting them to making coffee and scrambled eggs. Next day, in a car Luce managed to pry out of the American Express, the couple started for Paris. There was no time to gather together all their belongings, among them the books Luce had been traveling with. At the last moment he shoved one volume into his pocket. It was a translation of the *Odyssey*. Leaving Mrs. Luce to continue her reporting, he sailed back to New York, afire to alert his countrymen to the peril threatening the entire world.

Every morning after the British disaster at Dunkirk, while he was shaving, he would count the days to the September equinox, hopeful that if England could hold out under the German air raids until then, the weather would save her. In a radio appeal he proclaimed, ". . . we know we all have to prepare to fight . . . the problem which is troubling most of us is how to help the Allies right now in their back-to-the-wall struggle against Nazi conquest. . . . Suppose Hitler wins—this summer. . . . If we deal with the Third Reich on the basis of *appeasement* of any kind, it will follow as sure as night follows day that we will pay for it in blood and tears—in the bloody end of *our* democracy. We must deal with Hitler as an enemy—an enemy of Peace, our peace. . . . Now, secondly, suppose Hitler is not able to bring Great Britain and France to their knees—to his knees—this summer. Then the Allies are likely to win. But how soon they will win and how great their chances are of averting worldwide chaos—that will depend on how much help we can give and how soon we can give it. . . . But what about now,—what about now, this tragic desperate moment? There *is* something we can do immediately and do it better than ever again. We can stand up and speak our mind. We can strip off our false cloak of neutrality and announce to the world—to the brown men and the black men and the yellow men and to all the white men of the world—that we stand now and so long as any of us shall live continue to stand for democracy, for international law, for the sanctity of treaties, for freedom, for the individual rights of man, for the faith of our fathers. We can make it plain that therefore we as a nation, one and indissoluble, deeply wish that Hitler's attack may be beaten off, that we as a nation will continue to refuse to recognize the Nazi domination of free peoples, that we as a nation will continue to oppose, by whatever means seems to us best, the consequences of Nazi victory. . . ."

In a memorandum to *Time* editors he wrote, "First, as to the Road to War, the New Republic says: 'if we go to war it will be because a large number of good Americans want intensely to do so.' This was equally true in 1917. And recognition of this simple truth about cause and effect will sweep away at least a lot of the 'intellectual nonsense' which has been fashionable about how we got hornswoggled into the last war and consequently are likely to get hornswoggled into this one.

"But, secondly, what will make good Americans want to get into this war? Feelings of Right & Wrong, says the New Republic—and I agree and the same was true in 1917.

"And thirdly, what creates these intense feelings about Right & Wrong? What creates them are the facts as understood by people whom the New Republic in all sincerity calls the best people.

"Here is where we come in. Whether or not we are 'the best people' in the New Republic's opinion, which would be highly improbable, it is our function to present the facts. Now, what we must *not* do is to try to cook the facts so that they come out even or anywhere near even as to their moral implications as to the participants in this war. In my personal opinion the case is already closed. In my personal opinion the facts overwhelmingly convict Germany & Russia in their eyes. And if the facts will not so neatly absolve the Allies, neither will they absolve the United States. I am not so concerned that we should belabor the moral that arises from the facts. But I am deeply concerned that we should not draw any veil of darkness or confusion between the facts and the moral deductions from the facts.

"Fourth, granted that Germany & Russia are overwhelmingly convicted, does it follow that we should fight? There is, in my opinion, no one easy simple answer to this question. There are many answers to it. In its brief essay, the New Republic gives only one answer. Although it says its answer is based on the clear logic of experience, the New Republic's answer is actually an answer derived from age-old philosophical speculations on the Problem of Evil.

"There is, I am sure, a perfectly respectable philosophical answer to the New Republic's respectable philosophical answer. The New Republic, for example, has on other occasions not hesitated to 'fight' and to urge others to 'fight' the 'forces of evil' in the United States—and perhaps even in Spain.

"I am not one to deride philosophy. But it seems to me that those of us who are neither full-time philosophers nor full-time saints had best acknowledge that we are doomed to fight in one way or another and then concentrate on choosing the best battlefield for the least bad kind of a fight and for the best kind of a victory we can imagine."

He supported a plan, conceived by a group of interventionists, to aid Britain and he got word of it to President Roosevelt. The upshot was an invitation to both Luces to spend a night in the White House. After dinner, at which the only other guests were the President's secretary, "Missy" Le Hand, and his inseparable crony, Harry Hopkins, Roosevelt spun his wheelchair toward his study, motioning Luce to follow. The night was sweltering and Roosevelt shucked his jacket, showing, underneath his silk shirt, his powerful arms and chest. "A strong, tough guy," Luce would remember. He outlined his plan: to help defend British ships against the wolf packs of Nazi submarines that were stalking them, the U. S. should give England a fleet of overage destroyers. Roosevelt desired nothing so much as Hitler's defeat, but his initial reaction was that the American people would not tolerate such an involvement. In Luce's later hostility to Roosevelt he delivered a judgment with which few historians would agree: "The world credited him for saving it, but he hesitated to take any step until the people had moved ahead of him. He was overcautious, political. When his famous quarantine speech of 1937 against aggressors failed to catch on, he did nothing for two years. After Munich, when the question of defense expenditure arose, he was expected to ask Congress for a billion dollars more. He asked for only half that. At no point did he take the lead. I think he was isolationist." (Mrs. Luce once expressed her view of the President to Randolph Churchill. "All famous men have their characteristic gesture," she said. "Churchill has his V sign, Hitler his upraised arm, and Roosevelt . . . ?" She wet her index finger and held it up the wind.)

Luce pleaded that the American people would condone a gift of destroyers to England, once they understood the peril of Nazism. Let Luce, then, Roosevelt suggested, try to sway public opinion. *Time* and *Life* proceeded to do so, other publications followed suit, and in the fall Roosevelt delivered to Churchill fifty overage destroyers in exchange for U. S. bases on British possessions in the Western Hemisphere. "He delayed three months at that," Luce noted in retrospect.

During the Roosevelt-Willkie campaign of 1940, when Luce backed the Republican candidate, the President publicly accused *him* of isolationism. The crowning blow that forever after caused Luce to bridle when anybody mentioned Roosevelt came in 1943. Luce proposed to tour the

Pacific theater of war. He applied to Secretary of War Henry L. Stimson. Stimson referred him to General MacArthur's chief of staff, who granted the request. General Marshall then sent for Luce to tell him how heartily he approved his mission, and would he inspect the small islands where few troops were stationed and report back personally to him? Three days later, as Luce was eagerly preparing to leave, the assistant secretary of war, John J. McCloy, asked him to drop by. The President, he announced in extreme embarrassment, had overruled the generals.

Several months after, Luce, still furious, related the incident to Joseph E. Davies, the former American ambassador to Moscow. Incredible, Davies found it; there must have been a misunderstanding. In his opinion the President should appoint Luce to an embassy and he intended to recommend him. Curious to see what would happen, Luce feigned interest. The next time they met, Davies said he couldn't understand it, but there seemed to be some obstacle.

"I almost think it's my duty to go on hating Roosevelt," Luce said years after the President died. "I sometimes pray, 'Forgive me my sins as I forgive that son of a bitch his.'"

~ *thirteen* ~

Though the Luces occupied the house they owned in Greenwich so seldom that a butler once mistook a guest for Luce, Connecticut was their legal residence and in 1942 the erstwhile "kitchen maid of the New Deal kitchen cabinet" entered politics and won the state Republican nomination for Congress. Never before had Connecticut sent a woman to Washington.

Before the nomination was officially proffered Luce invited Felix Belair for a weekend, warning him to come prepared to discuss the advisability of Mrs. Luce's accepting it. Luce had already polled most of the New York editors and Belair talked it over with the Washington staff. Nobody thought she should run. "Instinctively, I guess," said Belair later, "we were trying to keep our lives uncomplicated."

In Greenwich he joined a gathering that included Herbert Bayard Swope and Bernard Baruch. After dinner the first evening, Luce went down the table asking his guests how they felt about the nomination. He himself clearly favored it and they all professed to agree—all except Belair. "My answer is no," he said. Luce demanded to know why. "Because when you married Clare, she married *Time*. For us to report the doings and sayings of Clare Luce as a congresswoman would probably be imposing on the credulity of our readers."

"No," Luce insisted, "because whatever *Time* prints will be believed because it is in *Time*."

Late that evening Mrs. Luce, looking for Belair, found him reading alone in the library. "That was an interesting conversation at dinner," she said. "I want you to know, Felix, that I'm not going to run."

Next morning, in the garden, Belair encountered Luce, who had been strolling there nervously since dawn. "You certainly messed things up," Luce told him. But he had no cause for anxiety. Mrs. Luce ran and defeated the Democratic candidate, Leroy Downs, by more than six thousand votes. Bumping into Belair in Chicago a few months after, Luce said, "Well, Felix, very well met indeed," and passed on without another word.

A pink rose pinned to her shoulder, redolent of a piny scent with which she sprayed her office as well as her person, accompanied everywhere by a cocker spaniel named "Speaker," the lady from Connecticut variously amused, piqued, captivated, and outraged her fellow legislators.

At her first press conference she braved tradition by

announcing her desire to serve on the Foreign Affairs Committee, an appointment granted according to seniority. When Roosevelt invited her, with reluctance and after considerable delay, to the customary White House buffet supper for freshmen representatives, she appended a long letter to her acceptance, mentioning various issues she wished to discuss with him. "There has been transferred to Congress, as if by swift contagion," she wrote, "the people's long delayed fury against the swollen and wasteful Washington bureaucracies that have lingered through the years."

The buffet, as the President's press secretary, Steve Early, coldly pointed out to her, was a social formality, not an arena for political contention. Roosevelt himself spoke only two words to her—"How's Henry?"

In her maiden speech before Congress Mrs. Luce coined a *Time*esque compound to deride Vice-President Henry Wallace's proposal to extend the freedom of the seas to the freedom of the air, permitting, in peacetime, the unrestricted flight of civil aircraft over all territories. "He does a lot of global thinking," said the lovely congresswoman. "But much of what Mr. Wallace calls his global thinking is, no matter how you slice it, still globaloney."

Mrs. Luce served two congressional terms, despite President Roosevelt's appeal to Connecticut voters to defeat her, and *Time* scanted neither her political nor her avocational activities. It admiringly reported her "globaloney" speech. It quoted at length her criticisms of the Administration. "Until 1937, Franklin Roosevelt was the world's outstanding isolationist. For years he was famed for blithe indifference to the oneness of the world in every chancellery in Europe and Asia. His public approval, for example of Munich is a matter of public record. . . .

"But after Munich the evil tidings out of Europe and Asia began to swamp the State Department . . . slowly, reluctantly, hesitantly, Franklin Roosevelt began to abandon his isolation. . . .

"Insensibly he began to adopt another nation's foreign policy . . . that of our nearest and most friendly neighbor —Great Britain. . . . And Mr. Roosevelt had no foreign policy for America before Pearl Harbor—and he has no foreign policy for America now."

Time hailed Mrs. Luce's re-election, publishing her photograph over the caption, "To factory girls a heroine," and repeated choice morsels from her campaign oratory. The coalition of New Dealers in the arts and in politics was "the whole Broadway-Browder axis." She dismissed Secretary of the Interior Harold Ickes as "that prodigious bureaucrat with the soul of a meat axe and the mind of a commissar." Of Roosevelt, "He is the only American president who ever lied us into a war because he did not have the courage to lead us into it. . . . The shame of Pearl Harbor was Mr. Roosevelt's shame."

Time also reported a summertime venture of the congresswoman as the title player in a production of Shaw's *Candida*.

∽ *fourteen* ∽

The Luces spent the Christmas holiday of 1943 in California with Mrs. Luce's daughter Anne, a student at Stanford University. Amid the turmoil of her protean career Mrs. Luce found it difficult to be an attentive mother. Often, when Anne came home from school, there would be no one but a chauffeur to meet her at the station. "If it happens again, I think I'll weep," she once said. But in her adolescent years mother and daughter drew closer together. Luce may have been a catalyst in the relationship. In his undemonstrative, inarticulate way he took a deep affectionate interest in his stepdaughter.

On January 11 Luce left San Francisco's Mark Hopkins Hotel alone for New York. After lunching with her mother, Anne and a classmate, Virginia Hobbs, drove back to the university in Palo Alto, twenty-five miles away. Mrs. Luce remained at the hotel to polish a political speech she was to deliver the following evening. As the two girls in an open convertible, with Virginia at the wheel, crossed an intersection near the campus, a car driven by a professor shot out of a side street and struck the convertible from behind. Both girls were thrown to the road. Virginia landed unharmed, but Anne struck her head and was killed.

Luce hurried back to San Francisco to accompany his wife and the body to their Mepkin plantation where Mrs. Luce wanted Anne to be buried. Stopping en route at Washington, he wrote Anne's obituary for *Time*'s Milestones section, identifying her as "the daughter of Mr. and Mrs. Henry R. Luce." "But, Harry, she wasn't your daughter," Belair pointed out. "That's the way it goes in," said Luce.

The Luces later built a memorial chapel in Palo Alto—St. Anne's Chapel—for which Mrs. Luce chose the dedicatory inscription from the Forty-fourth Psalm in Msgr. Ronald Knox's version of the Old Testament, "Thy beauty, now, is all for the King's delight; He is thy Lord. And worship belongs to him."

On a night long before, as the Luces were strolling home along Fifth Avenue past St. Patrick's Cathedral, he predicted, "If you ever become a convert, it will be Catholicism." Born to a Catholic mother and Baptist father, neither of them practicing, who divorced when she was ten, the stepdaughter of a lukewarm Congregationalist, educated in a High Episcopal boarding school, unhappy in her first marriage to an Episcopalian, she had subscribed to no formal religion. In efforts to understand the meaning of her existence and to relieve an inexplicable inner torment (". . . some vast uneasiness, restlessness, discontent, suffused the very interstices of my being. It spoiled every pleasure and heightened every pain and poisoned every relationship"), she explored a variety of panaceas—psychoanalysis; the teachings of the Russian mystic, Ouspensky; Alfred Korzybski's General Semantics; Marxism. The death of her mother, killed when a train hit her car crossing the track, the disappearance of her brother David in a plane over the Pacific, the suicide of four cherished friends—all within a relatively short span—increased her bewilderment.

Two years after Anne's death she took Catholic instruction from Bishop Fulton Sheen and was received into the church. The country's most publicized conversion, it perplexed her friends and prompted her detractors to derision. (According to a widely repeated jape, the Pope interrupts a doctrinal argument with Mrs. Luce to remind her, "But, Madam, I too am a Catholic.") Some associated her conversion with guilt feelings toward her daughter. We have her own explanation in a series of articles she wrote for *McCall's* magazine, entitled *The "Real" Reason:*

"The personal gift of Faith by Grace and the sense of personal sin and personal responsibility are certainly two of the major reasons I became Catholic. And yet, you can say, and rightly, that people of other faiths have also experienced God's grace and found relief for their sins on their knees, offering repentance, or on their feet, making retribution.

"Well, I suppose that the over-all reason, the one that

includes all the others and, therefore, one might say the real reason is, Catholic doctrine seemed to me the solid objective Truth. . . .

"My own mother had often said, 'I live in my children.' She had persuaded me, early, that her whole existence would somehow be justified in me. 'You,' she would say, 'are the real reason I was born'—because I would become all she had hoped to be. I believed my mother and I tried hard to justify her reason. And though she was killed before she was an old woman, my mother (or so she said) had felt justified. . . .

"Now I would do as my mother did: seek my justification, my salvation and the meaning of Life itself in the joyous and fruitful and meaningful life my own daughter would have. . . .

"The sudden death of my daughter sharply bolted the door on the last happy answer to the problem of my life. And hers. And perhaps of everybody's who believes life's 'real meaning' lies in 'living in others.' . . ."

Speaking privately of her conversion, she said, "The sight of boys dying in military hospitals was a decisive factor. Although they died no more bravely than others, they seemed more confident of the future, more serene. . . . Death makes you think of what's happening to others and what will happen to you. There are only five great questions to which all philosophies and all religions address themselves—what is love, honor, property, force, death? The answers define all systems."

As for guilt feelings, hers were general. "I am full of guilt. I feel crumby every night of my life. It comes of falling short of my own ideal of conduct. I have an ideal of how I should behave vis-à-vis my husband and my friends. But I fall hopelessly short."

Luce's friendship with Father John Courtney Murray and his frequent appearances in Catholic churches with his wife caused speculation as to whether he too might not embrace Catholicism. But nobody knowing his family background and upbringing could imagine it. "The day Harry Luce turns Roman Catholic," wrote Matthews, "I'll look out of my window and see streams of pigs flying past." Mrs. Luce once handed her husband a book by a Catholic proselytizer explaining how to convert people of various faiths. When Luce got to the chapter on Presbyterians, he chuckled. It said, in effect, don't bother.

⌾ *fifteen* ⌾

The sensibilities of the Time Inc. personnel were alternately bruised by Luce's brusqueries and warmed by his kindnesses. During a dinner in Bangkok with some local business leaders an argument arose over U. S. donations of surplus rice to India. It was a subject painful to the Thais who looked to India as a market for their rice. This led to a discussion of American farm subsidies designed to limit agricultural production. Luce considered them excessive and felt his government needed a better policy. A *Time* Far East correspondent traveling with him interjected his contrary opinion: the U. S. should distribute its surplus to poor countries like Thailand. Never hesitant to slap down an employee before strangers, Luce sneered, "There he is, Mr. Fixit, Mr. Fixit!" Yet the Thais' plight apparently touched him for he cabled his editors, BE KIND TO OUR SIAMESE FRIENDS.

George Abell, a general *Time-Life* utility man, spent a grueling year arranging a Luce-ordered photographic essay on the crowned heads of Europe. Denmark's sailor King proved particularly resistant because *Life* had ridiculed his tattooed arms. But Abell, a suave negotiator, won over all the monarchs. The task completed, he found himself sitting next to Luce in the airport as they both awaited their flight back to the States. Luce stayed buried behind a newspaper, addressing scarcely a word to him. In New York, however, he was unexpectedly amiable. He insisted on taking Abell to a performance at the Metropolitan Opera of *Rigoletto*. "You know 'La Donna è Mobile'?" he asked on the way. "Great aria. Great opera. Nice for you to see it." As they reached their seats, he explained, "The Duke, see, is in love with Gilda. . . ."

Walking by the office of a veteran *Time* editor, John Osborne, and seeing him sitting with his feet on his desk, a hole in one sole, Luce shouted for all to hear, "God dammit, don't we pay you enough so you can wear decent shoes?" He mockingly introduced Matthews, a bookish Princetonian, to the staff as "the Grammarian," an allusion to Browning's poem "The Grammarian's Funeral" ("Oh, such a life as he resolved to live,/When he had learned it,/When he had gathered all books had to give!"). Though the jest clearly affronted Matthews, he repeated it at every opportunity. "I guess I must have been clubfooted about it," Luce penitently admitted later. During a visit to Chicago he summoned the entire local bureau, some twenty people, to his hotel room for a conference. Arriving an hour and a half late, he demanded, without a word of greeting, "All right, what's wrong with the Chicago bureau?"

Oliver Jensen, a *Life* editor, had the misfortune to refer cavalierly in an editorial to sin, no laughing matter in Luce's book. "Do you know what sin is?" he raged at him. "It's a real thing and it has a definition. What is it?" Jensen feebly suggested, "Well, it's the opposite of good." "It's a specific thing. Look it up." Jensen consulted several dictionaries without finding a definition he felt would satisfy Luce. He dared not ask *him* for enlightenment, and thereafter he avoided the word.

Time Inc. adopted a certain caste attitude toward newcomers, an apartness and hauteur reminiscent of college fraternity upperclassmen. It mimicked but did not truly typify Luce's spirit. A young *Life* beginner, who felt himself totally ignored, shyly approached the managing editor with the plaint, "Nobody talks to me around here." "What do you expect me to do," said that sachem, "break a precedent?" The sufferings of those unable to attune themselves to the house mystique could be acute. During his first few weeks at *Time* Robert Jennings, age twenty-six, was bidden to lunch to meet the editor-in-chief. Two Martinis offered to him by the group of editors who had gathered before Luce appeared failed to allay his disquiet. Finally, Luce entered, acknowledged Jennings' presence with a nod and a mumble, plumped himself down across the table from him, and throughout most of the meal spoke exclusively to the editor on his right. Then he suddenly fixed Jennings with a piercing stare and tossed him a question about South American politics. Jennings, primarily a show business reporter, blinked wordlessly. "Read the magazine," said Luce. The neophyte did not measurably enhance his standing during a later staff conference involving *Sports Illustrated* when, asked by Luce what he thought of the new magazine, he replied, "It's pretty interesting, but there's too much stuff about clambakes in Bermuda." "Clambakes?" said literal Luce. "We've got no story about clambakes. Baseball, basketball . . ." "I don't care much about basketball," Jennings confessed. "Next," said Luce.

"I was a nervous wreck," Jennings recalled after he left *Time*. "I lived in the same nameless terror I had as a private in the army. I couldn't be my own man. I felt dead inside. I dreaded going to work."

But Luce's brusqueness was like that of an exigent yet devoted parent bedeviled by unruly progeny. Indeed, he thought of his organization as a family, and by the same token he tolerated a good deal of back talk and at times downright insolence. In an explosion of temper, when a Washington correspondent charged that *Time* was twisting its political news, Luce descended on the bureau chief, roaring, "I want that man fired!" "Who do you think you are—Beaverbrook?" said the bureau chief. Luce didn't and he subsided. The offending correspondent not only remained but survived to become a bureau chief himself.

When *Life*'s theater specialists, Tom Prideaux and Mary Leatherbee, prepared a picture spread on the musical comedy *Gypsy*, a tribute to the retired striptease queen, Gypsy Rose Lee, Luce, who had attended the opening, objected. He thought the show dull and vulgar. *Time*'s theater critic, Mary Leatherbee pointed out, was the only one to agree. "He has the right reaction," said Luce. "The other critics are corrupt." "Did you think they were corrupt when they praised *J.B.* [Archibald MacLeish's Biblical drama]?" Prideaux asked, knowing that Luce had invested in it. Luce's hardness of hearing suddenly grew harder. He seldom forced his tastes upon an editor and *Life* published the *Gypsy* story.

Among the most outspoken rebels in the Luce stable was Matthews. Luce once called him at home on his day off to reprove him for his handling of a political story, to which Matthews retorted that if ever he was disturbed again during his leisure hours, he would instantly resign. Luce apologized. He also apologized when Matthews, in response to a blistering memorandum about the labor leader Harry Bridges, which Luce distributed to half a dozen *Time* editors, shot back, "There are several possible answers . . . (1) tear it up and throw it in the wastepaper basket (as Alex did); (2) remonstrate with you (as John Billings did); (3) say nothing; (4) tell you to go to hell— as I am strongly tempted to do. . . . No decent human being would answer your memo by accepting it (I mean of course its tone and manner—*not* your views on Bridges). You have written it as if to dogs, not to human beings. And you have made a mistake. If you're really degenerating into a barking boss, you'll soon have behind you only the anxious, stupid, dishonest subservience that kind of boss can command. But you will no longer command my respect or my services."

For an issue of *Time* featuring a story about a soft-drink company Luce wanted a picture of its president on the cover. Matthews, who had an intellectually snobbish an-

tipathy to businessmen, said, with a curl of his lip, "What—
a businessman?" "Yes, sure, head of the company." "All
businessmen have faces like puddings." He held out for a
picture of the product instead and he prevailed.

Matthews later joined a six-man palace revolution with
the aim of rescuing Luce from what they felt was the
baleful influence of certain editors. After a series of secret
meetings to map strategy, they confronted him on three
separate occasions, the last in a private dining room at
the Players' Club. The year was 1941 and among the issues
they pressed him on was his policy toward the premier of
France's Vichy government, Marshal Pétain, whom one
opposition editor, to their dismay, had warmly praised.
They challenged Luce further with the question, "Under
what circumstances would you consider using *Time* as a
political instrument?" He replied, "If I thought the Republic was in danger." Matthews recounted the denoue-
ment in his autobiography: ". . . he handed us each a
copy of a memo he had written. As we read it, we saw
that he had lifted the argument to a general discussion
of journalism, its purposes and possibilities, and ended with
a statement of his journalistic faith. He had cut the ground
from under us. We looked at each other and shook our
heads. There was nothing left to say. . . ."

Luce's self-image of a paterfamilias would sometimes
give his interoffice memoranda an odd little parental tinge.
During one of his frequent returns to editing *Time* he
wrote "TO: ALL WRITERS (in an admonition against going
home too early), An oldtime custom was that TIME
writers should say goodnight to the Senior Managing Editor on Saturdays, Sundays and Mondays [the magazine's

weekend was then Tuesday and Wednesday]. It is my wish to revive this custom,—at least for this week and next. Object: to ensure the Acting Senior Managing Editor a peaceful repose."

Because of *Time*'s peculiar working schedule its employees saw much less of outsiders socially than did people with a normal weekend. As a result, they tended to romantic involvements with each other. Quite a few research girls married their editor. Luce, with his ingrained puritanism and conventional morality, worried about unorthodox relationships. He was appalled when a research girl divorced her husband, an editor, to marry the head of his department, all three of them continuing to work side by side. "Now what are we going to do about you?" Luce asked the discarded husband. "You can't go on working under that man." "Why not?" said the latter. "We're still good friends." Luce spluttered from shock, but finally resigned himself. "If you insist," he said. "I don't like it, though."

While quick to upbraid his cohorts, he would defend them against any alien derogator even when they were at fault. To placate a client infuriated by a *Time* slur, the advertising sales manager told him, "You wouldn't care if you knew what a bastard the writer is." Luce was irate when the appeaser reported the conversation to him. "Nobody," he burst out, "can say that about a *Time* writer!"

Luce tended to perform his kindnesses at a distance, through letters and gifts, for he shrank from displays of sentiment. When employees married, had a child, wrote a book, won some award, they would receive a graceful note from him. He established a tradition of sending, at the birth of each child, a silver Tiffany porringer. But on the random occasions when he felt impelled to make a paternal gesture in person the execution was apt to be awkward. A month after the wife of a *Time* Rome correspondent bore her first child Luce happened to come to town. The bureau chief phoned to advise the couple, "The boss is heading your way. He's on foot." She hastened to pretty up the infant and herself. Luce duly appeared, announced, "I'm here to see the baby," took a cursory look, commented, "Well, it's a baby," and fell to peppering the father with questions about Italian politics.

If open exchanges of warm feelings unsettled Luce, still less did he relish firing anybody. One couldn't, after all, fire members of one's family, however delinquent, any more than they could resign from it. One could only reprimand and discipline. But a parting was occasionally unavoidable. Then Luce would let a deputy wield the ax. Upon worthy veterans who had outlived their usefulness he preferred to bestow some face-saving title and relegate them to inactive duty, though many of his executives felt that a well-pensioned separation might be kinder. "Walking interoffice memos," a *Time* editor dubbed these displaced persons. Matthews, who became one of them before he finally quit, remarked about another who moved into his vacated Siberia, "If he looks at the wall, he'll see my initials."

To the top performers of his establishment Luce developed a strong, deep, possessive attachment, but only those in long residence grew conscious of it because he was incapable of articulating emotion. It lay hidden, disguised. These special relationships had the intensity of a love affair that remains unexpressed yet sensed on both sides, which was why, when a protégé ran counter to Luce's dyed-in-the-wool convictions, or left him, he felt personally betrayed. Of all his favorites perhaps the three he prized most were John Hersey, who came to prefer the freedom of independent authorship and wrote his masterly *Hiroshima* for *The New Yorker;* Theodore White, a dissenter from Luce's wartime China policy, who also turned to free-lance writing; and Emmet Hughes, who became a political commentator for *Newsweek*—and all three grieved him by their disloyalty, as he saw it. Passing Hersey on the street not long after *The New Yorker* had devoted an entire issue to *Hiroshima,* Luce nodded curtly and said, his voice edged with irony, "I just flew over *your* city." Time usually healed such breaches, but the interim was long and bitter.

With John Shaw Billings, one of the principal architects of *Life,* who retired after many years of yeoman service, there was no question of desertion, only battle fatigue. But the gratitude, affection, and regret that Luce undoubtedly felt, he could not put into words. When Billings announced his departure, just about all Luce found to say was, "All right."

A few employees came to a surprising realization about Luce. During the frequent absences of his wife on political business, his secretary would sometimes call Oliver Jensen, who then edited *Life's* entertainment pages, to inquire whether there were any private movie screenings of possible interest to Luce that evening. If Jensen said there were, Luce would ask to go along and invite Jensen to dinner beforehand. One evening, with James Agee, *Time's* peerless film critic, they watched a rerun of an old Buster Keaton comedy, "What are you fellows doing now?" Luce asked them afterward. They were both ready for bed. "I'm hungry. Let's grab a bite. I know a great place where they have real old-fashioned ice cream sodas." It turned out to be a dreary all-night cafeteria with a miscellany of derelicts hunched over their plates. Luce exclaimed over the authentic atmosphere and for an hour or so kept his companions captive. After several such evenings the simple truth dawned on Jensen. Luce was lonely. *Life*'s publisher, C. D. Jackson, made the same discovery. "He craved easy, relaxed comradeship, but he didn't know how to get it. He always put you on the *qui vive*."

～ *sixteen* ～

"How can you find good writers and editors who aren't Communists or fellow travelers?" It was a problem that troubled Luce throughout the war and early postwar years when a preponderance of American intellectuals leaned sharply to the Left. According to the arithmetic of *American Legion Magazine*, *Time* harbored forty-seven Communists. Whatever the figure, there were certainly some, for in 1939 they began circulating among the employees an anonymously written handout, *High Time*, "Published by the Communist Party Members at Time Inc." Purveying betrayals of confidential office talk and a general vilification of the management, it drew from Luce a memorandum to the entire Time Inc. personnel:

". . . I think that just as a gossip sheet it's a pretty amusing job of writing. I also think that the authors of it were disloyal to the organization and to all their fellow workers. I think so because:

"1) They have published gossip—already pretty sadly twisted by the time they got it—which will be further twisted as it passes from mouth to mouth and pen to pen. It damages the reputation of the organization and in doing so damages the basic earning power not only of the company, but of everyone who has a job in it.

"2) They have done more of the same kind of damaging in using TIME INC.'s name in partisan propaganda. A publication by 'The Communist Party of TIME INC.' is just as offensive as one would be by a 'Nazi Bund in TIME INC.' and far more offensive than a publication by 'New Dealers of TIME INC. Staff' or by a 'TIME INC. G.O.P.' I regard it as eminently fair to demand that all employees refrain from compromising the reputation for non-partisanship which we have all worked hard to earn.

"3) It has been a cardinal principle with us that editors, writers and researchers have a right to spout to one another their views—well considered, half-considered, or ill-considered—so that editorial give and take shall be honest and free. We have had people of all shades of political thought on our staff and I maintain the right of every one of them to speak to every other member of the staff with as much intellectual freedom—and carefreeness—as he would in his own family. I also maintain the right of members of the staff to gossip, kick, criticize and laugh about what others of the staff have said, done or written. *Free speech in confidence* is essential to group journalism. It would be intolerable if our editors had to feel that they could not open their mouths without having some half-uttered thought plucked out and used to stab them publicly in the back. It would be just as intolerable if any writer had to feel that if he repeated in the office what some other member of the staff had said, it might be twisted and publicly used against TIME INC.

"In the last few days I have received scores of written and verbal messages from people in every department of TIME INC. expressing their indignation and desiring to 'do something' about it. I think you will agree with me that one of the things *not* to do is to start a Red hunt. (Winchell is wrong again.) Nor am I going to ask anybody to mind his tongue when speaking to other members of the organization.

"We cannot get along on any basis except that of free expression toward one another in private and assurance that such confidence will not be violated. If anyone feels that he cannot make that confidence mutual on his part, he ought to resign. Certainly if the management discovers any employee making public gossip of matters that are properly confidential between members of the staff, he will be fired."

What complicated Luce's problem was the difficulty of distinguishing between secret Communists and open liberals, the latter composing the majority of his staffs. "We weren't very sophisticated. I didn't know what conspiratorial Communism was all about, or the techniques of infiltration. Clarification came with the Nazi-Soviet pact. Then you could see the quasi-Commies falling off the fence. We tried to identify the real Communists and if I knew a man was one, I'd fire him."

The advent of Whittaker Chambers in 1939, the year

following his renunciation of the Communist party, spread further confusion. Like many repentant ex-members, Chambers had swung to the opposite pole. "I was incapable of being a liberal," he wrote thirteen years later in his confessional book, *Witness*. He admitted his political past to Luce, though without disclosing that he had been a Soviet courier, and starting as a third-string book reviewer for *Time* at five thousand dollars a year, he rose within nine years to the eminence of a star writer for both *Time* and *Life* at thirty thousand dollars. "My debt and gratitude to *Time* cannot be measured. At a critical moment, *Time* gave me back my life. It gave me a voice. . . ." He used his new-found voice to sound alarms against what he considered the self-deceptive liberalism of his colleagues. Given an opportunity to write Russian and Communist news, he turned out copy so violently colored that the senior editor above him shifted him to Art and Cinema. The magazine's radio editor, John McManus, a future American Labor Party candidate, told Chambers in Luce's presence, "I should think your favorite movie would be *The Informer*."

Luce's judgment of Chambers fluctuated between admiration for his literary skill and expertise as a former Communist insider and mistrust of his editorial equilibrium. Faced with liberal and conservative views of an issue, Chambers rigidly excluded the latter. Nevertheless, in 1945, the ban against his handling Soviet stories was lifted and when *Time*'s Foreign News editor opted to work abroad, Chambers replaced him. "My assignment sent a shiver through many of *Time*'s staff, where my views were well known and detested with a ferocity I did not believe possible until I came to grips with it. With my first few Foreign News sections, the shiver turned into a shudder." And with cause. The department became known to its correspondents as "the bloody angle." Chambers totally rewrote, mangled, or junked any dispatches which seemed to him tainted by leftish sympathies. A Time Inc. vice-president, Allen Grover, circularized the correspondents for their opinions as to the editing of their reports. Nearly all of them deplored it. From Moscow John Hersey replied that out of the 11,000 words he had filed *Time* printed, by actual count, 168. The rest of its Moscow stories had been a Chambers recasting of material from newspapers, news services, and other sources. I'M JUST AN EXTRAVAGANCE, Hersey cabled. WHY NOT SEND ME HOME.

Chambers saw the protests as a conspiracy to destroy him. But the correspondents believed the reverse. He had repeatedly impugned their motives. A careful review of their dispatches exonerated them. Chambers was reduced to the Books section. His literary gifts, however, sent his stock soaring again and he wrote major articles, most of them nonpolitical, for *Life*. He stood at the apex of his success, financially and journalistically, in August, 1948, when the House Committee on Un-American Activities subpoenaed him, and he exposed the State Department's Alger Hiss as a former Communist agent. "It seems to me that you will not want me around here any longer," he told Luce. "Nonsense," said Luce. "Testifying is a simple patriotic duty." After he repeated his accusation in a radio broadcast and Hiss filed a libel suit, Time Inc. paid Chambers' preliminary legal costs, but since a federal jury convicted Hiss of perjury, no suit followed. Before the case ended Chambers talked to Roy Larsen. "I think that I should resign," he said. "Perhaps you should," Larsen agreed.

But his resignation was not voluntary. He longed to stay. Luce refused. "It's fallen through," Chambers brokenly told his *Life* colleague, Charles Murphy. "I'm going home. I'm sick." What Luce could not overlook was Chambers' failure to confess, when he joined *Time*, that he had served as a Soviet courier.

By 1952 staff problems involving Communism troubled Luce no more. Even Chambers declared in *Witness*, published that year, ". . . once it [*Time*] had reluctantly learned the facts of Communist infiltration, it acted with such tactful purpose that today there is not, as far as I know, a Communist on its staff."

⤳ *seventeen* ⤳

Luce had rejected objectivity as a journalistic ideal at the outset of his career. *Time* became a monument to subjective journalism. "Make a judgment," he would exhort his writers and editors. The ancient canon of the craft by which facts should be allowed to speak for themselves and opinions confined to the editorial page, he considered illusory. "Show me a man who claims he's completely objective," he said, "and I'll show you a man with self-delusions." Most journalists would agree. Which facts? The mere selection entails value judgments. No journalist can help but define, evaluate, interpret his material, and so, consciously or unconsciously, project personal attitudes. To report the facts in exhaustive, undiscriminated detail would, even if humanly possible, blur the story's significance, not to mention its readability. As Erwin Canham, editor of the *Christian Science Monitor*, pointed out, "The bare news event can be so misleading as to be false."

The real standard is not objectivity, but fairness. Has judgment resulted from facts, or have facts been manipulated to support a prejudgment? Under the system of group journalism created by Luce and Hadden, facts and opinions are so tightly interwoven that the reader cannot readily distinguish between them. The absolutism of *Time*, only slightly tempered by the years, was a manifestation of Luce's craving for tidy, simple formulations. Abstract thinking, speculation, ifs, ands, and buts, the gray areas between black and white, set him to fidgeting. A Far East correspondent, having made no headway discussing with Luce the complexities of Red China, dredged up from his memory a pithy comparison he had read someplace: "The Russians concentrated on production while the Chinese Communists are concentrating on social organization as a way of production." The correspondent was not sure what it meant, but Luce pounced on it and repeated it everywhere.

Luce was always clutching at concrete symbols to clarify a complicated situation. In the Italy of the fifties, for example, the ubiquitous Vespa motor scooter struck him as such a symbol of the country's industrial renaissance, the rise of a new middle class, and the decline of Communism, and for months, at staff luncheons and conferences, he kept referring to it. A typically Lucean bit of gimmickry in *Life* was a full-page photo of bicycles stacked outside a Saigon school, meant to prove that Vietnamese students were rich enough not to have to walk. The editors evidently never considered an alternative meaning, among at least half a dozen, that only rich children went to school in Saigon.

At a lunch party, given for Luce when he toured Formosa in 1960, the talk turned to the differences between the Formosans and the mainland Chinese. Luce would concede no differences, which was not only the official Chinese Nationalist line, but also, ironically, the Chinese Communist line. To prove his point, he pointed to a magazine picture of a Chinese-looking man sitting before a street sign in Chinese characters. Formosan or mainlander? he asked. Formosan, replied one of the guests, a local CIA man who could read the sign. "Well," said Luce, "he looks as Chinese as any Chinese on the mainland." "Yes, but . . ." the CIA man started to argue, then fell silent. Somebody else observed that Luce's logic was like saying Americans look like Englishmen; therefore Americans are Englishmen. A *Time* correspondent asked the CIA man afterward why he hadn't pressed his argument. "What's the use?" the latter said. "He's like his magazines. He oversimplifies everything."

In a *Fortune* manuscript about the Red Chinese economy *Time*'s Hong Kong correspondent, Stanley Karnow, wrote that its failures resulted from "successive years of mismanagement, confusion, natural calamities and population pressures—and perhaps the sheer unwieldiness of China itself." Luce scrawled across the margin, "Too many explanations. The simple answer is Communism." Where the author said Peking "exaggerated" in its claims of economic progress Luce changed it to "lied." For "official statements" he substituted "official lies."

As reflected in *Time*, this aversion to qualifying facts

generated an aura of Olympian omniscience. "Let Subscriber Goodkind mend his ways!" So Briton Hadden once answered an indignant letter-writer and hung a framed copy on his office walls. Though *Time* moderated the cocksnookery of its salad days, the cofounder's imperious words could still serve as its motto. "Who says so?" readers were asking long after Hadden died, and the Letters editor would reply, "*Time* says so." Arrogance ranked with bias as the offenses most frequently charged against the magazine. Luce shrugged off the first, but admitted to the second, dismissing the arguments for objectivity as meaningless platitudes. "If everyone hasn't brains enough to know by now that I am a Presbyterian, a Republican and a capitalist," he said, "I am biased in favor of God, the Republican party and free enterprise. . . . Hadden and I invented *Time*. Therefore we had a right to say what it would be. We're not fooling anybody. Our readers know where we stand. We're telling the story to the best of our knowledge and belief. No magazine tries harder to tell the truth."

~ *eighteen* ~

The truth, as *Time* saw it, enraged more readers than any periodical in the country. When Ralph Ginzburg, publisher of the tawdry magazine *Fact*, decided to print an article made up entirely of anti-*Time* letters, he got more than he could find room for, many from people who would probably not be caught dead with *Fact*. Thus, the critic, Eric Bentley: "More pervasive than *Time*'s outright errors in the misuse of truth. To lie without lying seems their general aim." The English playwright John Osborne: "*Time* is a vicious, dehumanizing institution." Leonard Rowe, attorney and educator: "As a teacher of semantics and propaganda, I find *Time* indispensable as a sort of laboratory manual and clinical exhibit for my classes." The University of Toronto professor, Marshall McLuhan: "Totalitarianism—engendered by the mass hypnosis of power, glitter, and the spectacle of regular ranks—rather than insight or intelligibility is the object of *Time*'s technical brilliance. Meanwhile the editors of *Time* stand at mock attention in the reviewing stand, thumbing their noses at humanity." Msgr. John J. Egan, director of the Archdiocesan Conservation Council: *"Time*'s recent cover story on Chicago's Mayor Daley contained gross and inexcusable calumny upon the Church's Negro position, and upon the person of Albert Cardinal Meyer. The story was unresearched, undocumented, and rife with unfounded libel." Sloan Wilson, author (who once worked for *Time*): "Any enemy of *Time* is a friend of mine." Irwin Shaw, novelist: ". . . it takes a stern exercise of self-discipline for me to keep my hands in my pockets when I pass the *Time* building."

Winston Churchill's irascible son Randolph used to commit his grievances now and then to leaflets which he sold for 1s. 3d. postpaid (fifty cents if delivered overseas by ship, one dollar airmailed), but distributed gratis to newspapers, all embassies, the entire Churchill family, and a list of notables which included the Archbishop of Canterbury, the Rothschilds, Aristotle Onassis, David Ben-Gurion. In the fall of 1962 *Time* nettled Churchill into penning "AN OPEN LETTER to the Right Reverend Bishop Fulton Sheen from Mr. Randolph Spencer Churchill, M.B.E. *Regarding the activities of Mr. and Mrs. Henry Luce and of 'Time' magazine.* The violence of the attack seems disproportionate to the immediate provocation, but doubtless it reflected a long maturing resentment. Lord Beaverbrook had chided *Time* for stating that "no Prime Minister in modern times has been a bachelor. "TUT TUT TIME," cabled the press potentate, "YOU HAVE FORGOTTEN ARTHUR JAMES BALFOUR." The Letters editor published the correction and alibied, "Well, Sir, it all depends on whether one considers 1911 modern times." This brought Churchill into the controversy. ". . . Your lame defense," he wrote, "might have been a little less lame if your gifted researchers had told you that Mr. Balfour ceased to be Prime Minister six years earlier in December, 1905. This would still have been a quibble, but less misleading. . . ." The editor footnoted Churchill's letter, "Gifted researcher says that Balfour was a member of Parliament until 1911, but concedes to Quibbler Churchill." There followed a Churchillian cable, "YOUR GIFTED RESEACHER STILL QUIBBLING STILL WRONG STOP BALFOUR MEMBER OF HOUSE OF COMMONS TILL 1933 COMMA STILL MEMBER OF PARLIAMENT AS EARL BALFOUR IN HOUSE OF LORDS TILL HIS DEATH 1930 WHAT WILL GIFTED RESEARCHER LAMELY SAY TO THIS. . . ."

She said nothing and the battle was joined. Churchill got off a letter to Mrs. Luce: "Dearest Clare, Here is a good example of the inaccuracy and suppression of Robinson's [sic] rag. . . . Surely this is what the Church of Rome would call 'sinning against the light'? If in doubt ask Bishop Sheen what he thinks about it. Robinson is a brand that might still be saved from the burning, though I doubt it. Such persistence in error on the part of someone who purports to be a purveyor of truth can only end in frying."

Receiving no reply, he wrote again, "Is Robinson beyond redemption? Has he passed the point of no return? . . . And what about yourself? I have known you a good deal longer than I have known Harry; but you do not condescend to reply. . . . Perhaps you and your gifted staff have been too busy attacking the President to deal with the correspondence of one of your oldest friends."

The same day, enlarging the target of his anger, he wrote to Luce himself, "Why do you allow your newspapers to falsify the truth and intrude into the private lives of other people, some of whom may have the misfortune to be your readers? Is it greed to be richer or an abortive quest for power? Why, when one of your papers makes a mistake, and your readers seek to correct it, do you falsify and suppress the truth? Why, Harry, why? What is the point of being rich and powerful if you can't tell the truth? . . .

"Why don't you let Clare induct you into the Roman Catholic Church? I am sure that Bishop Sheen could turn you into a Christian and explain to you the true values of life.

"It is more than thirty years since I first met you—nearly as long as I have known Clare. I have been distressed to observe the progressive deterioration in your character. Most people as they grow older and richer become more mellow. I grieve that this has not been your experience. Think about it Harry. Think about it seriously. Discuss it with Clare and the Bishop and you might still save yourself from the Presbyterian fire which you must presume awaits you. . . ."

Finally, Churchill wrote the open letter to Bishop Sheen, enclosed copies of the other letters and cables, and published the entire correspondence in one of his leaflets. ". . . Clare's failure to answer my letters is a matter between herself and myself. It is sad, however, that she would appear to approve collusively of the shocking way in which her husband's magazines are conducted:—more especially since she is still writing articles in one of them.

"Has she no influence over the man? Can you not stimulate her to use her radiant love of truth to inspire the publications of her husband, if not with a spirit of Christianity, at least with zeal for historical accuracy?

"Further, my dear Bishop, do you not find it rather odious that Mr. Luce's magazines should intrude so much into people's private lives, whereas the private lives of those who own newspapers are never intruded upon? . . ."

～ *nineteen* ～

Every year some two hundred to three hundred readers threatened to sue Time Inc. for invasion of privacy or libel. Few ever moved beyond threats, having been convinced by the corporation's house lawyer, or their own, that they had no case. During the four decades of Luce's regime 325 claims were actually filed. As with most publications, it was company policy never to settle, no matter what the legal expense, unless a wrong appeared incontrovertible, thus discouraging nuisance litigation. All told, it settled or, as the corporation's redoubtable counsel, Cravath, Swaine and Moore, preferred to phrase it, "honorably disposed of," less than 3 per cent by a public retraction, when the editors admitted error, or in cases of financial damage, remuneration. Of the cases tried it lost only nine. (Luce himself was never called upon to testify.)

To a man whom *Time* misidentified as a racketeer it offered $5000 in amends. He demanded $50,000. The court awarded him $5000. The biggest judgment, awarded in 1948 to a defamed clothing manufacturer, was $40,000.

The case of Hill vs. Time Inc., which dragged on for ten years, established an important precedent affecting people's right to privacy. In 1952 three escaped convicts invaded the home of James Hill, near Philadelphia, and held him, his wife, and their five children captive for nineteen hours. A writer, Joseph Hayes, wove the episode into a novel, *The Desperate Hours,* then into a play. To pictorialize its review of the play, *Life* posed the actors in the home, from which the Hills had moved to Connecticut. James Hill then charged *Life* with violating the family's privacy by giving the impression that the play was a true account of their experience. The picture story, *Life* countered, was basically truthful. A New York jury awarded Hill $50,000 compensatory and $25,000 punitive damages. A second trial without jury, ordered by the Appellate Division of the Supreme Court, went against the defendant, but compensatory damages only at $30,000 were awarded. That verdict was voided by the Supreme Court in 1967. Voicing the majority opinion, Justice William J. Brennan declared:

"We hold that the constitutional protections for speech and press preclude the application of the New York Statute to redress false reports of matters of public interest in the absence of proof that the defendant published the report with knowledge of its falsity or in reckless disregard of the truth.

"The guarantees for speech and press are not the preserve of political expression or comment upon public affairs, essential as those are to healthy government. One need only pick up any newspaper or magazine to comprehend the vast range of published material which exposes persons to public view, both private citizens and public officials. Exposure of the self to others in varying degrees is a concomitant of life in a civilized community. The risk of this exposure is an essential incident of life in a society which places a primary value on freedom of speech and of press.

"Freedom of discussion, if it would fulfill its historic function in this nation, must embrace all issues about which information is needed or appropriate to enable the members of society to cope with the exigencies of their period. No suggestion can be found in the Constitution that the freedom there guaranteed for speech and the press bears an inverse ratio to the timeliness and importance of the ideas seeking expression.

"The line between the informing and the entertaining is too elusive for the protection of [freedom of the press]. . . . Erroneous statement is no less inevitable in such case than in the case of comment upon public affairs, and in both, if innocent or merely negligent, it must be protected if the freedoms of expression are to have the 'breathing space' that they 'need to survive.' . . .

"We create grave risk of serious impairment of the indispensable service of a free press in a free society if we saddle the press with the impossible burden of verifying to a certainty the facts associated in news articles with a person's name, picture or portrait, particularly as related to nondefamatory matter. Even negligence would be a most elusive standard, especially when the content of the speech itself affords no warning of prospective harm to another through falsity. A negligence test would place on the press the intolerable burden of guessing how a jury might assess the reasonableness of steps taken by it to verify the accuracy of every reference to a name, picture or portrait.

"In this context, sanctions against either innocent or negligent misstatement would present a grave hazard of discouraging the press from exercising the constitutional guarantees. . . .

"Any possible difference with us as to the thrust of the constitutional command is narrowly limited in this case to the failure of the trial judge to instruct the jury that a verdict of liability could be predicated only on a finding of knowing or reckless falsity in the publication of the *Life* article.

"The judgment of the Court of Appeal is set aside and the case is remanded for further proceedings not inconsistent with this opinion."

❧ *twenty* ❧

The cofounders of *Time* adapted techniques of fiction-writing to news. *Time* stories had the narrative structure of the old-fashioned short story with a beginning, a middle, and an end. For example,

"The four-place Cessna 180 descended towards a landing at Wyoming's Minuteman Missile Site B-6. Down and down it went, faster and faster. Too fast. One of the passengers leaned towards veteran pilot Edgar Van Keuren. The pilot's eyes were open—but sightless. He was dead of a stroke."

With adjectives of characterization, action verbs, atmospheric nouns, *Time* infused more pungency into a single page than *The New York Times* would deem fit to print in an entire issue.

"[Richard Burton] is the demi-Atlas of this earth, the

arm and burgonet of men, the fellow who is living with Elizabeth Taylor. . . . When Burton's emotional life was particularly eruptive one day earlier this month, he drank half a gallon of cognac . . . the tympanic resonance of his voice is so rich and overpowering that it could give an air of verse to a recipe for stewed hare. . . . Amateur statisticians would have it that he has probably given some sort of lasting memory to 75,000 women in the last 20 years. . . . Once, after fluffing the same line repeatedly on a movie set, he lowered his head and rammed it into a wall. . . ."

Puns, *double-entendres*, and general word play came to typify *Time*, most conspicuously in its critical departments.

"A man [John Updike as a writer of light verse] who can dance a light fantastic without tripping over his dactyls is a treasure to be prized."

"In a triumph of style over substance it [the play, *The Chinese Prime Minister*], serves its mental hash like Beluga caviar, pours its intellectual eyewash like Dom Perignon."

"There is more to Sophia Loren than meets the eye and Director Vittorio de Sica is the man who sees it. In *Gold of Naples* he showed the world that Sophia is socko as a liedown comic. In *Two Women* he gave the girl an accelerated course in Duse and donts."

"Several ax murders later [in the Bette Davis movie shocker *Dead Ringer*] the problem appears to be: how you gonna keep Momma down on the farm when she has such a penchant for pruning."

Time style evolved partly from the physical limitations imposed by a small magazine aiming to cover all important news. Concision was essential. At their top performances the ace *Time* writers were capable of lapidary phrases that made a personality or an event stick in the mind:

"Winston Churchill, wholly British, half American . . ."

"Harry Truman was as sore as a hoptoad in a tack factory."

"It [the contradictory evidence in a murder case] all fitted like duck eggs in a light socket."

"The hand [of a Fascist author] that cradles the rock . . ."

But such verbal diamonds had to come naturally. Over-reaching produced only rhinestones. Among *Time*'s worst stylistic offenses were its variations on tired phrases like "It must be seen to be disbelieved," its tortured puns like "guilt-edged insecurities." Repeatedly used to avoid clichés, they became clichés themselves. As news writing went, however, *Time*, on the whole, developed a superior quality.

The polish it strove to impart to every story, together with its tight restrictions and deadlines of sometimes only a few hours, demanded solid gifts, and its two-hundred-odd staff members (Time Inc. employed 6700 people altogether) numbered some of the deftest hands in the profession. The magazines were a training school nonpareil, whose graduates adorned every branch of literature and publishing. They included John O'Hara, John Hersey, Hamilton Basso, James Agee, John Dos Passos, all three founders of *American Heritage* and *Horizon*—James Parton, Joseph Thorndike, and Oliver Jensen—the publisher of *Scientific American*, Gerard Piel, and the publisher of *Time*'s chief competitor, Lew L. Callaway, Jr.

⮈ *twenty-one* ⮊

Fairness, not objectivity. But was *Time* fair? As the Prince de Ligne replied when his wife asked him if he had been faithful to her, "Frequently." It depended on the area. When facts did not clash with preconceptions or prejudices, *Time* steered a fairly straight course. This generally applied to its "back-of-the-book" sections—Art, Music, Religion, Education, etc. But in its national and foreign news coverage, policy kept intruding and the facts had to fit policy. Once convinced of the truth, *Time* allowed no facts to alter it.

Below the managerial level droves of Luce's employees shared neither his political nor his philosophical outlook. Were they then occasionally obliged to betray their principles to keep their jobs? In an early memorandum to writers and researchers Manfred Gottfried tried to dispel any such suspicion. "Some may have come to *Time* from newspapers where it is taken for granted that employees should bow & scrape to the management's editorial bias as well as to its physical presence. For that reason, I know there are those among you who think altogether too much about 'writing for the boss.'

"*Time* never did and does not now demand servility, intellectual or otherwise, from the members of its staff. On the contrary *Time* does demand from every staff member the most forthright intellectual honesty and frankness in dealing with its editors and readers.

"As one who was with *Time* at the first issue, I can assure you that I have never known anyone to get far in this organization except with these qualities. In the beginning when Harry Luce and Brit Hadden had a staff consisting of three full-time writers and one researcher, it was natural that all four had full squawking rights direct to the top bosses on every point. Since then the staff has proliferated. I am aware that access to Harry Luce, Tom Matthews and myself is now limited in practice by the fact that we are often busy. But the old squawking rights still exist and are meant to be used. . . .

"Of course if you exercise your right of appeal the editors may overrule you—it is still the privilege of higher ranking editors to make the bigger mistakes that get into print—but you are not alone in that periodical frustration. The price of the degree of intellectual democracy that we try to practice is that virtually no one can ever have any story exactly as he wants it. . . .

"Since *Time* is a magazine that treats not only physical events but ideas as news, one of the jobs of the editors is to weigh these ideas and try as far as possible to help you report them in proper perspective. Your job is to consider and try to appreciate the editors' points—but not to accept them unless you yourself are convinced. If you still believe something else, it is your job to try to bring the editors around to your view. The object of the whole procedure is enlightenment, not dogmatism.

"It is quite true that the magazine has to have a generally consistent point of view, just as it has to have a generally consistent style, and a writer who goes to extremes (e.g. a convinced Fascist) obviously would not belong on the *Time* staff. We have never fully defined that point of view—mainly because our formal definition would inevitably shackle us. The magazine's point of view has to be broad enough to include many individual points of view among its writers just as among its readers.

"You cannot expect to be *Time*'s theater reviewer, for example, unless your general approach to the theater is in reasonable conformity to that of the editors. But if you are *Time*'s theater reviewer, the presumption is that you were hired and continue to hold that job because that reasonable conformity exists. And that being the case it is your job to say in your reviews not what you think the senior editor or the managing editor would like you to say but what you believe is the truth.

"The editors do not want any writer to write anything that he does not believe nor do they want any researcher to check any statement that she does not think is true. . . ."

But what if the editor can't be brought around? ". . . they have to trust their own judgment—that's what they are hired for. So it is their business to revise the story according to their own lights or get it rewritten by somebody who sees their point. This is done without prejudice to you. Your standing will suffer if you hold out for too many things which in retrospect looked cockeyed. But your standing will mount proportionally if you hold out for things which in retrospect turn out to be sound. . . ."

Luce himself came to dislike the term "group journalism." "Let's have no such denial of individual responsibility," he objected. While conceding that Time Inc. attempted to reach a consensus, he said, "It may be highly desirable to have in responsible positions men and women who are fundamentally not in sympathy with the attitudes and policies of the company. We like dissenters. . . ." He added, however, "Dissenters must be the exception rather than the rule. We must seek characteristic agreement leaving room for uncharacteristic dissent . . . the consensus must be formed and informed and reformed by the conscience of the individual. . . ."

Lecturing at the University of Oregon School of Journalism in 1955, Luce declared, "The owner-editor cannot honorably evade his confrontation with every aspect of truth in every aspect of his paper." But as a practical matter such omniscience became impossible. While the spirit of the overlord, emanating from the thirty-fourth floor, continued to permeate the furthest reaches of his domain, Time Inc. grew too labyrinthine for him to participate at every juncture. Advancing age alone precluded it. Because he delegated perforce a good deal of authority he had no prior knowledge of, and therefore no way of ruling upon, many deeds performed by his publications. His adjutants enjoyed enormous autonomy. Some, more royalist than the king, trying to anticipate his position, overshot the mark; others fell short of it.

Time's cool, tough, arch-conservative managing editor, Otto Fuerbringer, variously known as "the Iron Chancellor," "the Nerveless Wonder, "Otto Fingerbanger," might run the magazine for weeks without seeing or hearing from Luce, so that to a great degree it carried the slant of Fuerbringer's thinking. (Interviewing a likely job applicant, he said, "Before you join up here you should know that we are not the uptown edition of the *New Republic*.") From Fuerbringer the long chain of command stretched through two assistant managing editors, ten senior editors, each of whom headed one or more departments, twenty contributing editors (i.e. writers), seventy-three editorial researchers. The Luce news-gathering machine comprised thirty-eight bureaus and 390 part or full-time correspondents. Every employee was encouraged to make honest, independent judgments. But Fuerbringer's pencil was the last to touch a piece of copy, and except when Luce intervened, his was the final judgment.

The system was not designed to accommodate the non-organization man. It provided too narrow a scope for individual expression. There were no by-lines to gratify pride of authorship. Practically never did a story reach print exactly the way any one reporter reported it or any one writer wrote it. "If you had a real grievance," a European correspondent complained, "you didn't always know who to fight. You'd curse those bastards in New York. But which ones? You might have to horsewhip a dozen." When Matthews was managing editor, he couldn't refrain, being a stylish writer himself, from massive rewriting. The classic example was a story about Winston Churchill. Of the original writer's 359 words Matthews left 163 intact, including articles. More in jest than grief, Paul O'Neil, one of the deftest hands who ever turned a *Time* phrase, sent Matthews this mock lament for the mute inglory of the staff:

"Allow me to strike a chord or so on my splintered mandolin and sing a few stanzas about that nervous gladiator, the *Time* writer. The world knows little about him, and what it knows is generally incorrect. It is true that somebody in Corporate sometimes grabs one of him and holds him up to the pink window of the Publisher's Letter for the readers to see. But he is always equipped with a toupee and a thick coat of panchromatic make-up first and the world is given the impression that he just got back from Yucatan with a tan, and is going off to see Churchill as soon as he has lunch with Lana Turner at the Stork Club. There is also the FYI [*For Your Information*, the house organ] version of the *Time* writer—a man who seems to spend most of his time in Connecticut collecting antique automobiles and birds' eggs and cooking curries from recipes he picked up while he was an adviser to Generalissimo Chiang Kai-shek.

"Actually, he is an anxious looking fellow with thinning hair, whose stomach has assumed the knobby rigidity of a Mexican gourd from eating too much Union News food and from years of staring at the never ending piles of research, clippings, paper clips, unsharpened pencils and old copies of government reports which fill his in-box. He spends his days crouching in the blue tinted horror of his writing hutch like an incorrigible solitary, fumbling with paper and hating himself. Occasionally he swallows a pill. Occasionally he glares wildly out the window. But mostly he sits humped over his typewriter, smoking cigarettes and throwing them on the floor and staring morosely at the wall. He is waiting for his brain to work.

"Now this is not a pretty picture. But, like the club fighter whose work consists of getting his ears scrambled once a fortnight at St. Nicholas Arena, the *Time* writer has his points. He is durable and cunning and though he will probably never win the championship himself, he can, in his better moments, make the top men in his trade clinch, grunt and hold on for dear life. It is my contention that he is a unique and invaluable fellow. I am inclined to believe that the theory of Group Journalism is highly overrated, and that brigades of editors, researchers, advisers and assorted double domes, who are popularly believed to be helping the writer, are actually just riding around on his back, shooting at parakeets, waving to their friends and plucking fruit from overhanging branches while he churns unsteadily through the swamps of fact and rumor with his big, dirty feet sinking in to the knee at every step.

"As a writer he must be able to produce at least the illusion of literary quality, but no craftsman has been given so small a place in which to produce effects. He must use the tricks of fiction while working with fact, and if he distorts the actual timing and sequence of events to accomplish his purpose he must never do so without balancing his effects to also give the reader the smell of truth and the feel of reality. He is hemmed in on all sides, not only by restrictions of space but by restrictions of style and method. He is a kind of word mechanic who must yank odd-shaped chunks of raw fact off the overhead belt, trim it to size (often with his teeth), assemble his jigsaw of conflicting information into something with a beginning, a middle and an end, bolt the whole together with verbs and send it off through the hopper, glittering, polished and blushing with jeweler's rouge.

"He must do all this in a relatively short time. Furthermore, he is eternally surrounded by a ragged circle of secondary characters, buzzard-like creatures who waddle toward him with venal beaks and peck him cruelly when he begins to concentrate. Researchers, young women with enormous egos and a minimum of judgment, shrill at him from ink-stained mouths (they drink it). Office girls (either too fat or too thin for ogling) flap in and out piling paper and querulous notes on his desk. Window washers peer at him while dangling outside on the walls of the building.

"The *Time* writer's system must sustain other assaults. If he is a good one, he stays in his blue office year in and year out, feeling his hair dropping out, his internal organs disintegrating and his brain trembling on its blocks like a Bendix washer with an overload of soap chips. He must have something more than the bag of stock tricks he gradually accumulates with experience; he sells vitality and imagination and he must draw deeper, every week, to keep his copy sharp and fresh. Like any writer he must absorb more of the impressions of the world about him than he can record: he is like a storage battery which must be re-charged. But his is an artificial and high pressure kind of re-charging. He never sees the real, outer world. He is force-fed by paper. Good reporters, it is true, can give him the feel, smell and taste of what he is writing about, but for the most part he must supply these elements of stories from his own gizzard and nerve ends.

"None of this is written in a particularly carping or critical way. The average writer accepts the fact that *Time* is a high pressure operation. He doesn't see how it can be any different. He is, for all his muttering at certain policies, of the opinion that the magazine is good and that he is allowed to be a relatively honest man. But he suspects that his brains are going to pop out of his ears before very long. It seems to me that writers who are able to weather the vicissitudes of existence at *Time* and to reach a high degree of competence would be able to look forward to rewards other than they do at present. At *Time*, more than at most magazines, some writers contribute as much in my opinion to the finished product as many an editor. But making them senior editors is not quite the answer. A writer who is a senior editor is automatically caught up in all the ceremonial which seems to attend that high office. But he is an editor who is not an editor, a man who is living a lie, a general without an army, a sultan without a harem, a bull with no sloe-eyed Guernseys in his corral. What the hell is he anyhow? He doesn't know and nobody else does. Makes him nervous."

As the anonymous distillate of many minds moved up the assembly line to Fuerbringer, and frequently back down again for revisions, it acquired such uniformity of tone and viewpoint that a single mind might have produced it all. "The regimentation of ideas often becomes profoundly depressing," a contributing editor wrote to a friend on another magazine where he hoped to find a less inhibiting job. "It's getting to the point where almost every story must toe the line."

What correspondents filed from the scene of action the policy-makers thousands of miles away did not necessarily heed. *Time* drew upon a multitude of other sources— newspapers, wire services, official statements—and if their own man's dispatch contravened policy, they might ignore it altogether. Such was the decision that led to the Mohr *cause célèbre* in 1963. Of Charles Mohr, chief of *Time*'s Southeast Asia bureau, Luce once said, "I like passionate reporters and I especially like Mohr." From Saigon, in September, 1963, Mohr reported that the Vietnamese war was being lost, and he sharply criticized the Diem regime, a view in which the majority of his Saigon colleagues concurred. This contradicted the rosy official Pentagon view which *Time* shared. A young contributing editor, Gregory Dunne, was directed to write another version based on optimistic sources. He refused to touch not only that story but any story about Vietnam. More tractable hands took over. According to the resulting article, Diem's army was "fighting better than ever."

Fuerbringer went further. Summoning a writer from the press section, he dictated the gist of a story describing the *modus operandi* of American correspondents in Saigon. One background source already reposed in the *Time* files. Mohr had furnished it six weeks earlier. But in line with Fuerbringer's view the writer delivered an impeachment which included, by implication, *Time*'s own representative, Mohr.

". . . the press corps on the scene is helping to compound the very confusion that it should be untangling for its readers at home.

"Much of its failure can be traced to its solidarity. Foreign correspondents, wherever they are stationed, are tempted to band together into an unofficial club. . . . In Saigon, however, more than mere sociability brings the U.S. correspondents together.

"The country is completely alien to their experience. It lies in the middle of nowhere. . . . None of them speak the language with any fluency. . . . At the battlefront, both U.S. military observers and the Vietnamese brass blandly tell the newsmen stories that blatantly contradict evidence obvious to the journalists' eyes. . . .

"Such uncommon pressures unite the newsmen to an uncommon degree. . . . When they meet and unwind—in the field, in their homes or in the camaraderie of the Hotel Caravelle's eighth floor bar—they pool their convictions, information, misinformation and grievances. But the balm of such companionship has not been conducive to independent thought. The reporters have tended to reach unanimous agreement on almost everything they have seen. But such agreement is suspect because it is so obviously inbred. . . . Such reporting is prone to distortion. . . .

"The Saigon-based press corps is so confident of its own convictions that any other version of the Viet Nam story is quickly dismissed as the fancy of a bemused observer. Many of the correspondents seem reluctant to give splash treatment to anything that smacks of military victory in the ugly war against the Communists, since this would take the sheen off the theory that the infection of the Buddhist troubles in Saigon is demoralizing the government troops and weakens the argument that defeat is inevitable so long as Diem is in power. When there is a defeat, the color is rich and flowing. . . ."

Time's chief of correspondents, Richard M. Clurman, knew Mohr would resign when he read the story and he hated to lose a good man. Failing to dissuade Fuerbringer, he tried in vain to reach Luce, who was watching a football game in Atlanta. So he cabled Mohr, forewarning him of the blow about to fall and asking him to meet him in Paris. At Clurman's entreaty Mohr agreed not to quit with one proviso: *Time* must publish his own refutation.

Clurman hurried back to New York to attempt the impossible. There he found Luce in a state of surprise and confusion. He wished to lose neither Mohr nor his proficient managing editor. He suggested a compromise: let *Time* publish a follow-up story more sympathetic to the press corps. Fuerbringer complied, but the result failed to mollify Mohr. Though the second story saluted "the hardy band of U. S. correspondents . . . energetic, ambitious, convivial, in love with their work," it repeated the original offense. They were "such a tightly knit group that their dispatches tended to reinforce their own collective judgment, which was severely critical of practically everything." Mohr resigned and shortly joined *The New York Times*.

~ *twenty-two* ~

No section of *Time* showed greater bias than National Affairs. The staff might be preponderantly Democrats, with a sprinkling of left-wingers, but what reached the reader generally gilded the G.O.P. Luce's fealty to Republicanism came a close third after God and country, and, indeed, all three were related in the continuum of his ideals. "Why don't we admit Roosevelt is winning?" an editor asked the week before his second electoral victory. "Because it might help him win," said Luce.

On the political stage, as viewed through *Time*'s tinted spectacles, the Republican actors were mainly shining knights, the Democrats knaves and buffoons. To project the desired image, the magazine resorted to such artful devices as the allusive word, subtle insinuation, highly selective quoting, sleight-of-hand juxtaposition of facts, sweeping generalizations based on the unknowable opinion of "the average man" and "millions of Americans." It depicted George E. Allen, when he was Truman's unofficial adviser, as "roly-poly . . . like a pneumatic rubber hose . . . a clown." But nine years later, under the Eisenhower Administration, the same man had miraculously acquired dignity. ". . . the President chatted quietly with golfing companion George E. Allen, Washington lawyer and friend of Presidents." Under Truman, the taxpayer, calculating his returns, "did not do the job happily." But somehow under Eisenhower it had "become more and more unfashionable to criticize the income-tax level." Truman's message to Congress on the State of the Nation "made little news." Eisenhower's had "sweep and calm and balance." A Truman swing around the country was "an ancient device whereby a President can pay his expenses from his $40,000 travel allowance instead of from the party treasury." When Eisenhower took a similar fence-mending trip, *Time* commented, "From time to time, the President of the United States must travel around the country." When Truman evaded reporters' questions about a second term, he was "just acting deliberately mysterious. It has become an unprofitable inquiry and a stale joke." Eisenhower "skillfully refused to commit himself. . . . Adroitly, he fielded questions. . . ."

As governor of Illinois, Adlai Stevenson drew a bouquet. He "sent state police out to stop commercial gambling downstate. . . . Lopped 1,300 political hangers-on off the state payroll . . . men like Adlai Stevenson have dedicated themselves to a . . . proposition: that the U.S. is not a static pattern but an experiment, among other things—in good government." But when Stevenson became a presidential candidate, *Time* disclosed a different record. "He never so much as slapped the wrist of the Cook County Democratic organization, the most corrupt and powerful of existing big-city machines. . . ."

Few events ever drove so deep a wedge between *Time*'s upper and lower strata as Stevenson's first bid for the presidency in 1952. The majority of the editorial staff revered the Democratic candidate, none more than Matthews, a fellow Princetonian. "The distortions, suppressions and slanting of its [*Time*'s] political 'news,'" Matthews charged in his autobiography, "seemed to me to pass the bounds of politics and commit an offense against the ethic of journalism." Fuerbringer, then assistant managing editor, wrote a cover story on Stevenson which Matthews considered "a clumsy but malign and murderously meant attack." As *the* editor, ranking even above managing editor, he had the power to revise it. Fuerbringer went to Luce with both versions. Luce reluctantly passed Matthews' version, but forbade him to edit any more political stories. An Eisenhower cover story, scheduled for the following week, he said he would edit himself. Lest somebody tamper with the approved Stevenson story, Matthews sat over it late into the night until a research girl stuck her head in the door and jerked her thumb, meaning the issue had gone to press.

Not long after, as the votes piled up for Eisenhower, Luce sauntered gaily through the office, hands in pocket, hat on the back of his head, whistling. "Look at him," said the tearful research girl. "Only gravity is holding him down." Passing Matthews' door later, she saw him at his desk with the lights out, covering his face with his hands.

Time's treatment of Stevenson had aroused such acrimony among its staff that Matthews advised Luce to make some conciliatory gesture. So Luce bade everybody to a dinner at the Union Club. He evidently forgot its purpose, however, because midway through the dinner he rapped on his glass, rose, and announced, "In case any of you don't know who I am, let me introduce myself. I'm your boss. I can hire and I can fire." In the question period that followed an editor asked, "Do you feel *Time* has been harmed by its extreme partisanship?" "I don't think circulation has been affected," said Luce.

Matthews was determined to resign, but Luce persuaded him to reconsider and suggested that he explore the feasibility of starting a British edition of *Time*. As great an anglophile as Luce, Matthews succumbed to temptation. After four months in London he finished an enthusiastic report and delivered it personally to Luce in Rome. Then he went back to London to await the decision. It came two months later not from Luce but from a business administrator and the decision was No, whereupon Matthews cabled Luce, WHY DID YOU KEEP ME STANDING ON TIPTOES SO LONG IF YOU WERENT GOING TO KISS ME?

Returning to New York to wind up his affairs, having determined to live permanently in London, he had a farewell dinner with Luce.

". . . I decided that I might as well get a few things said. These, as I remember them, are the few things. 'Harry,' I said, 'now that you've got America how do you like it?' . . . There must have been a reply, or at least a spate of words, but what it was I cannot tell you. Anyhow I regard that as one of the few blows landed during the entire bout. As a dead-game sport, I can now admit that he jarred me once; he said (or words to this effect), 'By what right do you put me on the moral defensive?'

"I remember bringing one haymaker right up from the floor: I told him that he was kidding himself about the power of the press; the press had no power of *accomplishment*, though it did have a negative power—to debase taste, harm individuals, etc. That should have laid him out, but it never fazed him. What an iron jaw! . . .

"I did feel that one of us ought to say something about the final severance of an association that had lasted 24 years—and as he obviously wouldn't say anything, I did. . . . I just said, as I remember, that in some ways it was a wrench to leave an organization you'd given so much of your life to, or words to that effect, and that I was sorry to be saying goodbye. He seemed to agree that that might well be so. Anyhow, we shook hands on the sidewalk. . . ."

Some years after, a member of *Time*'s London bureau, Raimon von Hofmansthal, who liked both men, told Matthews that Luce was in town and they ought to get together again. Matthews agreed. So von Hofmansthal went to Luce. "Harry, wouldn't you like to see Tom?" After a long pause Luce said, "No." "At least," von Hofmansthal told Matthews, "he thought about it."

But they did meet again by chance in New York and a few evenings later Luce, to Matthews' amazement, accepted an invitation to dinner. "I felt again some of my old fondness for this grizzled tycoon whose hard-shell opinions hadn't become any softer." When Matthews confessed that his wife, Martha Gelhorn, had prompted the invitation, Luce made a courtly little bow and said, "Please tell Martha I am grateful to her."

It was with distress that Matthews followed from afar *Time*'s coverage of the 1956 race between the Stevenson-Kefauver and the incumbent Eisenhower-Nixon slate. *Time* called Senator Estes Kefauver "the professional common man." It quoted a "friend" of the senator as saying, "He is the type of fellow who if he was campaigning and came across a farmer pitching manure would take off his coat, grab another pitchfork and start to work." Then, the shiv up the hilt: ". . . pitchfork in hand, Vice-Presidential nominee Kefauver was all set to start work on the key part of his Democratic campaign." He campaigned with a "poor-mouthed, Southern drawl," his handshake was "limp," his speeches "dull, platitudinous, primerlike," and he kept an extra shirt in his briefcase because "he perspires heavily."

By contrast to that unattractive image, Richard Nixon emerged as a firm hand-shaker, "a man of consistent principles, whose values are as sound and fundamental as any in the U.S.," while Mrs. Nixon always looked "chic, fresh, interested and pleased." For an endorsement of Nixon's single-minded sincerity *Time* referred to an anonymous aide. " 'His whole life is now dedicated to being Vice-President. . . . There just isn't anything else.' "

And what motivated Stevenson to run a second time? "The presidential virus is not easy to shake off." But

Eisenhower "sincerely and devotedly" wanted "to continue the job."

For a Democrat, John F. Kennedy fared well at *Time*'s hands while a presidential candidate. Possibly Luce's long friendship with the family explained it in part. (He wrote the preface to the young Kennedy's 1940 book, *While England Slept,* pronouncing it "remarkable," and in the White House Kennedy told a *Time* correspondent, "I like Harry Luce because he reminds me of my father.") It also happened that illness kept Fuerbringer away during the campaign, and his replacement, Thomas Griffith, was an editor of a different kidney.

After the Iron Chancellor resumed his command in January, 1961, President Kennedy had little cause to love *Time*. Appraising his first hundred days, the magazine found scarcely a single act or a single quality meriting commendation. Its hostility pursued him beyond the grave. The issue following his assassination mingled grudging praise for a few undeniable accomplishments, but concluded that his Administration might be known "less for the substance of his achievements than for its style . . . his 'image' was all-important. Few presidents have ever been so preoccupied with their public relations. . . . His critics claimed that he placed politics over principle. . . ."

But to one of the dead President's habits *Time* accorded the friendliest attention—he studiously read *Time*. The publisher's promotional letter, which prefaced each issue, spoke glowingly of Kennedy's "special feeling about *Time*," and quoted him as saying he considered it America's most important magazine. The letter so incensed a *Newsweek* editor that he wired Luce, THERE IS NO AC-

COUNTING FOR TASTE BUT PERHAPS THERE SHOULD BE HOW TYPICAL OF TIME TO BLOW ITS OWN HORN WITH KENNEDY'S LAST BREATH.

Toward President Johnson, in the early days of his Administration, *Time* was relatively amiable. It played up the Texas folksiness, the raucous jollity, but with more amusement than derision. On the Republican side, *Time*'s preconvention coverage seemed to favor William Scranton of Pennsylvania, and in an adulatory *Life* article Theodore White wrote, "A self-assured aristocrat, Scranton makes the politicians come to him. . . . When he moves through a room, the eyes of dowagers caress him, girls wriggle. . . ."

The nomination of Barry Goldwater brought doubt and soul-searching to the Luce publications. For a while it seemed that the Republican tradition would prevail. *Time*'s cover story had a tone distinctly favorable to Goldwater, particularly when contrasted to the general press reaction. *Life* ran a two-part story on the financial affairs of Lyndon Johnson which unstintingly detailed the Johnsonian bent for accumulating private wealth in public office.

Then, as Republicans directed mounting criticism at the press for anti-Goldwater bias, a *Life* essay entitled *The Difficulty of Being Fair to Goldwater* examined the inconsistencies of Goldwater's statements, and hurled some sharp barbs. "A [political speech-writer's] biggest thrill comes when he sells the boss not just some language but an idea. This is a thrill which comes often to Goldwater speech-writers."

Life gave Johnson its endorsement. He "has proved himself a very effective president," and has "begun to find the consensus that will keep the country unified," said the editorial. ". . . As for Senator Goldwater and the brand of Republicanism he espouses, we do not think a landslide defeat would be unjust to either."

But if reason dictated support of Johnson, taste recoiled before his style. His sentimentality, his boisterousness, his wild-Western recreational habits scarcely fitted the Lucean ideal of presidential comportment, and *Time* highlighted some of those tendencies. Its story on the campaign windup was filled with samples of the President's overblown oratory. He was "carried away by the wonderfulness of it all" as he spoke of the Great Society. . . . "In Los Angeles, where tinsel dreams are mass-produced, Lyndon sounded every bit as utopian." Piling quote on Claghornian quote, the article reported that the President "talked, talked, talked. . . . Much of it was pure corn, or just plain tasteless." After missing his lunch in Milwaukee, *Time* noted slyly, Johnson stopped at a grocery for "a little hunk of baloney."

In contrast, while *Time* dissented from Goldwater's views, it clearly liked the cut of his jib. Here was a well-bred gentleman, and even while criticizing him, it maintained a respectful tone. The senator's lunches went unchronicled. His final campaign utterances, as *Time* reported them, were a straightforward summation of the G.O.P. case.

Then again, Luce himself declared in a 1961 address to the Magazine Publishers Association, "By now, the term Great Society has become the object of Bronx cheers and other catcalls, both highbrow and lowbrow. As for me, I have just reread [President Johnson's Ann Arbor speech projecting the Great Society], and I esteem it now, as I did when it was made, as one of the ten or twelve great milestones in American history."

✑ *twenty-three* ✑

By and large *Time*'s editor-writers were an imaginative crew with strong egos. How then did they reconcile themselves to the required submersion of individuality? The range of motives, from cynicism to conviction, was much the same as in any corporate structure. For some no conflict existed. They approved the group system, they respected the Luce concepts, and they accepted the sacrifice of ego in the spirit of a marine who puts the corps ahead of any individual. Some, not wedded to the system, found enough escape hatches to satisfy their consciences. Never, it is true, were they asked to write a word against their beliefs. While some did so, Luce would probably have fired them had he known it. When the writer's superiors slanted his copy, he could take solace in the knowledge that it left his typewriter bearing the truth by his lights.

The queasy writer could even refuse to work on a particular story without risk of dismissal. He could request reassignment to a less sensitive policy area. Of course, if he remained consistently unreceptive to the Luce wave length, he was unlikely to survive. But in practice few stories outside national and foreign affairs created serious clashes between policy and the individual. Other writers, able to compartmentalize their minds, considered their private opinions irrelevant. They thought of the story as a commodity to be sold, like any other commodity, and they packaged it as attractively as their talent allowed. And still others, the downright cynics, prized foremost Time Inc.'s agreeable working conditions and salaries—up to twenty-five thousand dollars a year for a senior editor.

The corporation was a munificent employer. Under a retirement plan, for which it paid the entire cost, and a profit-sharing plan, to which it contributed 5 per cent to 10 per cent of salary, staff members of long service could look forward to a cozy future. Time Inc. further offered five weeks' vacation, free life insurance amounting to two years of salary, health insurance, of which it paid 60 per cent, loans at 3 per cent, and under an education benefit plan, half the tuition of after-hours courses that any employee cared to study. For top key employees, who earned in salary, fees, and bonuses between $90,000 and $130,000 a year, the retirement and profit-sharing plan plus a stock option plan yielded an accrual of many hundreds of thousands. To a newly promoted editor who thanked him for the size of his salary raise, Luce said, "Why not? I was poor once and I didn't like it. Why should you?"

∾ *twenty-four* ∾

The way it works: a case history.

At about 7:15 on the morning of Friday, November 1, 1963, Otto Fuerbringer is shaving with an electric razor in his Greenwich, Connecticut home. The chore must be finished before the half-hour strikes lest the buzz of the razor drown out the 7:30 news broadcast from his bedroom radio, an inviolable prelude to his daily duties as managing editor. The big news this morning comes from Saigon. Lieutenant General Duong Van Minh of the Vietnamese army has led a revolt against President Ngo Dinh Minh and his brother, Ngo Dinh Nhu, who ran the secret police. With the deadline for next week's issue barely thirty-six hours away, Fuerbringer decides to pull the cover story already completed (Calvin Gross, superintendent of New York's public schools) and substitute General Minh and his *coup d'état*.

By 9:45 A.M., as Fuerbringer's secretary serves him a cup of tea at his tidy desk on the twenty-fifth floor of the Time & Life Building, preparations for the "crash" cover story are under way. . . .

But to start with the previous Tuesday, the beginning of the week for *Time*'s front-of-the-book sections, as Monday is for the back:

11:30 A.M. The office of Henry Anatole Grunwald, senior Foreign News editor, whose secretary, a comely East Indian, wears a shimmering sari. Around his desk sit a battalion of writers, researchers, employees of the news bureau, the picture bureau, the map department, the morgue—fifteen in all, variously armed with clipboards, notebooks, long pads of lined yellow paper. "I don't know how all of you feel this morning," says Grunwald, a chubby, owlish man, "but I feel terrible. Late night . . . Well, who's got it?" Michael Demarest, an elegantly tailored writer whose youth in London has given his speech a slight Mayfair inflection, produces a story list. It has been winnowed from an immense harvest of suggestions cabled or airmailed by *Time*'s thirty far-flung bureaus and 260 "stringer-correspondents," and transferred, according to content, to sheets tinted blue or shocking pink. Additional sources include a world-wide compendium of news tips addressed "personal and confidential" to the chief of correspondents, Richard M. Clurman, and a Washington report "for limited and confidential distribution only. Must be returned in envelope after reading to Room 2401 [Clurman's office]."

Having set a tentative agenda, Grunwald ticks off an item—"JAPAN. ATTEMPT TO KIDNAP EMPEROR'S DAUGHTER

FOILED; LOOK AT KIDNAPPING AS NATIONAL PASTIME." "Who wants it?" Demarest nods. Grunwald picks twelve stories altogether, apportioning them arbitrarily, when nobody volunteers—INDIA. NEHRU UNKNOWN IN COUNTRYSIDE; TRAVELS IN PUNJAB . . . TURKEY. NATIONAL OUTRAGE OVER MURDER OF GERMAN COUPLE . . . EUROPE. HAND-KISSING ON THE RISE. . . . Grunwald will later determine the space allotments. At this stage almost no story is sure to reach print. As the week advances, the writer may have to abandon his task halfway through and start afresh with more urgent news. Edward Hughes, who is fated to handle the week's most arduous foreign story assignment, tentatively draws ITALY. NENNI SOCIALISTS PREPARE TO ENTER COALITION WITH CHRISTIAN DEMOCRATS and DAHOMEY. ARMY OUSTS PRESIDENT MAGA. The scheduling session breaks up around noon. So have the preliminaries in the offices of the senior editors of the other front-of-the-book sections, The Nation and Business (and the day before in the eighteen back sections, Art, Books, Cinema, etc.).

Hughes, a calm, reflective, pipe-smoking southerner of forty-two, came to *Time* in 1954 from a reporter's berth on the *Wall Street Journal*. He graduated from Centre College in his native Kentucky and, following a year of Army service, took postgraduate courses in history and international politics at Harvard. For three years after joining *Time* he headed its Johannesburg bureau and for the next three its Bonn bureau. He reads and speaks French, German, Russian, and a smattering of Afrikaans. Recently separated from his wife, he lives alone in a five-room apartment fifteen blocks from his work.

Before lunch he confers with the researchers assigned to

him, a different girl for each story. Theirs will be the austere duty of challenging every word he writes for which they can find no verification. With some writers the resultant friction kindles hot fires. "*Time*," lamented an early staff member, consists of creative male geniuses surrounded by female assassins." The wielders of the knife need to enjoy their role for its own sake, there being no room at the top for females in Time Inc. Because of certain writers' looks, brains, charm, disposition, or prestige they are more popular than others among the researchers, and a good deal of jockeying goes on for assignment to the favorites. Upon the head researcher of each section devolves the Solomon-like responsibility of fairly distributing the honors. Hughes ranks high, since he is even-tempered, unpretentious, and receptive to correction which, he acknowledges, may save him from the readers' scorn.

After reviewing with Hughes the situation in Italy and Dahomey on the basis of prior knowledge and the day's newspapers, his researchers attack the task of gathering raw material. They clip stories from five or six newspapers. They consult *Time*'s Bureau of Editorial Reference where seventy-eight people compile and index a continually changing mass of some 45,000 books, files of 900 magazines and technical journals, 18,000 folders on American and foreign companies, 225,000 biographical folders, 100,-000 subject folders from "acupuncture" to "zirconium." By phone or in person the researchers interview local fonts of information.

Meanwhile, from the news desk "snap cables" speed to the foreign bureau chiefs, SCHEDULING YOUR SUGGESTIONS FOUR AND SIX. These have a way of reaching them just in time to disrupt their dinner. They, in turn, rouse their correspondents who then spend the evening trying to establish contact with people privy to the facts. By the time the bureau chiefs open their offices next morning, a telex machine, activated in New York, has transmitted the full queries. The correspondents hustle.

For the writers awaiting material Tuesday is relatively quiet. Hughes goes home at five. Wednesday he picks experimentally at the Italian story, but still lacking enough details, he gets away at seven. Thursday, following a revised scheduling conference, Grunwald reshuffles the story list. He assigns Hughes to a new European development, U.S. WITHDRAWING REGIMENT FROM WEST GERMANY; COMMENTS BY NORSTAD, BROWN AND COUVE DE MURVILLE, as well as SOUTH AFRICA. SABOTAGE CHARGES AGAINST ELEVEN DISMISSED BUT THEY ARE RE-ARRESTED, and he transfers to Demarest, whose schedule is light, Hughes's Dahomey story. Finishing the South Africa story (which will never run) in three hours and postponing the other two, Hughes leaves at nine.

As he crosses the threshold, the morning after delivering his copy, the writer's eyes move by reflex to his in-box containing one of the ten duplicates. If it bears a notation from the senior editor, "See me pls.," or, worse, if a phone call follows, "Got a minute?", trouble looms. Whether pleased or dissatisfied, Fuerbringer—who communicates his verdict to writers through the senior editors, according to protocol—is bland, smiling, low-keyed. Like many of his predecessors, with a *Time* occupational habit influenced perhaps by the Lucean manner, he tends to leave his comments dangling and fall back on some interpretive gesture not readily understood by newcomers. Manfred Gottfried seemed to be screwing the top on a Mason jar in a mysterious pantomime whose precise significance hardly anybody could grasp except that one knew something was amiss. Fuerbringer will mildly observe, "I think it's all there, but . . . ," then twist his hands as if wringing out a wet towel. Tighten the story? Squeeze it dry?

He may bounce an unsatisfactory product back to the author for drastic revision, have other hands rework it, or, in extreme cases, scrap it. But no such clouds darken Hughes's Friday morning. Instead a thunderclap rends the air when Fuerbringer switches the cover story to General Minh (at a loss in the Gross cover photograph, already run off the presses, of seven thousand dollars) and Grunwald taps Hughes. Demarest takes over Hughes's original assignments and, as an adjunct to the Minh story, a third writer whips up a short sketch of "The Last of the Mandarins," namely, the Ngo Dinh brothers.

In the *Time* scale of achievement a successful cover story is equivalent to a soldier's battle stripes. Hughes has done thirteen so far. (Duncan Norton-Taylor, who became *Fortune*'s managing editor, holds the record with some sixty.) External signs of approbation from the powers above, however, are rare and traditionally restrained, the wildest enthusiasm being conveyed by the notation on the copy, "Well done" or simply "Ah!" Luce himself has been known to go so far as to note, "Very well done." The highest accolade the writer's colleagues can bestow is to gather at the copy desk to read his latest story, as they often do, for example, when Henry Bradford Darrach, Jr., one of the country's wittiest and most influential film critics, turns in his weekly review. But the approved posture for *Time* writers excludes any outward show of eagerness. Nonchalance, detachment, cool strike the proper key. Feet on desk, shirt sleeves rolled up, tie loosened. At the same time ambition should drive them ever onward and upward. Every man is expected to buck for the senior editor's command, though without obvious strain. One can, to be sure, abide contentedly in the same minor slot, but those who so prefer are never quite considered the genuine article. As Napoleon's soldiers were said to sleep with a marshal's baton under their pillows, so the bona fide *Time* type sleeps with a senior editor's pencil under his.

As his harness mate on the cover story Hughes draws Margaret ("Cissie") Boeth, a pretty, raven-haired Mississippian with a college degree (a prerequisite for a *Time* researcher's job) from Hollins in Roanoke, Virginia. She has a husband, Richard Boeth, a *Newsweek* editor, and a nine-months-old baby. The working hours of husband and wife prevent them from seeing very much of each other or the baby, whom they employ a young English girl to tend. With her research completed on three stories assigned to her at the beginning of the week, Mrs. Boeth had planned to visit her hairdresser. This is now out of the question. From the reference files she fetches all entries on Vietnam for the past ten weeks, every relevant *Time* story since the spring, and a year's accumulation of Vietnamese political history and biographical data about the military and government figures involved. To these she adds, at Hughes's request, a series of Sunday articles by *The New York Times*'s astute Saigon correspondent, David Halberstam. Poring over the lot, she circles the most arresting portions with a red pencil. In her absorption she forgets to eat lunch. Hughes sends out for a cheeseburger. Usually on Friday Mrs. Boeth meets her husband for dinner, but she calls him at *Newsweek* to tell him she can't get away. Later, in a nearby cafeteria, she bolts an order of roast beef.

Hours earlier Clurman has cabled and phoned to the Far East. At the Hong Kong airport *Time* reporters brandish back copies of the magazine to catch the eye of fugitives from Saigon and stop them for interviews. In riotous Saigon itself correspondent Murray Gart, who witnessed the rebel attack lying flat on his belly on a rooftop two hundred yards away, bangs out a ten-thousand-word dispatch and rushes it to the cable office. But the overloaded channels can't handle it. From Los Angeles, where Madame Nhu has ended a tour of the States, come her furious accusations. ("There can be no coup," Hughes will quote her as saying, "without American incitement or backing. . . . I believe all the devils of hell are against us, but we will triumph eventually. . . . I cannot stay in a country whose government stabbed me in the back.") *Time*'s Washington bureau files the news as received by President Kennedy, and the general government reaction ("For better or worse, Minh is now Washington's man, and his success or failure will be America's success or failure"). The picture editors assemble a mass of photographs from which Fuerbringer eventually chooses seven to accompany the text, and the crack cartographer, Robert M. Chapin, Jr., draws a map of embattled Saigon, after cabling the *Time* bureau there to make sure he locates each site correctly. By 10:30 P.M. *Time*'s Chicago printing plant, one of six scattered around the country, has engraved the cover photograph of General Minh. But from Gart there are only a few garbled scraps.

Out of the material at hand Hughes starts spinning a provisional narrative. It may do in a pinch, but it lacks the incisive detail, the touches of color, that give a story vitality, and for those he needs Gart's eyewitness account. His cell-like office is so small that for convenient reference he scotch-tapes to the wall the data Mrs. Boeth has fed him. Fuerbringer's "squawk box," linking him to Grunwald's office, never stops squawking. "Be sure we tell what the U.N. mission is doing in Vietnam. . . . How about a box on the generals? . . . There's a good quote in the *Times*. . . ." As Hughes toils away, Grunwald keeps popping in to pass on Fuerbringer's directives along with some of his own. After waiting until midnight for Gart's dispatch, Hughes taxies home. For researchers detained late at night *Time* provides rented Cadillacs to drive them safely home, and for suburban dwellers, hotel accommodation. On closing nights a fleet of Cadillacs, flanking the exits, makes a glittering show.

(And where is Luce this week? Invisible yet present. Though he has formulated no specific policy line toward the Vietnam developments, he calls assistant managing editor James Keogh with some ideas about *Time* covers in general. Having recently returned from the World Council of Churches in Greece, he talks to Grunwald about the next Greek elections. *Time* should, he feels, report them extensively. There are also his impressions of Queen Frederika, whom he has long admired, that he wants to convey to Grunwald and they arrange to lunch together. With

Fuerbringer Luce discusses the Gross cover story, now put off to the following week.)

Saturday, 10 A.M. During the night both Ngo brothers have been killed. More fragments from Gart. They keep dribbling in all morning and Hughes fits a sentence here and there, like pieces of a jigsaw puzzle, into what he wrote the day before. Not until 3 P.M. does the Associated Press call to say that Gart's big dispatch has come over its wire. In desperation, after failing to file through American Embassy channels in Saigon, Gart had flown to Bangkok, a three-hour trip, used the AP facilities there, and flown back to Saigon. Hughes braces himself for the final sprint. Grunwald gets a copy of his first "take," with three more to follow, at four o'clock. At 8:30 the last page leaves Hughes's typewriter. But his travail is far from over. He pours himself a bourbon and water from Grunwald's supply (he will replenish his glass at the rate of one shot an hour for the rest of the night), eats a roast beef dinner brought to his desk from the restaurant above, and sits waiting in a daze.

The play now shifts to Mrs. Boeth, who up to late afternoon has been fidgeting in her cubicle, anxious to start her checking. At length she receives her copy of the first take, and scanning it word by word, she checks it against her sources. Over each word she marks a dot, red to indicate such library sources as the *Britannica, Webster, Who's Who,* black to indicate *The New York Times,* some authority she has interviewed, a correspondent's report. Having learned to rate the correspondents' reliability, she double-checks those she has found wanting. If convinced she can accept the writer himself as a source, she marks the word with his initials. Always at her back stand the specters of libel, the informed reader's ridicule, and the displeasure of Essie Lee, chief of researchers. In these frenzied closing nights the *Time* fact factory reverberates with the plaintive cries of Mrs. Boeth and her sisters as they try to track down obscure trivia. "How do you determine the sex of a panda? Where did George Washington return General Howe's dog under a flag of truce? What became of the Haitian Declaration of Independence? Which Siamese twin was on the left?"

Fortified by a bourbon highball and a sirloin steak, Mrs. Boeth tackles the next takes. "Those 'ng's' and 'nh's' in Vietnamese names," she sighs, "you can slip up so easily." Confronting Hughes, she points to a misplaced quote— "Diem said that in a speech, not to Gart"—and an event out of chronological sequence, and by way of proof she produces a *Times* clipping. She could find no source for a description of Saigon's boulevards as "tree-lined." "I've been there," says Hughes. "Well, in the photographs they don't look tree-lined to me," she insists. He finally convinces her and she marks the phrase "E.H." But "red-brick cathedral" she will not accept. A color shot shows it to be brown. Hughes yields. "And seven Buddhist monks didn't burn themselves alive," she persists. "It was six. The seventh was a woman." "So she was," says Hughes.

No checking is final until a copy bears Grunwald's and Fuerbringer's initials, and one or both may first request editorial changes or insertions, necessitating further checking. Grunwald, in fact, wants Hughes to add a sentence about an abortive plan for Diem's escape as well as a more vivid description of the palace guards. Mrs. Boeth receives the last initialed take at 12:30. From her weary hands it goes to a copyreader, who combs it for infractions of spelling, grammar, syntax, and the house style rules, then back again to Grunwald. Only when the senior editor, having satisfied himself that neither checking nor copy-reading has altered any shade of meaning, circles his initials, is the story ready for production. At 4:30 Sunday morning, after a bourbon nightcap, Mrs. Boeth departs. This time her husband is in bed asleep.

A last delicate bit of surgery remains to Hughes. He must adjust the length of his story to the available space, giving the printers some leeway. This procedure is known as "greening" and "killing." With a green crayon he brackets optional cuts and with a red crayon obligatory ones. Dawn is near when the Chicago plant confirms the final fit by teletype. It is drizzling, but Hughes walks home to clear his head. He eats a slice of cake, drinks a glass of milk, and sleeps until noon. A company Cadillac takes Fuerbringer to Greenwich.

Even Monday morning is not too late, though it can be costly, to nail an error before the magazine is completely distributed, because, owing to time differentials, the Chicago and Los Angeles printing plants start their runs later than those in the east. Very early every Monday morning, the day before most newsstands sell *Time*, when the staff doesn't work, a curious mode of delivery takes place in Greenwich. A truck from the Old Saybrook, Connecticut plant, rolling toward New York with a load of the magazines, stops at the Greenwich railroad station. There a taxi driver waits with his window down. The trucker hands him eight copies. The taxi then drops one off at Fuerbringer's house and the rest at the houses of the other top Time Inc. men who inhabit the area. Thus, with their breakfast, they get their first look at the finished product. One May morning in 1965 Fuerbringer spotted a hideous boner that sent him flying to the phone to rouse Robert Boyd, the senior editor in charge of production. *Time* had identified a photograph of the assassinated Santo Domingo dictator, Trujillo, as that of ex-President Juan Bosch. It was Boyd's last-minute inspiration to minimize the expense of a new plate by phoning to the later-starting plants a simple change of captions.

~ *twenty-five* ~

Incredibly, despite all the elaborate precautions, blunders plague *Time*. Probably no issue, in fact, escapes them totally. According to a common complaint of people with specialized knowledge, they seldom read a story in their field that can meet rigorous standards of accuracy. Leaving aside errors of interpretation, value judgment, bias, and oversimplification, they speak only of simple, verifiable facts that somehow get muddled. How can so many eagle eyes let slip by such bobbles—to cite but a few among hundreds—as "Management Consultant John Diebold, the man who invented the very word 'automation' . . ." (a Ford Motor Co. vice-president, Del Harder, invented it); icosahedrons are "two-sided solid figures" (they have twenty sides); "Dr." as the title of a British surgeon (they are always called "Mr."); the French *pourquois* twice in the same story (the word has no *s*); "Amy Vanderbilt, official etiquette consultant for the U. S. State Department . . ." (no such function exists); The New York Hilton Hotel provides its guests with "free parking" (it charges $4.75 per twenty-four hours)?

Various explanations suggest themselves—the complexity and high speed of the editorial machine; a defect inherent in journalism by committee; the occasional inattentions of exhausted researchers. Some *Time* errors, however, are hard to absolve on the grounds of accident.

Aiming a shaft at a favorite target (March 16, 1959), *Time* reported, "Pennsylvania liberal Democrat Joe Clark took the Senate floor to recommend a balanced budget—liberal Democrat style. . . . Nowhere did Clark suggest where costs be cut." A closer scrutiny of the record would have shown that the senator actually said, ". . . some of the bills proposed for agriculture by Democratic Senators from farm states . . . would result in considerable economies below the more than $3 billion in this year's price support operations. I am also sure that through further unification of the armed services, better management of procurement and other means, the Defense Department could save considerable sums."

To *Time*'s put-down the senator retorted from the floor, "If *Time* magazine were selling applesauce instead of a weekly publication, it would not be able to call itself, as it does, 'the weekly newsmagazine,' because the Federal Food, Drug, and Cosmetic Act of 1938 would prohibit it. That act requires the truthful labeling of goods for sale."

Referring to one of forty-two students who traveled to

Red China (August 26, 1957), *Time* perpetrated six errors in seven lines. ". . . Sally Belfrage, 17, raised in Manhattan by her British father, Cedric Belfrage, editor-in-exile of the Communist *National Guardian* who was deported from the U.S. in 1955 and who now works for Moscow radio. Sally is touring Communistland at the behest of devoted father Cedric 'to absorb both Eastern and Western atmosphere.' " Miss Belfrage was twenty and raised in Croton-on-Hudson, New York. Though decidedly left-wing, the *National Guardian* was not Communist. Belfrage never worked for Moscow Radio. His daughter's trip was entirely her idea, and its purpose, to gather information for a book, which the New York house of Reynal published the following year under the title *A Room in Moscow*. The quote attributed to her she never uttered. "The only achievement in accuracy," she recalled, "was the spelling of my name, which was sufficient to make the rest of the smear stick."

In 1962 Columbia University's *Journalism Review* asked 203 members of the Washington press corps which of ten magazines* they relied on most in their work. *Time* headed the list (33.5 per cent) with *U.S. News & World Report* and *Newsweek* placing second and third. But on the question of fairness and reliability *Time* got only 9 votes as against 75 for *Newsweek* and 66 for *U.S. News & World Report*. The *Review* noted: "It was a revealing exercise. Not only did 24.1 per cent of the correspondents fail to list any news magazine, but 16.9 per cent wrote

* *Time, U.S. News & World Report, Newsweek, The Reporter, government publications, Harper's, Business Week, The Economist, The New Republic, Fortune.*

'None' and some of them decorated the margins of the questionnaire with such comments as 'Are you kidding?' and 'No such animal.' . . .

"It should be mentioned there is nothing necessarily strange about relying upon a news magazine without trusting it. A magazine, as well as a newspaper, can provide leads to stories.

"The case of *Time*, however, offers a special insight into the Washington press corps. *Time* is widely read by the correspondents, it seems clear, because of its crisp cleverness. Two of the correspondents who wrote 'None' in the space available for listing the fairest and most reliable news magazine added, 'But *Time*'s the only one worth reading,' and '*Time* has the only literate writers.' One correspondent who dislikes *Time* intensely confessed that he could not bear to miss an issue. He paid for a subscription to it, then discovered that he could get each issue a day earlier by buying it at a newsstand. Unable to wait for his subscription copy, he began picking it up at the newsstand. 'Then,' he said, 'I cuss my way through it.'"

❧ *twenty-six* ❧

Luce's curiosity was obsessive. He engorged facts, the trivial as well as the momentous, his attention to people quickened or flagged according to what they could tell him that he didn't know. Anybody with expert knowledge he would pump dry. The wife of a *Life* editor whom he was berating for arriving late at his house for dinner—"It's always *my* people who are late!"—turned aside his wrath by tossing him a fact as one might quiet a bawling infant by popping a candy into its mouth. "Did you know," said the clever girl, "that airlines won't carry a woman seven months' pregnant?" Luce's tirade stopped dead. "What's that? What's that?" "In case of premature birth, of course." Curiosity once led him to a psychoanalyst's couch, but the first hour was the last. "The fellow didn't tell me anything," Luce complained.

Slaking his thirst for facts became a recognized means of acquiring status in the organization. "You couldn't make a general statement with Luce," said one long-sufferer. "You couldn't say a dozen men got off a plane if there were eleven, and he'd want to know who the eleven were." Some employees, unable to stuff themselves with sufficient information, developed considerable ingenuity at faking or evading answers. In anticipation of a Luce visit to Denver the *Time* man there, unfamiliar with the names of all the surrounding mountains and surmising, correctly as it turned out, that Luce would ask, invented them. A Texas correspondent, recently transferred from Peru, was driving Luce through an oil field in a Jeep. "What are the Peruvians up to?" Luce asked out of the blue. Having no notion, the Texan picked a deep rut in the Jeep's path and took a teeth-rattling jolt. Every time Luce broached another imponderable the Jeep hit a rut. The ride ended with Luce badly shaken and for once silent.

Frank Grimes was a noted Abilene editorialist, an impressive figure, pole-thin, given to black clothes and a black string tie. No sooner had he met Luce at a Dallas party than the publisher opened fire. "Mr. Grimes, they tell me you write great editorials. Why is that?" Stupefied, Grimes reached for a bourbon. A moment later: "What are the people in Texas thinking about?" Grimes downed another drink. "Are they religious? How do they feel about God?" He drove the editorialist to speechless intoxication.

Dining with his Chicago staff one evening in 1945, Luce suddenly asked its chief, Penrose Scull, "What's happened to Chicago? Where's all the old renaissance crowd—Hecht,

MacArthur, Hansen, Masters?" The names meant little to Scull, but he ventured a brave bluff. "Why, nothing's happened to them. They just moved to the suburbs." In the awkward silence Luce dropped the subject. Shortly after, Scull was assigned to a less demanding post.

The ordeal of Serrell Hillman, then a newcomer to the San Francisco bureau, ended more happily. During the fall of 1951 word came from New York to expect both Luce and his wife. All seasoned hands being engaged in the preparation of a *Life* color spread on a University of California football game, the bureau chief, Al Wright, burdened Hillman with the duty of meeting the Luces at the airport and ushering them around town. Panic assailed the novice. A confirmed city-dweller, without a car, he seldom visited the outskirts and knew nothing about the shipyards, factories, and housing developments lining the highway, sites sure to fire Luce's curiosity. Wright, on the other hand, drove the route to work every day and he reassured Hillman. "Get out your notebook," he said, "and I'll describe everything Luce can possibly see between the airport and the hotel." His encyclopedic knowledge filled a fat notebook and Hillman spent the next several nights memorizing every note.

On the crucial morning he set out in a chauffeur-driven Cadillac, full of confidence, with soaring daydreams of impressing Luce and thus shooting up the organization ladder. Suddenly, his memory began to fail. He reached for the notebook. He had left it at home. Too late to turn back. Sickened, he stared blankly to the right and left of the highway. He recognized nothing. He approached the arrival gate like a condemned mounting the scaffold.

With the Luces ensconced in the back seat, Hillman braced himself for the worst. Eyes glued to the rearview mirror, he could see Luce's probing gaze, a flood of questions forming on his lips. In an inspiration born of despair, Hillman turned to Mrs. Luce, whose new play, he remembered, had opened in Boston. "Please tell me about the play, Mrs. Luce," he said. She was delighted to and for the rest of the drive he kept her talking. Luce never got in a single question.

Once at the center of town, Hillman relaxed. Here he was on safe ground—or so he imagined. Mrs. Luce thrust him back into panic by asking, "What's that building?" Though Hillman knew it as well as his name, the answer eluded him. He feigned a coughing fit. The chauffeur saved him. "It's the opera house, Mrs. Luce."

Whenever Luce traveled, as he tirelessly did, the strain upon his news bureau personnel was severe. Not only must they be prepared to appease his voracious appetite for information, they must arrange for him to meet important, knowledgeable people, and without waste motion. In his hectic impatience he accepted no delays except perhaps those caused by acts of God. To reconstruct some typical episodes from the lifelong Luce odyssey:

London. The postwar austerity phase. Miss Honor Balfour, an Englishwoman working for the *Time* bureau, reproaches him, "We happen to be your main ally. Instead of spending three or four days here in London, viewing us through the Martini haze of Claridge's windows, or getting the picture from Winston Churchill and Lord Beaverbrook, why don't you go out into the provinces and look at the grass roots for a week or so?" "Right," says Luce, "I'll take you up on it."

He is back the following year, eager to take a ten-day trip through the provinces. Miss Balfour, a Lancastrian who has twice run unsuccessfully for a seat in Parliament, steers him to her native province for a taste of its bleak, wintry moors, with their dour inhabitants. Near Manchester she books him into a "family and commercial hotel" lacking central heating and private bathrooms. Out of a thick "muggen" cup he drinks his morning tea already poured by the chambermaid, who tells him, "Ah don't know if yer takes sugar, but Ah've put in two anyway."

After meeting the area's big industrialists, he lunches and sups with local trade union leaders and small mill-owners. "Oo's yon bugger yer bringin'?" one horny-handed worker asks Miss Balfour. She discloses the name. "Luce? Never 'eard of 'im. Wot's 'e do?" Publishes magazines, he learns. "Aw well, let's 'ave a look at 'im. 'E can 'ave a piece of our minds."

At the end of the tour, Luce, that Anglophile since boyhood, exclaims with emotion, "Yes, indeed, Britain *is*, repeat is, our chief ally! And no wonder she's what she is! A great people!"

A late staff dinner in London. "Africa," an editor remarks, "is on the eve of a great transformation." Luce pricks up his ears. "Who's got a map?" At that time and place nobody. "Clear the table," he commands and, with all hands pitching in, he draws a map on the tablecloth. "Now, what's the constitutional situation here . . . and down here? . . ." Luce has discovered Africa. The Q & A lasts until early morning. Not long after, *Life* publishes a special issue on Africa.

Paris. A tête-à-tête with de Gaulle. Luce speaks no French, but understands it. They spend an hour together. The general lectures him on America's mistakes. Speaking of the Russians, he declares, "After all, they are essentially Western and the time will come when they will want to be part of the West. Communism must be fought now, but it will go away." "There are two kinds of Frenchmen," Luce says later, "those I can understand and those I can't. De Gaulle with his beautiful diction and clear mind belongs to the former."

To celebrate *Time*'s fortieth anniversary, the Paris bureau hires, at a cost of $4600, a *bateau-mouche*, the same that once bore Queen Elizabeth up and down the Seine, and invites 180 celebrities to a nighttime party on the river, among them Prime Minister Pompidou; Pierre Lazareff, publisher of the newspaper *France-Soir;* the singer Juliette Greco; the Comtesse de Ribes. . . . The hour of embarkation is 7:30. At 8:15 barely half the guests have arrived. Luce nevertheless gives the order to shove off.

Moscow. Luce to bureau chief Israel Shenker, "Are people happier here?" Shenker can't say.

Geneva. Before the Reformation Monument with its gigantic statues of Calvinist theologians—Calvin himself, Farel, Beza, John Knox. "Great, aren't they?" says Luce to the Time Inc. man with him. "Yes, fine-looking men, but would you want to lunch with them, Harry?" "How do you mean?" "They look so rigid, so inhuman. Would

211

you really want to lunch with them?" "Well, no, I guess not," but he sounds unconvinced.

Zurich. The airport. Luce has appointments in Vienna, but because of bad weather no planes can land there. He tears up to the booking counter. "What planes *will* be taking off?" "Where to?" "Anywhere." The booking agent smiles gently like a man humoring a lunatic. "There's a flight to London in an hour, to Paris in forty minutes, and to Amsterdam in twenty minutes." "Give me a ticket to Amsterdam." There must be statesmen in Amsterdam whom he can talk to profitably. The Swiss stringer seeing him off phones his Amsterdam opposite number. By the time Luce lands, about an hour later, the impossible has been accomplished; an audience awaits him with the prime minister.

Aloft over the Alps. April. Luce discovers the Alpine spring and writes to *Life*'s managing editor, "We ought to do something about spring here." Next year a photographer-researcher team hover over the area in a helicopter, the expedition costing $46,000, but spring is late that year and the colors lack enough *Life*-like verve for publication.

By car through Austria. The scenery dazzles Luce. "We have bigger mountains and forests at home," he remarks to his companion. "Why is this so beautiful?" "Because it's man-made. Everything has been cultivated and tended for centuries. Only the rocks were made by God." The explanation offends Luce, for whom America is God's special country.

Hamburg. He wants to meet Rudolf Augstein, editor of the flourishing *Time* imitation, *Der Spiegel*. Preparing

Augstein for the encounter, Frank White, the Bonn *Time* man traveling with Luce, advises him, "Don't bother with shop talk about business details. What interests Mr. Luce is economics and politics." Luce's first question, after a long, hard stare: "Do you write your own direct-mail subscription letters?" "Why, no," says Augstein. "I have a special man for that." "Well, it's the heart of the business. An editor should do it himself. I always did."

"A good foreign correspondent is first of all a good tourist," Luce contends, and he believes that a requisite of good tourism is to buy the products and eat the food of the country. In Hamburg's posh Atlantic Hotel, with its French cuisine, he tells the waiter, "Go get me something typically German." "But, *Monsieur* Luce—" "No, it should be *Herr* Luce." The waiter helplessly suggests filet mignon. Studying the menu, Luce growls, "Dammit, where's the apple strudel?"

Bonn. Gift shopping with Mrs. Frank White, he inspects Germany's famous Rosenthal china. Mrs. Luce has an affinity for the color pink. A pink rose always festoons her breakfast tray. Luce wonders, "Does this stuff come in pink?" The salesman shows him some. He chooses a breakfast set for two. "If I get more, Clare will be tempted to have people in for breakfast. It's one of the few times we have alone together." Mrs. White points admiringly to a 125-piece dinner service. "All right, I'll have that too." Next day it is delivered to the Whites.

Rome. Passing through after a tour of the Near East, Luce wants to discuss his observations with Eugene Cardinal Tisserand, Secretary of the Sacred Congregation of the Eastern Church, and an authority on Arabic culture.

Correspondent William Rospigliosi arranges it. Luce informs His Eminence, "A religious revival is brewing in the Near East."

"Oh," says the cardinal, "I was not aware of it."

"Just got back. Pretty sure I'm right."

"I have spent some years in that part of the world. How long were you there, Mr. Luce?"

"Fortnight."

"Really! How enterprising of you to learn Arabic for such a brief stay."

"Don't speak Arabic."

"You mean you got by on your French alone?"

"Don't speak French."

The cardinal's irony grows sharper, but like a brave bull stuck full of banderillas, Luce stands his ground. (And events prove him partly right. A wave of pan-Arabic nationalism, if not religion, soon sweeps the Moslem world and Nasser emerges.)

Preceding a later, longer Luce sojourn in Rome, George Jones, the bureau chief, takes too literally a cable from New York telling him not to disrupt the office routine on Luce's account. Nobody meets the voyager at the airport. He phones the bureau. "I'm terribly sorry," says Jones, "but we're right in the middle of a cover story." From the Hotel Hassler, Time Inc. Vice-President Allen Grover, accompanying Luce, makes a second call. "When Mr. Luce is in Rome, the bureau must be mobilized," he tells Jones. "Mr. Luce comes first." Rospigliosi hurries to the hotel to repair the damage. Luce receives him with an air that says, "If you're so much on your toes, let's see what you know." Interviews with high government officials, which might have appeased him, can't be arranged at such short notice. Something of a historical scholar, Rospigliosi proposes a tour of the Forum. At the Arch of Titus a brass band is playing. "Who are they?" Luce asks. Rospigliosi risks a guess. "The Air Force band." His heart sinks as Luce steps closer. By rare luck, it *is* the Air Force band. Characteristically, Luce is more impressed by Rospigliosi's glib guess than by his eloquent recital of Roman history. Anybody can find the latter in books, but it takes a good reporter to command such a trifling detail about the city he covers.

In the Mediterranean aboard la Belle Creole *with Mrs. Luce.* Owned by the Greek shipping magnate Stavros Niarchos, it is the world's biggest private yacht. The object of the cruise: skin-diving, enthusiastically pursued by Mrs. Luce, but of no appeal to her husband. Niarchos runs short of liquor. Nearby a U. S. Navy fleet is maneuvering. Mrs. Luce dons pink slacks—"Always pink for the Navy," she notes—jumps into a motor launch flying the American colors, heads for the flagship, and returns bearing ample liquor supplies.

Tokyo. Eisenhower has just defeated Stevenson, for whom most of the *Time* men here, like most *Time* men everywhere, voted, and Luce wonders how much the average Japanese understands about the election. In a restaurant with the bureau chief, Dwight Martin, he instructs an interpreter to ask a waitress if she can name the candidates. The interpreter summons one. "She say Eisenhower-san and Stevenson-san." "Good. Now ask her who the voters were for." Martin chuckles wickedly as the interpreter replies, "She say Stevenson-san." "They've been brainwashed!" cries Luce.

He calls on Ambassador Douglas MacArthur II for a rundown on current U. S.-Japanese relations. "I'll try to sum it up under six headings," says MacArthur, and delivers a two-hour exposition. Luce listens with ferocious concentration, not missing a syllable. When MacArthur finishes, he says, "Very interesting, Mr. Ambassador, but you mentioned six headings. You've only covered five."

New Delhi. The local bureau's Don Connery, ex-Harvard, an adept at Time Inc. gamesmanship, not only satisfies Luce's curiosity on every question, but conquers him with a monumental written assemblage of facts about India. Luce forwards them to *Fortune* with a covering letter telling the editors, "If I say anything that contradicts Connery, he is probably right."

⚞ *twenty-seven* ⚟

The fruit of Luce's journeys were memoranda to his lieutenants prescribing policy and often embodying reportage
as perceptive as any his magazines printed. No stenographer
could follow the pell-mell rush of his spoken thoughts.
One girl who tried in the early days quit on the spot,
crying, "He's crazy!" He couldn't type a first draft either,
being manually inept. He required a pencil to slow down
his thought process and marshal it into an orderly sequence.
Consequently, he seldom dictated, not even a letter, but
left it to "Miss T.," as he called Corinne Thrasher, his
secretary, to decipher his scrawl. The procedure was set
from the day, in 1930, when she first came to work.
She had barely sat down to her desk before Luce, just
back from Russia, burst through the door and deposited
a manuscript which he had written on both sides of flimsies

while riding a Russian train. "If you can read my hand-writing," he said, "we'll get along all right." She stayed twenty-eight years.

Some of Luce's memoranda, ranging from brisk commands to dissertations, the recipients treasured as collector's items for the glimpses they afforded of his teeming, probing, paradoxical, arrogant and humble, cold and passionate mind. The classic of Lucean brevity, considering the importance of the subject, was addressed to Allen Grover: "See me about Hitler. H.R.L." At an assistant managing editor he fired the sardonic query, "Would it be possible to have all TIME writers and correspondents instructed on the improper use of the word 'fortuitous'?"

"TIME is full of a lot of commonplace writing," he admonished Alexander, Billings, and Fuerbringer (March 12, 1953).

"In 1922 Walter Lippmann warned us against 'journalese.' There's a lot of 1953 journalese in TIME—vis:

"1) taking 'another longer look' (Page 50 of this issue) or taking a 'hard look.'

"2) 'bit'—as in the statement on Page 54 of this issue that London's voice [George London, the operatic basso] is 'a bit light.'

"Please abolish these two tiresome idioms and advise your Senior Editors to freshen up their language."

In similar vein, referring to a business story (June 25, 1962): ". . . it says that the Bruce company had 'net income' of $25 million. It would appear from the following sentence that the statement should have read 'net sales' or gross receipts or just 'sales.' But maybe I have spots in the eyes.

"Spots or no, I am confirmed in my suspicion that most journalists, including LIFE journalists, don't know one damn thing about business—and this suspicion pains me.

"I await now the explanations. Perhaps you will tell me that in the new sophistication of Harvard economics, my vocabulary is out of date and that Messrs. Billings and Breen (and their copy editors) know what they are talking about—and always did.

"In which case I will retreat mumbling back to my corner and order three more beers."

As Luce, the generator of magazine ideas (August 21, 1961): "I suggest the only thing to do is to insist that every cover of LIFE shall say 'IMPORTANT.' . . . My current example . . . is that some week in November we should have *Rembrandt* on the cover—apropos that $1,000,000 sale. We could have either Rembrandt himself or a great story-telling Rembrandt painting. The cover would, of course, be supported by a magnificent Rembrandt show inside.

January 15, 1962. "*Bringing Up Children*. I don't recall we have had anything notable on this subject in a long time. Could be a picture story. How one set of parents brings up their children—in pictures. Then commentary on alternatives, pros and cons . . .

"*Labor*. Plain and simple, let's photograph a big Labor Union. Maybe Steel. Maybe Electrical Workers. They say 1962 is good to be a year of front-page Labor news. Let's see a union. I'd like to meet my fellow-citizen, the big union Laborer, who seems to be making life difficult and expensive for me in so many ways. . . . And incidentally, why does the laborer want shorter hours? What's he going to do with his leisure? Become a race-track bum or an alcoholic?

"*Mariology*. . . . Wasn't there some idea of doing it this Easter? (Perhaps *not* the best time because so divisive.) What is the 'month of Mary'? Is it May? August celebrates the Immaculate Conception, I think. . . . Pictorially, of course, it's rich.

"*Music*. We are all aware of the tremendous increase in consumption of music in the last 20 years—records, hi-fi, highbrow and lowbrow. There's been much more consumption of music (good music) than of Art. Of course, Art is our national specialty because the pages of LIFE can show Art and they can't play music. Still we could and should do some pretty big stuff on Music. . . .

"*College newspapers*. Might be interesting.

Same day to *Life*'s editorial writer, John K. Jessup. "*Gambling*. Shouldn't we take up specifically Bingo? This is the (Catholic supported) 'good' family gambling game. It's become a source of corruption. All organized gambling does. Worse than corruption is the stultifying of the mind —see what happened in England. I am against bingo— especially as it is advertised as the nice harmless form of gambling.

"Much better play for highest stakes is bridge or poker —which take some brains and even some 'character.'

"*Traffic*. I am 100% with you in opposition to curbside parking. It's ridiculous. . . .

"*Merriam-Webster* [the dictionary]. We should denounce the hell out of it."

April 3, 1962, from Phoenix. "The key word is: Religious Illiteracy.

"A story of how little today's Christians know about their 'faith' and about the Bible is a real good shocker. And I mean church-going Christians and their children.

"Such a story is plain and simple—and doesn't involve 'metaphysics.'"

August 13, 1963. "There are only 30,000,000 sheep in the U.S.A.—same as 100 years ago. What does this prove? Answer??? . . .

"Postscriptum: today I read in TIME that Krushchev was swinging in his hand two plastic containers of fertilizer and it was said that Krushchev 'seems drugged with the problem of agriculture.' I also read that a group of American experts say that agriculture is turning up in Russia and the satellites. There are even noises to the effect that things are better in Communist China. . . .

"Postscriptum: do you know who the largest chicken producer in the U. S. is? I know a man who has 3,000,000 chickens. Does that make him the biggest?

"Postscriptum: the farm implement companies are having a very good year—a piece of intelligence I did *not* read in TIME.

"*Conclusion* from all this: None.

"Except I think there are a lot more good stories (and items) in Agriculture than the Editors of TIME, LIFE and FORTUNE find."

August 21, 1962. "Speaking of *Lord of the Flies* [William Golding's novel]:—How does its popularity with the young fit with our theory of The New Breed?

"How does Salinger [J. D. Salinger, *The Catcher in the*

Rye] fit with the increase of serious work in the colleges?

"And how do both fit with the purposefulness of the Peace Corps? Would Zen Buddhists be Peace Corpsmen?"

As Luce, the watchdog of the American Proposition and the Republican party (January 15, 1962, his third memo of the day): "Incidentally, one of the points that could be made is that we're pretty sick and tired of the monotonously cheap and easy attacks on our society—whether in novels or by those dreadful socio-economists like Mills. What really requires some knowledge and imagination is to show how 'attractive' structures of social life can be developed. In the times of the Fabian Socialists and all that, the critics of 'capitalism' at least pointed to a happier world—via socialism or whatever. Even psychiatry came along as a kind of gospel of hope—but now it's simply a tool for making 'adult' movies respectably pornographic. . . ."

May 8, 1962. "In view of the many things 'wrong' with the U. S. economy, there is, could be, a very strong Republican case. (By 'wrong' I mean things out-of-balance, dislocated, distorted, unnaturalness piled on unnaturalness.) But instead of coming to grips with what's wrong, what do Republicans say? They talk generalities about 'creeping socialism' or conduct wailing wall exercises about 'cost-wage' squeeze—introducing a slight degree of anti-Laborism (but let's don't lose any Labor votes!) Or, from time to time, they will pick up on a little scandal like Billie Sol Estes, or a goof of the administration. Or, at the Republicans' current best, Senator Goldwater will crack jokes. I am bored to tears with the conventional Republican talk and while I appreciate jokes, they are hardly a substitute for a 'platform.' (I am also not carried away by a Rockefeller saying that he will do it better, cheaper.)

"For a lot of practical reasons—for all the practical reasons in mind—I do not see how the Republican Party can make the kind of exciting sense I'd like it to make.

"A third party? Well, you know how impractical *that* is.

"So I guess we just have to wait for the distortions and dislocations to get worse. Am I now reverting to a pessimistic view—contrary to last Friday? No, I rather think we'll muddle through.

"Muddling through is wonderful—the only trouble is, it's so goddam boring."

As Luce, the policy-maker (August 24, 1949): "STRICTLY CONFIDENTIAL TO THOSE TO WHOM THIS POLICY MEMO IS SENT." "I send you herewith a tentative summary of what I think may be considered to be the policy attitude of TIME Inc. publications on broad questions of public policy. . . . After receiving your comments, I will consider what to do next." There followed seven single-spaced pages covering in part what Luce saw as the two great trends of the preceding six months—"Truman's failure to get practically any of the Truman (domestic) program adopted," and "in Europe, the political trend away from socialism and emphatically away from 'dirigism.'"

Luce commended a *Time* article for containing the outlines of the kind of speech Truman ought to have made on Asia. He then enumerated his specific policies toward various countries and issues. *Europe:* Continuation of the

Marshall plan but insistence that Europe put its "contiguous houses in order according to sound principles of industry and commerce"; military defense of the West must be under U. S. leadership. *Germany:* "On the one hand we want due precautions against the 'rise of German nationalism' but on the other hand we want Germany, like any other people, to develop their individual capacities to the utmost. . . ." *Hong Kong, etc.:* "The American role in Asia is to liquidate imperialism and to help establish self-government based on constitutional order." *"As to our own America:* We have taken a fairly strong and consistent stand against Statism."

September 21, 1961, five months after the Bay of Pigs disaster. "Should Kennedy proclaim a State of National Emergency? I think he probably should *not,* but I would support him if he did. Instead of proclaiming a national emergency, what he should do is to proclaim that he will cut down on all spending that does not have an immediate bearing on our survival in the next few years, and that he will spend whatever is needed to secure survival. I am afraid that Kennedy will find it easier to proclaim a national emergency than to do what I recommend."

~ *twenty-eight* ~

During its fortieth reunion the Yale class of '92 voted the Reverend Henry Winters Luce the classmate who had led the most successful life. Acute intestinal pain, later diagnosed as a sympton of stomach ulcer, had forced him to leave China in 1925. Hoping to avoid surgery, he endured prolonged medical treatment and a dreary diet. As he traveled the country seeking, as usual, money for his beloved Chinese colleges, he had to pump out his stomach at night before he could sleep. An operation proved unavoidable. Three weeks after it he was on the move again, fund-raising. He also taught Oriental religion and philosophy, first at Hartford Seminary, then at Princeton. In 1935 he ventured a last trip to China. When he returned, he and Mrs. Luce made their home in Haverford, Pennsylvania with their daughter Emmavail and her husband,

Leslie Severinghaus, the principal of Haverford School. In 1940, while lecturing at Princeton, he had a stroke that left him partially paralyzed but still able to move around. The doctors told his family that he would live as long and more happily if they let him pursue his customary activities. Thereafter he always carried, in case of emergency, a paper giving his name and address.

On only two major issues had the minister and his older son ever seriously differed—Catholicism and prohibition. The aim of the Catholic Church, Dr. Luce maintained, was not truth, a position inadmissible to Henry R. Luce. He welcomed prohibition because he condemned drinking on moral and religious grounds. His son, however, considered the Volstead Act unconstitutional. It was one reason he supported for the presidency, to his father's dismay, a repeal candidate as well as a Catholic, Al Smith. Luce further deplored the social deformity resulting from prohibition. "People got preoccupied with it," he said. "How to make bathtub gin, who was a good bootlegger—all the drinking and all the talking about drinking absorbed too much intellectual energy." After repeal Dr. Luce entreated him in vain not to accept liquor ads. At the same time Luce, ever concerned for the welfare of his Time Inc. family, fretted about the heavier drinking members. In an effort to reform them by example he renounced for a while even a single luncheon cocktail and those lunching with him had to settle for water. "I came to see that my father had a point," he said. "So much damage was done."

Regarding the Far East, there was no disagreement. Decades earlier, when most Americans who thought about

Japan at all thought of her as a nation of quaint flower arrangers and tea ceremonialists, Dr. Luce had foreseen the rise of Japanese imperialism. China, he pleaded, was America's natural ally. Now he kept badgering his son-in-law, "When are you school people going to wake up to the fact that America's future lies in the Pacific?" He was ailing the day the Japanese bombed Pearl Harbor, five weeks after his seventy-third birthday. In bed that night he wrote to a friend, "We are entering a new great period in world history. We must believe that at long last all will work out for a total larger good." He died next day. To Theodore White, who offered his condolence, Luce, dry-eyed, his jaw set, said, "He lived long enough to know that we and the Chinese are on the same side."

The bulk of Luce's little-publicized philanthropies commemorated his father's devotion to China, the Presbyterian Church, and education. Dispensed through the Henry Luce Foundation, whose assets exceeded $1,500,000, they included grants to the Chinese Institute of America, designed to promote cultural ties between Nationalist China and the U. S.; the United Board of Education in China, the culmination of Dr. Luce's efforts, which grew to support six Far East Christian institutions; Union Theological Seminary; Yale; and Wellesley College. At Union Theological the foundation established the Henry W. Luce Visiting Professorship of World Christianity. At Tunghai University on Formosa the foundation built, at a cost of $150,000, the Luce Memorial Chapel. Luce's sister Elizabeth, dedicated the chapel. Afterward Chiang Kai-shek told her, "You are a member of the family. The Luces belong to China."

Dr. Luce's influence pervaded his son's career. The Jovian arrogance of *Time* reflected the editor-in-chief's inbred mission to teach, reform, pass judgment. Filial sentiments played a major part in Luce's quixotic espousal of Chiang, what Time Incers came to call "Harry's aberration . . . Harry's flight from reality." The involvement dated from the Japanese invasion of China in 1931. When they occupied Yenching University, in Peking, with its tablet over a pavilion gate bearing Dr. Luce's Chinese name, *Ssu-I-Ting* (The Pavilion of One Who Seeks Righteousness), it was to Luce a desecration of his father's lifework. In Chiang, the Christian warrior, he saw the instrument to restore and perpetuate that work.

To be sure, Chiang earlier, when trying to crush the independent war lords and unify the country, had allied himself with the Chinese Communists and accepted Soviet aid. But in 1927 he abruptly changed tack, staging a bloody coup against the Reds. The ensuing civil war raged on even in the face of the common foe, Japan. For a time Chiang put up no resistance to the invaders, diverting his troops to the subjection of the Communists. He never succeeded. Under the leadership of Mao Tse-tung, they escaped in the epic "Long March" to the northwest and there behind mountain fortifications established their own Red republic. As ruler of the Nationalist government, Chiang accomplished some measures of unification. He also committed the Kuomintang to social reforms and democracy. But Japan's renewed assault, together with harassments of the war lords and the Communists, prevented any solid progress. The Communists had long been clamoring for a united front against Japan. Chiang finally agreed and Mao placed his guerrilla forces under the nominal command of the Kuomintang. Throughout the life of the new alliance, however, the signatories schemed to undermine each other.

In 1938 Theodore White graduated from Harvard *summa cum laude* and won a Frederick Shelton fellowship whose recipients could pursue any study in any country they wished. He chose the language and people of China. The following year he got a job with the Kuomintang information office in Chungking. John Hersey, roving the country for *Time*, met him there and was so impressed that he recommended him to Luce. As a result, White remained for the next five years *Time*'s only military and political correspondent in Asia. His early dispatches from the battle front appeared under his by-line, a rare privilege for a *Time* beginner. (During the war the magazine partly abandoned its tradition of anonymity on the grounds that journalists who risked their lives deserved public recognition.)

Six months after Pearl Harbor the Luces paid their first visit to Generalissimo and Madame Chiang Kai-shek, of whom Luce wrote in a *Life* article, illustrated with photographs by Mrs. Luce, "We had our big appointment—tea with Madame Chiang and, possibly, The Man Himself . . . we left knowing that we had made the acquaintance of two people, a man and a woman, who, out of all the millions now living, will be remembered for centuries and centuries." Both Luces took to White at once. They brought him back with them to America and put him up during part of his stay in their Greenwich home. "Teddy White," Luce said long after, "was one of the most remarkable reporters ever." He developed for him those intense, paternal, emotionally charged, though submerged feelings that made the break, when it came, so bitter.

After White got back to China, his reports, indicating admiration for Chiang as a valiant soldier, continued to please the home office. The change began with the Honan Province famine of 1943. "Two million people died," White recounted later. "No one in the West knows what a famine is. I rode through it on horseback for two weeks. You didn't allow any personal feelings to enter. You must suppress every human instinct you have to stop and help. You spur your horse on because if you stop they slash at it and eat the flesh off."

What turned him against Chiang was the plunder and savagery of his army and the corruption of his government. He predicted the collapse of both. Within a few months peasants by the thousands were deserting to the Japanese. They would eventually rally to Mao Tse-tung. White managed to file an uncensored account of the famine which *Time* published. Chiang demanded his dismissal. Luce refused. "Basically we were always pro-Chiang," he later explained almost apologetically, "but there were bad guys as well as good guys in his government. There was corruption and we had to report it."

General Joseph W. Stilwell, whom the U. S. had proposed as commander of all Chinese forces, warned Washington that unless it got rid of Chiang the country would fall to Mao and Communism. Instead, Chiang was allowed to force Stilwell out. White wrote a story denouncing the evils of the Kuomintang and appended a ten-thousand-word letter of political analysis for Luce. Stilwell had it flown to America to escape censorship. But to Luce Chiang was still "The Man Himself," *chevalier sans peur et sans reproche,* who could save his country from both Japan and Communism. *Time* ignored White's story, running instead a cover story on Stilwell by Whittaker Chambers, which colored the general slightly red. By way of response to White's letter, Luce relieved him of further political correspondence and restricted him to combat stories. From the war zone White in his fury reported that Mao alone was effectively fighting the Japanese. Had he then become a Red partisan? So Chambers suggested and Luce believed him.

Toward the spring of 1945 Luce himself arrived on the scene. To fit the trip into his overladen schedule, he had canceled a prior engagement to visit Brazil at the invitation of President Getulio Vargas, tactlessly explaining in a cable, DEEPLY REGRET UNABLE TO ACCEPT CHIANG KAI SHEK WANTS ME TO COME TO CHINA MY FIRST LOVE. He was joined in China by a *Life* writer, Charles J. V. Murphy, sent ahead to take a fresh appraisal of Chiang. Before Luce left him to his task, they completed a whirlwind tour of thirteen cities in twenty days. At a press conference in Shanghai most of the foreign correspondents treated Luce like an enemy of the Allied cause. In Tsingtao, on the coast, he was appalled to learn that the governor general's garrison there consisted of barely a hundred Japanese prisoners of war, while the Communist guerrillas under arms numbered some hundred thousand. Why? Because, according to Chiang, the Communists had conserved their strength by not fighting the Japanese.

As a boy Luce had spent summers by the beach at

Tsingtao and he longed to see it again. He dragged Murphy away from a beachside inn in the middle of lunch to climb a hill for a better view. "What do you think of it?" he asked, contemplating the vista through a mist of boyhood memories. Murphy saw only a seedy, overcrowded stretch of sand, dotted with hovels. "It looks like Far Rockaway to me," he said. Luce didn't speak to him again for days.

Murphy produced a four-part series for *Life*. By then the Japanese had surrendered, the Kuomintang and the Communists had resumed civil war, and General George C. Marshall had gone to China with the rank of ambassador and a plan to effect a coalition between Mao and Chiang. *Life* never published the series. There were two main reasons. First, editors and executives implored Luce to drop his pro-Chiang policy which they felt was staining the image of Time Inc. Second, Luce thought Marshall might possibly succeed. But Murphy's series was laudatory to Chiang and hostile to the Marshall proposal. Any coalition that embraced Communists, he believed, could only bear poisoned fruit. So for the first time Luce wavered in his attachment to Chiang and killed the series.

He regretted his lapse when Marshall's mission failed. During a staff conference twelve years later he said, "Every now and then an editor has to review his mistakes. My greatest mistake was not publishing Charlie Murphy's articles on Chiang." And still later, "We had an obligation to restore Chiang to power just we did towards de Gaulle. Why didn't we? Because Marshall wasn't backing Chiang a hundred per cent. He tried to make a deal."

Upon White's homecoming, shortly before the Japanese

surrender, he met a glacial reception. Luce behaved like a trusting parent betrayed. "I think you're using *Time* for what you can get out of it," he said. White rejoined, "*Time* used me. I proved my loyalty in China." He obtained a leave of absence to write his first book, *Thunder over China*, which exposed the malignance of Chiang's regime. When the question of White's next post arose, the chief of correspondents, Charles Wertenbaker, proposed him to succeed John Hersey as Moscow correspondent. But Luce, convinced that White had swallowed the Communist line in China, feared he would do the same in Russia. The fact was, White detested Stalin as much as Chiang. He received a message from Luce through Wertenbaker. "Will Teddy accept any assignment I choose to give him in the future? If the answer is Yes, I'll talk to him. If it's No, tell him there's no place for him in the organization." The answer was No. Within a few hours of transmitting it, White learned that the Book-of-the-Month Club had selected *Thunder over China*, which meant a financial cushion of seventy-five thousand dollars. He wrote a rather wistful farewell letter to Luce. Luce replied in kind, regretting the breach.

White heard from him again in 1956 after *Colliers* magazine, for which he worked, collapsed. "Well, Teddy, what are you going to do now?" White knew what was coming. "I don't want to be on anybody's payroll ever again," he said. The bitterness was gone on both sides and eventually, as a free lance, White contributed articles to *Life*. "Harry and I were both old enough or tired enough to realize that we agreed on many issues."

A series of *Time* correspondents followed White to

China. A few tried, but none succeeded in building up Chiang as the Churchill of the Far East. *Life* editorials periodically called for all-out aid to Chiang. Luce underwent another transient period of disillusion in 1949 when the Generalissimo, routed from the mainland by Mao, withdrew to Formosa. John Osborne wrote an editorial expressing sympathy. Luce recast it, declaring, in effect, that Chiang's defeat must now be recognized and accepted. "We've got to get this off our back," he told Osborne. "But, Harry, we can't chuck him after supporting him all this time." Luce looked shocked and sad.

The next year he recovered from his disillusion as Chiang, having established dictatorial rule on the island, was promising to rconquer the mainland. *Life* acclaimed President Truman for sending the U. S. fleet to protect Formosa. "Of all the world's leaders Chiang is the one who fought Communism longest—one of the few who has never been taken in by Communist camouflage. He is ready and able to work closely with America in both military and economic affairs. His goal is a democratic China." And in 1951 *Life* announced, ". . . the Nationalists survive—they refuse to die the death predicted for them by the mistaken prophets of yesterday. Second, the total victory of Communism in China which these same prophets proclaimed as an accomplished fact in 1949 and 1950 has simply not occurred. Instead the Chinese Communists are struggling to hold what they have. By their own accounts they are fighting to suppress discontent and rebellion in many parts of China. All the U.S. government has to decide is whether to let the Nationalists do whatever they can to compound this resistance and roll back Communism in China . . . we have only to respect the unique tenacity and courage of Chiang Kai-shek and in his long struggle against Communism. . . ."

◦⁓ *twenty-nine* ⁓◦

In at least one respect Calvinism and Marxism are alike. According to Engels, "Freedom is man's decision to support the objective trend of necessity." The Calvinist's supreme privilege is to implement God's will, assuming he can recognize it. To Luce the American political instrument of providence was the Republican party, and in 1951, after eighteen years of Democratic rule, he dedicated himself to its restoration. For a time he had favored Robert Taft as the Republican presidential nominee. He still considered Taft's intellect superior to Eisenhower's, but the party took precedence over the individual and Eisenhower, he believed, could carry it to victory. William Schlamm thought Eisenhower a dolt and he told Luce so. "You know my feelings about Taft," said Luce. "If you can show me that he has a better chance, I'll support him." Schlamm couldn't.

In addition to charting Time Inc.'s pro-Eisenhower course, Luce actively politicked in the thick of the convention fray. So did Mrs. Luce. Her qualifications as a razor-wielding hustings in-fighter were solidly established. Speaking at the previous Republican convention, she described the opposition as "less a party than a podge . . . a mishmash of die-hard, warring factions. . . . Take the extreme Right or Jim Crow Wing of the party, led by lynch-loving Bourbons . . . anti-Semitic, anti-Catholic, anti-foreign. In short, antediluvian. . . . Then there is the Left or Moscow Wing of the party. This is currently master-minded by Stalin's Mortimer Snerd, Henry Wallace . . . the Center, or Prendergast Wing. This is run by the wampum and boodle boys, the same big city bosses who gave us Harry Truman in one of their more pixilated moments. . . ." Now she aimed equally slashing lunges in I-like-Ike speeches (forty-seven of them on radio and television), wrote peppery articles extolling his virtues, and struggled indefatigably to inspirit waverers.

Her feminine charm, when she chose to exert it, could pierce the horniest hide. During a trip to Dallas a year earlier to speak before a Catholic woman's group she met at a party the crusty, thrifty, politically medieval old oil Croesus, H. L. Hunt, and without even intending to, totally conquered him. A conservative Republican woman and a beauty to boot! Hunt was beside himself. He waited for her next day outside a beauty parlor to escort her wherever she wished and invited her to lunch in his office. Hunt didn't believe in such effete luxuries as restaurants, nor-

eating an apple out of his desk drawer. He ordered a hamburger for Mrs. Luce and fetching a toothbrush glass from his bathroom, poured her a shot of bourbon. "I never drink during working hours myself," he said.

When business brought Hunt to New York not long after, one of his first acts was to call Mrs. Luce. "I'm so sorry," she said. "I'm just leaving for the country with Harry." "Harry who?" "Why, my husband, Henry Luce of *Time*." "Henry Luce," said Hunt. "He's a Communist."

At the convention Luce, abetted by an elite corps of Time Inc. stalwarts, helped scuttle Taft. He then granted C. D. Jackson and Emmet Hughes leaves of absence to serve Eisenhower as campaign advisers and speech writers. They stayed on for many months after he became President. Hughes obtained another leave in 1955 to perform the same services. In 1960 he left Luce for good, though on friendly terms, to act as Nelson Rockefeller's political adviser, and in 1963 he went to *Newsweek*. That spring Luce turned violently against him. The provocation was a book Hughes wrote, *The Ordeal of Power*, revealing what he had seen and heard in the White House and attacking Eisenhower and most of his entourage. Reviewing it, not in Books but The Nation, *Time*, with Luce's knowledge and consent, gave it rough treatment. Under the heading, "The Valet's View," it lashed Hughes for apostasy and abuse of the President's confidence. Thus ended another long, close association between Luce and one of his golden protégés.

But nothing could shake Luce's faith in Eisenhower's ability to lead the country, not even when the President had a heart attack. During a dinner party at the Luces, shortly after, John Osborne was sitting between Connecticut's Republican Senator Prescott Bush and Allen Grover. In defiance of everybody else's conviction Luce said, "Ike isn't going to give up the presidency." Bush whispered to Osborne, "Harry's being a damn fool," and in Osborne's other ear Grover said, "This is Harry at his worst. He can be so blind." Osborne asked Luce on what grounds he based his certainty. "I just know it," he said. "Ike won't give up." The doubters failed to reckon with Luce's prescience. Eisenhower, of course, finished two terms.

As the *Passionaria* of his first campaign, Mrs. Luce was in line for a political plum. Long before, in fact, during the party's dark hours, Eisenhower had told her, "If I do get to be President, you're one of the people I want on my team." Luce let it be understood that he desired nothing for himself, but for his wife he expected a front-rank post. Not that political ambition had never possessed him. At various times he had eyed the Senate and the Cabinet. He sought opinions as to his chances from knowing Washingtonians as well as from his staff. They were equally discouraging. Osborne told him that too many politicians hated him, and, moreover, his absence would disastrously weaken the corporation. Matthews said, "You're one man who shouldn't run. You would have to divest yourself of all your magazines." Luce eventually stifled his urge. But in all likelihood, had it come to a test, he could not have borne to renounce journalism.

Eisenhower asked Mrs. Luce what appointment she fancied. Delegate to the United Nations, she said modestly, but he felt she merited a higher office, and he broke a precedent. Though no woman, American or foreign, had ever been entrusted with a major ambassadorial post, he offered her Italy. She happily accepted, but would the Secretary of State, John Foster Dulles—"Old Sourpuss," as she called him privately—agree? She confided her misgivings in a letter to Luce, then visiting Chiang Kai-shek on Formosa. "Don't worry about Old Sourpuss," he answered, and wrote to Dulles saying how much he hoped his wife would receive the honor. Dulles didn't demur, and in February, 1953, Eisenhower announced his choice. According to *Time*'s glowing account, "Last month the Gallup poll reported that [Mrs. Luce] ranked fourth in U.S. favor as the world's most admired woman (Front runners: Eleanor Roosevelt, Queen Elizabeth II, Mamie Eisenhower). . . . News of her appointment brought statements of approval in Congress and from the Italian press. . . ."

The picture was not quite that bright. In Italy Latin masculinity was wounded. A number of Roman dignitaries appealed to the outgoing ambassador, Ellsworth Bunker, to prevent such an insult to a great nation. Only minor ones like Denmark and Luxembourg, they protested, got women ambassadors. Nor were all the American Embassy officers elated at the prospect of female command. In America many Protestants voiced their fears of Catholic influence. The Senate, nevertheless, confirmed the appointment, and on March 5 Chief Justice Frederick Vinson administered the oath of office.

Luce could scarcely contain his pride. In a suite at Washington's Carlton Hotel he gave a small victory dinner attended by Time Inc. higher-ups and prominent politicians.

He was holding forth even more volubly than usual long after the last course. The wine had been copious and his listeners were growing visibly uncomfortable. At length, with a flourish, he said, "And now I invite you to use the ambassador's bathroom."

❦ *thirty* ❧

Luce resolved to stay at his wife's side and they left together for Naples, diplomatically choosing an Italian liner, the *Andrea Doria*. On the whole the press and public received them warmly, though one magazine portrayed Mrs. Luce in a composite photograph as Cleopatra embracing Antony and another printed the American flag trimmed with lace. (During a wave of anti-Americanism in Italy the following year she ordered the Stars and Stripes hoisted above her residence against the advice of her domestic staff. "You just raise it," she told them. "I'll see about the lace later.") The horde of reporters who clambered aboard the *Andrea Doria* as she docked surrendered at first sight—what Italian ever resisted a beautiful woman? —and when she made an elegant little speech in carefully practiced Italian, they exploded into shouts of *"Brava!*

. . . *Benevenuta, Signora Lu-che!*" Some thousand Nea-
politans added their huzzas as she descended the gangplank
waving a white-gloved hand. "'The biggest reception,' reported *Time*, quoting the *New York Daily News*, 'any
American Ambassador ever got.'"

Upon settling into the seventeenth-century Villa Taverna, the official American ambassadorial residence, Luce
told *Time*'s Rome correspondents, "I'm here to do everything I can to make Clare's mission a success, including
pouring tea if I have to." He did, in fact, not long after,
while Mrs. Luce was conferring behind closed doors
with Admiral Arthur Radford, chairman of the Joint
Chiefs of Staff, offer tea to Mrs. Radford. To run Time
Inc. business from Rome without embarrassing either the
embassy or his own employees, he established a separate
office two doors away from Communist party headquarters. Despite its lurking resentment, Italian officialdom was
effusively cordial. So that Luce might accompany his wife
to diplomatic functions the Foreign Ministry stretched a
point of protocol and named him honorary minister.

Mrs. Luce's success was spotty. Her popularity among
Italians continually waxed and waned. She overcame a
great deal of hostility by applying her exquisite sense of
the affecting public gesture. When a flood devastated
the southern coastal town of Salerno, killing some hundred
people and wrecking thousands of homes, she hastened to
the scene, getting there a day ahead of the prime minister,
Alcide de Gasperi, to comfort the bereaved, hold fright-
ened children in her arms, and visit every bedside in every
hospital. She also arranged for a delivery of fourteen military truck loads of American supplies. A few days before

243

she was to board an American plane on her first home leave, a *Linee Aeree Italiani* jet liner crashed at Idlewild. She immediately changed her booking to LAI. When de Gasperi died in 1954, she sacrificed another vacation at home to attend his funeral. Notified by the embassy's public affairs officer that Joe DiMaggio was having a drink in a sidewalk cafe on the Via Veneto, she joined him and they walked the famous thoroughfare together to the noisy delight of the populace. Millions of Italians were moved by the new ambassador's innumerable acts of sympathy and generosity. "Signora Luce," attested an ardent admirer, "had a Madonna-like presence that touched the Italian soul." She also took care not to inflame anti-Catholic sentiment in the States by too close contact with the Vatican. During the first two years she sought no private papal audience. (Recognizing her in a crowded public audience, Pius XII wagged a discreet friendly finger at her as he made the sign of the Cross.) To a U. S. senator who requested her to arrange a private audience for a group of his constituents, she replied, "This embassy has no official relations with the Vatican."

But the ambassador's meddling in Italian politics, a necessary diplomatic activity if subtly performed, angered, at various times, the Right, the Center, and the Left, and sometimes all three at once. In her first major public utterance, shortly before an election, she declared that "if the Italian people should fall the unhappy victims of totalitarianism, totalitarianism of the Right or Left, there would follow, logically and tragically, grave consequences for the intimate and warm cooperation we now enjoy"— an honest statement of U. S. policy toward Italy, but one never intended to be so bluntly expressed. De Gasperi's coalition of Center parties, which Washington favored, lost ground and the press on both sides of the Atlantic blamed Mrs. Luce's indiscretion. Actually, her implied threat had no substantial effect on the election results. Italy's leftward drift continued, the Communists holding 143 seats in the Chamber of Deputies and controlling more than a third of the electorate, a reality with which Mrs. Luce never quite came to grips.

In equally blunt speeches—"brutal blackmail," a Catholic labor party called them—she kept warning industrialists that the U. S. would cancel contracts with any plant where Communist workers predominated. Most plants had such a majority. She managed to get canceled an $18,000,000 munitions contract with Milan's *Officina Vittoria Meccania* and a $7,528,000 contract with a Palermo shipping firm. She wielded more power than American ambassadors normally did because she had direct access to Eisenhower and would sometimes go to him over Dulles' head. "If only the Italian voters were rational," she complained to that nimble anatomist of his country, Luigi Barzini. "Are they more rational in Connecticut?" he asked.

The Communists, expectedly, mounted the most savage assaults against her. Their leader, Palmiro Togliatti, spoke of her in Parliament as an "old lady who brings bad luck to everything she touches." The party organ, *L'Unità*, spread the rumor among superstitious peasants that she had *il Malocchio*—the Evil Eye. During a courtesy call at the Villa Taverna the Soviet ambassador, Bogomolov, thinking perhaps to dishearten her, remarked, "You see how difficult the Italian problem is. They are so unruly."

"Yes," she retorted, "I can see the problem you will have once Italy goes Communist."

In the spring elections of 1955 she backed Amintore Fanfani, a Christian Democrat, at the time slightly to the left, but one she respected for his brilliance. She arranged a private meeting in the home of correspondent Rospigliosi. "You should be prime minister," she told Fanfani. "You must oppose Gronchi." Giovanni Gronchi of the same party, whom she considered pro-Communist, was her particular bête noire and she never troubled to conceal her distaste. "If Gronchi wins," she proclaimed at a press conference, "it will be disaster." The disaster happened. She watched the counting of ballots from the diplomatic gallery, and the moment Gronchi's victory appeared certain she walked out, close to tears.

Luce's services to his wife were not limited to the domestic or social scene. Enabled by his prestige to see anybody he chose whenever he chose, he made unofficial contacts in her behalf which the ambassador could not judiciously make herself. Occasionally he carried a message from her, which she preferred not to send through the State Department, directly to the White House. In his frequent encounters with Italy's big businessmen he fostered her prescriptions—and his—for curing the country's ills. Italy, in effect, got two ambassadors for the price of one, and some throught the price too high. "Theology interested Harry above everything," Barzini recalled. "He brought to every problem the outlook of an eighteenth-century Anglo-Saxon Calvinist. Italy fascinated him because he saw it as a country of sin, corruption and the devil."

The Italians scarcely knew how to take Luce with his stanchless, and to them, naïve, curiosity, his puritanism, his demand for simple solutions. "There's no problem in Italy that a little common sense won't solve," he was always saying. What the country needed to bridle the Communists, he insisted, was an undiluted Right administration (a conclusion he had also reached in Greece during his intimacy with its king and queen). He had little understanding for the political flexibility of a banker like Giovanni Fiummi, who favored an "opening to the Left," with the object of drawing the Socialists away from the Left toward the Center. This necessitated more social reforms, a kind of New Deal. It did not mean that Fiummi favored the Left. Luce had still less possibility of understanding the nature of Italian socialism since hardly any of its leaders spoke English.

A luncheon party of important Romans wondered whether Luce was pulling their legs when, having learned that the Italian common man loved hunting rabbits, he suggested that hunting licenses should be made contingent on proof of anti-Communist affiliation. Noting the blank looks, he turned to the *Time* man with him. "They don't get it," he said and repeated, "Let them be Communists if they must, but don't let them hunt rabbits." Still silence. "They just don't get it." In a literary discussion he likewise stunned two exceptionally erudite ladies when he asked them, obviously believing they could patly settle the centuries-old argument, "Who's the better writer, Racine or Corneille?"

Luce's Roman years were in many respects the most serene and satisfying he had ever known. They were certainly the most leisured. "He had often said," Barzini wrote, " 'Some day I will go to Europe, to Asia, anywhere, and study one country, not just move from place to place. Learn the language, get to know the people, their philosophy of life, their hopes, past and present.' " Luce had no ear for languages. He tried to learn to speak Italian, as Mrs. Luce ably did, hiring one Signor Vanucci for daily lessons, but his constant interruptions to ply the teacher with questions about the "man in the street" instead of the grammar made progress tortuous and he soon gave up. He could read Italian haltingly and he plodded through the entire Italian version of the Bible. He especially enjoyed expounding the American Proposition to civic groups. "Luce unconsciously fell into the role of a Henry James character," Barzini wrote, "the honest, straightforward American, defending and promoting the simple ideas Americans abroad believe to be theirs above all: courage, private initiative, responsibility, honesty, independence from government aid and interference. . . . His speeches and his private conversation carry great weight." He acquired a fondness for the polar bears in the Rome zoo and frequently brought them food. When Matthews came to Rome to submit his prospectus for a British *Time*, Luce earnestly told him, "The zoo keepers have some sort of cake the bears like better than the stuff I bring, but I'm going to find out what it is." Sundays, in addition to attending Presbyterian church, he would accompany his wife to Catholic Mass. Behind the embassy stood the Church of the Carmelites and in its chapel Bishop Sheen sometimes celebrated Mass privately for Mrs. Luce and her suite. In one sermon he conjured wives to obey their husbands. Observers detected more pleasure in Luce's countenance than in Mrs. Luce's.

She taxed her energies to the limit. On her desk, flanked by the American flag and her ambassadorial pennant, she kept a framed copy of her favorite prayer, "Lord, Thou knowest I shall be verie busie this day. I may forget Thee. Do not Thou forget me.—*Lord Astley before the battle of Edgehill*." Her popularity took a sharp upturn following the settlement of the explosive Trieste question, for which she had striven from the early days of her appointment. Since 1948 the Free Territory on the Adriatic, once Italian soil, had been the scene of murderous riots and near-war between Italy and Yugoslavia. It was then under United Nations administration and partitioned into Zone A, held by Anglo-American troops, and Zone B, held by the Yugoslavs. In 1953 the U. S. and Britain announced their withdrawal from Zone A and its restoration to Italy. Marshal Tito promptly threatened war if Italian troops entered the zone. A year of diplomatic wrangling ensued, accompanied by more bloody disorders. The Anglo-British negotiators proposed to surrender a little larger slice of the territory to Tito, but so little that Italy would not balk.

It was one of the occasions when Luce transmitted an appeal from his wife directly to Eisenhower. A letter from the President to Tito produced a dramatic change. Its contents remained secret, but *Time* surmised that a threat of withholding shipments of U. S. wheat to Yugoslavia may have turned the trick. Under the final settlement, for which Mrs. Luce was largly credited, Italy got Zone A, which included the city and port of Trieste; Yugoslavia, a slightly expanded Zone B and the right to rent or buy wharfage from the Italians. The prestigious Milanese newspaper *Corriere della Sera*, among others, saluted the American ambassador, "Nobody will ever know how much Italy owes to this fragile blonde creature."

During their first year of residence the Luces had been largely ignored by Rome's "black" nobility, a status determined by the number of popes a dynasty has produced. Luce was eager to know them, not for snobbish reasons— if any snobbishness ever motivated him, it was intellectual —but because they interested him as an archaic social phenomenon. Rospigliosi, himself the scion of aristocrats, proposed Luce for membership in the rarefied *Circola della Caccia* (Hunt Club), to which only position can open the doors. While the proposal lay under advisement, *Time*'s Robert Neville wrote a cover story that offended the houses of Buoncampagna, Orsini, and Torlonia (the princes of the last two families alternated as assistants to the papal throne). They suggested that perhaps Luce would care to repudiate the story. Instead he instantly withdrew his application to the *Circola della Caccia*. But in 1954 *Principessa* Isabella Colonna, possibly because of Trieste, invited the Luces to a party at the Palazzo Colonna. Thereafter all resistance crumbled and the Luces were everywhere sought after.

On her fifty-first birthday the ambassador received a mystifying cable from her husband in New York, HAPPY BIRTHDAY TO MY MADONNA OF THE ROSES. Its meaning was clear when she stepped into her private salon, already adorned by a full-length portrait of herself in a green Chinese gown. There was newly hung a Florentine painting of a madonna and child against a background of roses.

One story *Time* printed about Mrs. Luce at her behest (July 23, 1956) had unforeseen repercussions that sent her popularity plummeting again. It began, overdramatically as events proved, "One of the best kept secrets of U.S. diplomacy has been the cause of recurring illnesses of Clare Boothe Luce during her three years-plus as Ambassador to Italy. Last week the secret came out: she was poisoned."

The story, almost a full page long, proceeded to the alarming clinical symptoms. "Day after day, she found herself feeling vaguely ill and tired . . . bone-gnawing fatigue set in. Nervousness and nausea followed. At an art festival in Venice a friend askd her to waltz. She found her right foot was benumbed, she almost had to drag it in dancing."

Medical examinations, while she was in New York, disclosed "severe anemia" and "extreme fatigue." After two months' rest she returned reinvigorated to Rome. But "all the symptoms reappeared and some new and frightening ones developed. Her fingernails became brittle, broke at a single tap. She began to lose blonde hair by the brushful. Her teeth were noticeably loosening. Worst of all for a diplomat, she had become irritable. . . . CIA and embassy officials quietly went to work. U.S. and Italian employees were quickly investigated. . . ."

The clues? "Within a week [they] pointed to the rose-covered bedroom in Villa Taverna. The villa's service quarters are immediately above the bedroom, and the ambassador had noticed heavy footfalls as they went about their chores . . . her breakfast coffee had always tasted bitter and metallic . . . the repairman [working on a defective bedroom record player] had reported that its mechanism was clogged with whitish dust and particles of paint. . . . The agents went to work on the room, found other lodes of white dust in the folds of draperies, in cosmetics, in crevices and corners of furniture."

Time finally relieved the suspense. Nobody had been trying to assassinate the ambassador after all. "Quick tests showed a high content of arsenate of lead. The source of the deadly fall-out: the painted roses of the ceiling. . . . The conclusion: for 20 months Ambassador Luce had been breathing arsenate fumes, had been eating food and drinking coffee powdered day after day with the deadly white dust."

The Italian press, variously mistranslating *Time*, glossing over crucial facts, or simply fictionalizing, implanted the notion that Mrs. Luce believed herself to be the intended victim of murder. Reader reaction was divided between anger and mockery.

History may perhaps be able to assess the pluses and minuses of Mrs. Luce's ambassadorial career, but considering the elusive Italian character ("To govern Italy is not only impossible," the writer Curzio Malaparte told Mussolini, "it is useless"), and her own mercurial temperament, her achievements were of no mean order. At the end of her appointment in 1956, Italians of every class paid her homage.

Some months before her departure she told an embassy officer, "We need more publicity at home. It would be good for the foreign service." When no unusual publicity resulted, she scolded him, "You've stalled me long enough. If you won't see to it, I'll put it up to the U.S.I.S.

[United States Information Service], and if they won't do it, I'll go straight to the President. And who do you think will win that fight?" The unobliging officer was bemused to read, four years later, in the first of the monthly commentaries that Mrs. Luce contracted to write for *McCall's* magazine:

". . . Many of my correspondents . . . press the question of a woman for Vice-President." No woman as yet, Mrs. Luce quickly conceded, was qualified, but "there is not a male politician alive—and running—who does not know that women are in politics to stay. Without 'the women's vote,' no male candidate can get elected. Today all practical male politicians, eager to garner women's votes, ask themselves: 'How can a deeper involvement of the American woman in politics best be accomplished?'" and she quoted Eleanor Roosevelt, "'Women cannot be expected to show great interest in politics until the men of both parties have proved their willingness to give women equal opportunity for participation at *top policy-making levels*.'" The italics were Mrs. Luce's, as they were in her answer to the question, How could the politicians prove such willingness? *I suggest they they could prove it by working to create the office of 2nd Vice-President and signifying their intention to fill that office with a woman.*"

With the Kennedy-Nixon contest nine months away, Mrs. Luce concluded, "If this suggestion were adopted by any male candidate today, I predict that his chances of election, if nominated, would be much enhanced and a woman Vice-President would be nominated in 1964."

In 1959 Eisenhower nominated Mrs. Luce ambassador to Brazil. The Senate Foreign Relations Committee approved 8 to 1, the lone dissident being Senator Wayne Morse, Democrat, Oregon. Morse was also the most vociferous objector in the minority of eleven when the Senator confirmed the nomination. He denounced the intemperance of Mrs. Luce's past campaign oratory and the blunders of her Italian ambassadorship. Luce, meanwhile, gallantly preparing once again to assist his wife's mission and looking forward to studying another foreign country, had requested *Time*'s Rio de Janeiro bureau to find him a separate office. But it was not to be. No sooner confirmed than Mrs. Luce surpassed in mordancy all her previous rebukes to her political foes. "My difficulty, of course," she said at a press conference, "goes some years back and begins when Senator Morse was kicked in the head by a horse." Eight years earlier, during a Virginia horse show, the senator had sustained a mild injury to his jaw inflicted by his own entry. Mrs. Luce's implication, he retorted, was consistent with "an old, old pattern of emotional instability."

In the White House, the State Department, and the Senate doubts arose as to whether the unseemly skirmish had not destroyed Mrs. Luce's diplomatic usefulness. Senator Frank J. Lausche, Democrat, Ohio, who had voted for her confirmation, declared from the Senate floor that her remark revealed "an absence of rationality so serious" that had she uttered it before the voting, he would have opposed her.

The storm burst at an awkward moment for Luce. Not long before, *Time* had printed a story about Bolivia in which it repeated seriously an ancient joke of South American politics. The way to solve Bolivia's problems, *Time* quoted an anonymous "U.S. Embassy aide" as saying, was to divide it among its neighbors. The story incited anti-American riots. In La Paz mobs stoned the embassy, burned the American flag, and accidentally killed a native boy. The embassy denied that any aide had made the offensive suggestion.

Amid the furor over his wife's appointment as ambassador to one of Bolivia's neighbors, Luce issued a public statement, "For twenty-five years in the course of her public life my wife has taken not only the criticisms provoked by her own views and actions but also many punches which were really intended for me or for the publications of which I am editor-in-chief. The attack of Senator Wayne Morse is perhaps the most vitriolic example of this. . . .

"As an ambassador she will not be able to defend herself from vendetta politics at home which makes common cause with anti-Americanism in South America. I have asked my wife to offer her resignation. . . ."

She took the advice.

～ *thirty-one* ～

The impression persisted that Mrs. Luce influenced Time Inc. policies. But when that appeared to be the case, it merely indicated concurrence, not influence. If the magazines seemed occasionally to mirror her views, it was only because Luce shared them in the first place. "My wife and I agree broadly on most things, but not entirely," he told an interviewer. "We have argued plenty. If we ever basically disagreed, I don't know what the situation would be." He hastened to add, "Time Inc. obviously does not promote her political fortunes."

It obviously did not in the 1964 presidential campaigns, when Mrs. Luce stumped for Barry Goldwater, partly, she declared, because he had been unfairly treated by both his competitors and the press. "When Ambassador Lodge announced he was leaving Saigon to help Scranton, not one newspaper, not even *Time* questioned it, even though everybody knew it wasn't true. He was leaving to help himself. I don't know what the real case against Goldwater is except he wants less federalism." She weighed and finally rejected a return to public life as senatorial candidate on the Conservative party ticket. Yet she had no grounds to complain of neglect by her husband's publications. During her Italian phase *Time* had printed more Italian news than ever before or since, and it continued to quote her witticisms and report her activities, though perhaps no more than other periodicals.

Mrs. Luce's own writings for various magazines did not always delight her husband. Though *Time* had found some kind words to say about the power behind the Diem throne, the beauteous Madame Nhu, it never voiced such unqualified approbation as Mrs. Luce did in an article for the ultra-right-wing *National Review* entitled "The Lady *Is* for Burning." Absolving "this fragile little creature who has been so scornfully dubbed 'the Dragon Lady'" from charges of nepotism, vote-stealing, demagoguery, Catholic bigotry, the persecution of Buddhists, and compromising the Vietnamese war effort, she upheld Madame Nhu and her family as their country's true defenders against Communism. The Buddhist monks who incinerated, or as Madame Nhu jeeringly phrased it, "barbecued" themselves, moved Mrs. Luce to a harsh witticism. They "not only gained 'face' for the temple, but Nirvana or Paradise and sainthood for themselves," she wrote. "For at least three of the monks who were over age 70, this must have seemed a rather good deal."

When Mrs. Luce met Time Inc. editors socially, she

was apt to have in mind some cause she wanted publicized or some story looked into. Now and then, especially if Luce concurred, she might succeed. But the editors tended to keep their guard up. Upon her retirement from Congress, Luce undertook to write the story so as to spare the staff embarrassment. He paid her a restrained tribute. But Fuerbringer returned a first draft with the suggestion that he tone it down. Luce tried again. He rewrote it four times before Fuerbringer approved. "Otto," a former *Time* editor surmised, "had sensed instinctively that Harry would admire him for it."

Nor did the editors treat Mrs. Luce's own submissions as sacrosanct. A writer going into the Foreign News editor's office one day found him embroiled with Luce over an article by Mrs. Luce on the Far East. The editor judged it unsuitable. Luce, waving the typescript aloft, insisted it was fine. But in the end he gave way; the article was rejected. When, during the war, *Life* published color pictures Mrs. Luce had taken of the Flying Tigers in Burma without giving her a credit line, she protested, "Harry, this is carrying reticence too far."

In moments of pique she was known to refer to her husband's employees as "Harry's people." Whenever any of them wrote a book, she would give Luce a leatherbound copy with the phrase stamped on the spine, "On Time's Time." The collection grew to number several novels that caustically depicted a Luce-like publishing empire.* To an editor of *Sports Illustrated*, when he introduced

---

* *Ralph Ingersoll*, The Great Ones; *Charles Wertenbaker*, The Death of Kings; *William Brinkley*, The Fun House; *John Brooks*, The Big Wheel.

himself to her at a party, Mrs. Luce remarked, "Ah, yes, *Sports*. The only good things in it are Charles Goren on bridge, which I suggested, and my articles on skin-diving."

The tone the Luces took with each other in public had the formality of institutional figures—the Publisher and the Stateswoman. Uninterruptible by anybody else, they deferred to each other, though at times with visible strain. At social gatherings they competed to score dialectical points and to rivet the attention of their listeners. Here Mrs. Luce, with her gift of crystalline expression, had an edge on her husband, with his gropings, short cuts, and tangential flights. "What Harry means," she once put in at the conclusion of a tangled Lucean discourse, and she neatly condensed his thesis. Yet they were as dependent on each other as the monarchs of two allied kingdoms besieged by a common foe.

After years of turbulence such as individuals so strong-willed were bound to generate between them, they settled with age into a close, sure companionship. ("It's curious," she once told a friend, "how things that are annoying at first in marriage become endearing.") They derived more pleasure from disputation than most couples do from agreement. In the heat of political argument, their favorite arena, she never sought refuge behind her femininity, and he accepted her as an intellectual peer. They tried to contend within a strict rational framework. It was a game they played zestfully, free of animus, a game whose rules outsiders couldn't understand. Mrs. Luce, typically: "Mao Tse-tung is the greatest ally America can have." Luce: "What is your basis for that?" Mrs. Luce: "He is a bulwark against a Soviet takeover of Asia." Luce: "Let's explore it." And the game is on. They have chosen sides—A vs. B. If she seemed to sway toward his position, he would be disappointed, like an eager fencer whose opponent backs off too soon.

But Luce could no more articulate his emotional feelings for his wife than those he harbored for the stars of the Time Inc. firmament. He could open his mind, but not his heart. The dead whom he held dear, his father and mother, his stepdaughter Anne, he seldom mentioned except in impersonal terms. Words of endearment came hard to him. When his wife accused him, as wives will, of not loving her, he would rejoin with a question in the vein of a Socratic dialogue, "Why am I here?" The deed, if not the word, however, betrayed a depth of feeling, as when he gracefully adapted himself to the role of consort to the ambassadress, or when in Phoenix he attended two churches daily, the second to escort her to Mass. He was a lavish giver of gifts—a college education to his Greenwich gardener's daughter; Time Inc. shares to members of his family; to his wife, houses, paintings, and jewelry (the most treasured, a gem-encrusted gold cigarette case to which he added another gem at each accomplishment of her career)—but one who recoiled from effusions of gratitude. With his own indifference to possessions, he taxed his wife's ingenuity when she wanted to make him a gift. She felt she probably pleased him one birthday with an antique enamel box inscribed, "All the joys of life are not worth the pangs of love."

They observed certain domestic rituals of indefinable but, to them, fond meaning. Though Luce said of television, "It corresponds to some dark side of the human psyche," they regularly followed the adventures of Perry Mason. Neither could explain exactly why. For an hour every night before retiring he would read aloud. The choice was eclectic—anything from a thriller to a theological treatise. Every morning a maid would set up a folding table in Mrs. Luce's bedroom and Luce, barefoot and wearing a dressing gown—he fancied crimson—would join her in a substantial breakfast. Invariably he read his newspaper between bites, invariably she would chatter, and invariably he would grumble, "Why don't you let me finish my paper?" In a cage by the sliding glass doors opening on the heated swimming pool, Coco, a pet cockateel, would at some point erupt into gravelly song, usually *Stars and Stripes Forever*. "Coco," Luce would admonish it, "you flatted again."

❧ *thirty-two* ❧

A curious instance of Luce's need to combine idealism with pragmatism accompanied the birth pangs in 1955 of *Sports Illustrated*. It was the only Luce publication that did not germinate from some high-minded concept. *Fortune* proposed "to give business a literature of its own," *Life* to help mankind "see and be instructed." The considerations that engendered a sixth magazine were primarily material. Waiting to be tapped was a new, leisured, moneyed market grown up since the war. At the same time the corporation had accumulated a reservoir of technical resources and talent larger than its existing publications could absorb. Why not use the surplus creatively and profitably?

But why sports? Why "Muscles," as the magazine came to be called around Time Inc.? No area was more remote from Luce's personal tastes. The playing fields of Hotchkiss and Yale had held little lure for him. He was a buoyant but unstylish swimmer. He played a vigorous, slashing game of tennis, but without finesse. In singles against his wife, a born tactician, he was known to have been trounced. (A *Time* editor whom they pressed into service as a referee refused to officiate again because they constantly disputed his decisions.) Luce once returned a *Time* editor's baseball story with the marginal comment, "I have no interest in sports, but this could make me a fan."

As subject matter for the new magazine, he had pondered numerous alternatives—short stories, poetry, art, do-it-yourself. Of almost irresistible appeal to Luce, with his passion for uplift, had been a monthly "think" magazine proposed in 1945 and known by the working title of "Project X." He appointed William Schlamm to run it, but Project X never got beyond the dummy stage. "Personal, intellectual journalism simply couldn't fit into the Time Inc. scheme of things," claimed Schlamm, who became a politically conservative writer and lecturer on economics and politics. "Luce didn't choose to buck the system he had created. He is both the creator and a victim of that system." According to Luce, the trouble was, "Too many people got involved. They mulled it over too much."

As Luce explained his final choice, no matter what other projects he contemplated, "the compass needle swung back to sports." Among the experiences that decided him was a television wrestling match he chanced to turn to. "Who'd ever look at that?" he asked the editor with him.

"Millions of people," said the editor.

"Is that so?" said Luce. "This is a market we ought to capitalize on."

At an executive meeting he met no resistance to the

prospect of a sports magazine. The main question raised was not whether to publish it, but when and how. Marketing surveys by Time Inc.'s promotion experts fortified the decision. They learned, for example, that of all the women's ready-made clothing sold in department stores, almost a fourth was sportswear. So the mighty Luce machine, which had never yet produced a failure, moved into high gear.

One can hardly imagine a Hearst, a Pulitzer, or a Beaverbrook worrying about the "philosophical justification" of a commercially promising enterprise. But Luce's conscience made stern demands. No lofty principle being inherent in "Muscles," he could not rest until he had superimposed one. During a prepublication luncheon conference, he asked each staff member in turn what *he* thought was the magazine's philosophical justification. It was an awkward moment. Nobody had been thinking in such exalted terms. Hems, haws, and confused mumblings greeted the question. A promotion man suggested, unhappily for him, the last *raison d'être* that Luce could ever accept: modern society was materialistic and anti-intellectual and the magazine seemed ideally suited to that spirit. The temperature in the dining room dropped.

An editor struck a more Lucean note. Whereas most sports writers tended to talk down to the fan, treating him as something of a bum, the new magazine would treat him as a gentleman. "Well, that's exactly right," Luce said. Another editor quoted a television baseball announcer who, when asked why he devoted his career to a mere game, replied, "If I can give just a little happiness during the day, a little something to take people's minds off the terrible shape the world is in, I think I've made a good contribution." The editor added, "As far as I'm concerned, that's the philosophical justification."

Luce raised the tone of the discussion with a reference to the Socratic idea that the unexamined life is not worth living. The sporting life, he said, is one to examine.

In a talk to the business staff he soared still higher. "Sport has aspects, too, of creativity. Man is an animal that works, plays and prays. As a boy, I remember reading a book titled *Four Things Men Live By*. These four things were Love, Work, Play and Prayer. No important aspect of life should be devalued. And if play does correspond to some important elements in spiritual man, then it is a bad thing for it to be devalued. And sport has been devalued. It has become a lowbrow proposition. It does not get serious attention.

"The new magazine will be a re-evaluation of sport—not an over-evaluation—to put it in its proper place as one of the great modes of expression. . . ."

As a summation of his thoughts about the relation of sport to the human spirit, Luce cited a passage from Goethe's *Faust* in a context nobody but he would discover:

Only he deserves his liberty and life
Who must conquer them each day anew . . .
Such is the turbulent scene I long to see,
To stand on free soil among free people,
Then to the fleeting moment I could say:
Stay, you are so good.
The traces of my earthly days
Then could vanish into eternity.

The year after the magazine appeared Luce virtually equated it with national survival. In an open letter to the head of an important advertising agency, he declared:

"We have the H-Bomb and we have SPORTS ILLUSTRATED. These are the two instant symbols of our fears and of our hopes.

"Let me explain. Last night a few of us sat up 'til a late hour talking about the Spirit of Geneva. Is it good? Bad? One or two of the brethren thought it was very dangerous. So the talk—pretty knowledgeable talk—went round and round. Finally one of my wisest colleagues said: 'Look, the President of the United States has to proceed on *two* assumptions. He has to assume that H-Bomb war is "inevitable" and he has also to assume that peace is possible.'

"There, in a nutshell, it seems to me, is where we are—all of us. Even as you work up brilliant advertising and merchandizing plans, you keep your citizen's eye cocked on our Military Estimate and the election returns in far countries. These items will determine whether Burnett & Co. is in business at all x years from now. But you also write those ads. You, like the President, not only assume that peace is possible, even probable; more than that, you live and work as if it is, right now.

"But what does peace mean for the American in mid-twentieth century? Meat and potatoes, sure—and more meat and potatoes. But it means a lot more than that because meat and potatoes (even in surplus) can be taken largely for granted. Peace in America in mid-twentieth century means enjoyment of life, the pursuit of Happiness. It means in short, SPORTS ILLUSTRATED.

"What? Is Sports the goal of life? Certainly not. There are far deeper things to be pursued—Art, Religion, Good Morals, all the high 'ideals.' But if you ask most any American what he's going to do with peace-time—leisure, —what's he going to do next weekend, what's he going to do next winter, next summer, what's he planning now for his pursuit of happiness—one sure part of the answer (and a large part) will be something to do with Sport. He and she are going to Florida to lounge on the beach—and fish or sail. He and she are going to Alaska to shoot a bear. He and she are going this weekend to the football game. And they're going to Arizona because there they get not only scenery but golf. Meanwhile, their son is writing home about being substitute tackle on the Freshman team; their daughter has unaccountably got hold of a bow and arrow and junior is taking tennis lessons. And Cousin Fred has, of all things, bought a racing horse. And this is what they talk about when they've finished with the H-Bomb and with how Mary got engaged to John. *The greatest common denominator of leisure activity and of human conversation among Americans pursuing happiness is—Sport.* . . .

"We have the H-Bomb and we have SPORTS ILLUSTRATED. To put your money, now, on SPORTS ILLUSTRATED is to put your money on the hopes of the American people in a very simple, human way—in a way universally understood and richly appreciated. . . ."

After a lifetime of ignorance about sports Luce began his education with the aid of the knowledgeable buffs among his employees. Nerving themselves for an orgy of questions, they took him to ball games, prize fights, horse races. Sidney James, whom Luce appointed publisher of *Sports Illustrated*, took him to his first major league baseball game in 1954, the day the Dodgers beat the Giants and won the pennant. When the crowd stood up for the traditional stretch after the seventh inning, Luce said, "Well, guess that's it. Got to go now." James explained to him that the game wasn't over.

Life's managing editor, Edward K. Thompson, was Luce's mentor at his first Madison Square Garden basketball game. Both teams represented Catholic colleges and when any player stepped up to the free-throw line he would cross himeslf.

"What's that mean?" Luce wanted to know.

"They're asking for divine help in sinking the shot," said Thompson.

"But how can one tell which side God is on?"

In the third quarter the winning team, which was thirteen points ahead, began freezing the ball.

"Why are they doing that?"

"It's a defensive play. They don't want to endanger their lead."

Luce immediately identified himself with the other team. "Charlie Stillman has convinced me that you can't survive by hoarding your money," he told Thompson. "You have to spend money to make money. That team which is ahead will lose."

It did, too.

As for *Sports Illustrated*, after dropping some twenty-three million dollars the first five years, it went on to become a big money-maker.

∽ *thirty-three* ∽

Spring, 1960. In the corridors of world power seventy-three-year-old Chiang Kai-shek is practically a cipher, but not to Luce. Accompanied by Editor Roy Alexander and *Time*'s Hong Kong correspondent, Stanley Karnow, Luce alights on Formosa to attend the Generalissimo's third inaugural ceremony as President of the Kuomintang. A deathless bit of apocrypha is the reply ascribed to Karnow when Luce, losing sight of the porters, asks, "You don't think they've lost our luggage, do you?" "You never know. They lost the mainland."

Next morning the trio drive to the movie theater where the grand celebration is to take place. Chiang has procured his re-election through some intricate constitutional juggling. Luce is unhappily aware of the extra-legality. He would in any event have preferred Chiang to retire and, as an elder statesman, tour the States, possibly under his sponsorship. But wanting always to believe in Chiang's popularity, he takes the big turnout of officials and well-wishers as proof of it. He appears moved. See, he notes, how the people love and respect Chiang; perhaps it's all for the best that he should retain authority.

A banquet in the presidential residence. The room resounds with toasts to the "return to the mainland." At first Luce nervously skirts the subject, confining himself to expressions of good luck. Madame Chiang's comments, couched in her fluent, Wellesley-schooled English, further disconcert him. "Well, Harry, we've got to get those Communists out of the State Department." He grunts noncommittally. To Chiang, however, he listens with passionate attention. They communicate through an interpreter, for Chiang speaks only a Chekiang dialect that few of his compatriots can understand and Luce long ago forgot his Chinese. Skeleton-thin in his tight military tunic, his head shaved, skilled in Oriental intrigue, but blind to the realities of the world beyond, an anachronism wholly possessed by his dreams of reconquering China, the aged warrior is a figure out of never-never land. Yet Luce questions him seriously.

"What are your plans, Mr. President?"

"We will attack the mainland."

"When do you think you might attack?"

"Soon, very soon."

"Do you have any idea when?"

"The moment is approaching."

"How do you propose to move?"

"There will be an uprising."

"How do you know? Where do you get your information?"

"I know, I know."

A few days later Chiang summons Luce to his council chamber to resume the dialogue. After the futility of the dinner interview, Luce indicates to Karnow en route, that his enthusiasm has waned. But once in Chiang's presence he hangs on every oracular word.

"Mr. President, what are your feelings about the future?"

"I see danger near the end of this year. The American elections. The Russians may attack. A very dangerous period."

"Very interesting, Mr. President. What makes you think so?"

"End of the year very dangerous."

"Yes, Mr. President, but why?"

"We must be prepared for a very dangerous period."

Roy Alexander, who tarried at the hotel, is waiting in the antechamber. "What did he say, Harry?" he asks, as Luce emerges. "He says we've got to be careful around the end of the year."

At a cocktail party Alexander is cornered with a Catholic missionary who has spent thirty years in China. "He tells me," he informs Luce afterward, "that Mao Tse-tung is a very intelligent man." Luce glares. "So what do you want us to do—give up?"

During dinner with a group of old China politicos, among them a former foreign minister, Wang Shih-chieh, the conversation turns to the civil war and General Marshall. Luce damns the general as the author of China's fall, but Wang, curiously, defends him. Luce, his eyes blazing under their bristling brows, claims he knows better. "Harry, I've never told you this before," says Wang, almost certainly improvising. "When I was in Washington, Marshall asked me what I thought about a certain man as ambassador to China. And who do you think he mentioned? Harry Luce." The editor-in-chief is floored. "Marshall said that?" "Yes he did, Harry." Luce huffs and stammers and mutters incomprehensibly. At length he allows that maybe Marshall wasn't all that bad, misguided maybe, naïve, but a patriot. . . .

~ *thirty-four* ~

"Benevolence and righteousness are my only themes," said the Chinese sage, Mencius, whom Luce's father liked to quote, "why must you speak of profit?" The most doctrinal Presbyterian need shun neither profit nor power, providing he pursues them, not for self-gratification, but the welfare of others. Pitfalls yawn at his feet, however. To maintain power, with even the noblest ends in view, may sometimes demand the temporary abandonment of smaller principles.

In 1961 *Life* printed a short item about the Christian Anti-Communist Crusade, an ultra-right movement organized in Los Angeles by a former Baptist revivalist named Frederick C. Schwarz and backed by West Coast industrial potentates. With sawdust-trail fervor Crusade orators clamored for such actions as an end to foreign aid, severing diplomatic relations with Russia, investigating the U. S. State Department to weed out leftists, and "a practical program for the seizure of power by anti-Communists abroad."

Time had been the first national magazine to carry a full exposure of the John Birch Society. Though Schwarz professed disapproval of the society, on many issues Crusaders and Birchites stood shoulder to shoulder. Known Birchites, moreover, aided the Crusade's steering committees, and Schwarz had never repudiated them. His chief backer, Patrick J. Frawley, who headed Technicolor, Inc., Schick Safety Razor, and Eversharp, once publicly thanked the Birchites for their loyal support. According to the *Life* report, the Crusade was "a new kind of 'revival meeting' serving nonreligious ends . . . Schwarz preaches doomsday by Communism in 1973 unless every American starts distrusting his neighbor as a possible Communist or 'comsymp' (Communist sympathizer)."

In Los Angeles the earth shook. "Whoever pulled that sleazy stunt," roared Schwarz, "is working for the Communist criminal conspiracy." Raging protests from California big businessmen overwhelmed the magazine. They threatened to boycott its advertising pages. Luce had defied many such threats in the past. Henry Ford, for example, infuriated by *Time*'s fair coverage of the auto workers fighting to unionize his Baton Rouge plant in 1937, withheld all advertising for three years—a loss of millions to Time Inc. The ire of the Wisconsin McCarthyites cost the corporation $100,000 worth of ads. But now Luce faltered. Along with most magazines *Life* had suffered heavy reverses. They stemmed from multiple causes—television's big bite out of the advertising dollar, fiercer competition among magazines for the remainder, rising production costs, the 1958 recession. In 1961 *Life* showed a loss of some two million dollars.

If any correction was due Schwarz, the normal place for it would have been *Life*'s Letters page. But reluctantly Luce, the pragmatist, conceded the need to make handsomer amends. C. D. Jackson flew west to appear on the same platform with Schwarz at a rally in the Hollywood Bowl. He exceeded his mission. Before fifteen thousand cheering Crusaders he not only tendered an abject apology, but aligned *Life* with Schwarz in the struggle against Communism. "Knowledge is power," said Jackson, quoting Sir Francis Bacon. "You have here with you a man who has dedicated his life to helping disseminate that knowledge, and therefore to helping endow our nation with that power. That man is Dr. Fred Schwarz and, like all dedicated men, he will be subject to oversimplified misinterpretation. Regretfully, my own magazine recently published such an oversimplified misinterpretation. I know that you are not interested in how that happened, but I hope you will be interested in my statement that I believe we were wrong and I am profoundly sorry."

When the cheering subsided, he urged his listeners to read a book Schwarz wrote, "one of the best books analyzing the Communist menace I have ever read." At a private Hollywood meeting the former actor George Murphy, vice-president of Technicolor, a stanch Crusader, and later Republican senator from California, crowed that he had made Luce come crawling on his hands and knees.

Two weeks later *Life* repaired its tattered pride in an

editorial reaffirming its hostility to the radical Right. But for Schwarz it reserved a pat on the head. He himself was "well-informed" and his Crusade attracted "respectable support," even if it also attracted "people who are too superheated to teach or learn anything."

Bishop James A. Pike of California's Episcopal diocese was so puzzled by Luce's policy on this and other issues that he wrote to him asking, "What do *you* think?" Luce replied with a reminder of *Time*'s record as a foe of the ultra-Right. As for the Schwarz affair, "It was regrettable that C. D. Jackson, who is an uncompromising 'libertarian,' should have been understood to have apologized [sic]. The mistake we made about Dr. Schwarz was to imply that his motives were largely commercial. Such an assumption of motives was stupid in any case, and it required a decent expression of regret. But, in view of many distortions of our position, we owed it to ourselves to make it clear that we were not foreswearing our own long-standing, extensive, and often painful, opposition to Communism."

Elsewhere in the letter Luce explained, "We stand in the great liberal tradition—with what some theologians might call Christian presuppositions. My own political hero was Theodore Roosevelt, who, fallible though he was, did not hesitate to assert that 'righteousness' is relevant to politics and all the public affairs of men and actions."

~ *thirty-five* ~

For some months before 1958 Luce suffered from inter-
mittent chest pains. A stoical man, he attached no importance to them, though they proved to be *angina pec-
toris*. In the winter of 1958, while with his wife in Phoenix,
he was felled by a pulmonary embolism, complicated by a
coronary occlusion. "*Life* goes to a party," he murmured
as an ambulance sped him to St. Joseph's Hospital. The
party lasted three weeks and his doctor, Hayes Caldwell,
put him permanently on a drug to prevent blood clotting.
The true nature of the attack, which he kept secret from
even his closest associates, was probably a factor in has-
tening his plans for the future of Time Inc. He had always
thought of it as a young man's organization. His measure-
ment of youth, however, lengthened with his own increasing age. When interviewing John Hersey as a prospec-

tive employee, he noted, "Nobody here is over thirty. At forty we'll all retire and let the young take over"—a heady outlook for Hersey, who had just graduated from Yale. Luce himself was then thirty-five. Five years later he was saying the same thing, but he had advanced the retirement age. And so it went through the years. "I'll never retire," he finally told Miss T. "I'll die at my desk."

A year after his heart attack he invited the corporation's editorial director, Hedley Donovan, to dine alone with him at his River House apartment. A taciturn, scholarly, vigorous man of forty-two, politically an independent, Donovan had risen fast. In 1945, while scouting for fresh talent, Vice-President Eric Hodgins compiled a list of Rhodes Scholars who had chosen journalism as a career. One he couldn't find was Donovan. Yet at that very moment Donovan was knocking at *Fortune*'s door in quest of a job. After they finally met, Hodgins reported to *Fortune*'s managing editor, "I think Donovan is a remarkable young man and that taking him on the staff at an intermediate level on a three to six months' trial basis would be a very good gamble."

Donovan was born in Brainerd, Minnesota, the son of a mining engineer. He attended Minnesota public schools, graduated *magna cum laude* from the University of Minnesota with a B.A. degree in history and a Phi Beta Kappa key, and for three years studied history at Oxford as a Rhodes Scholar. For five years after that he was a reporter on the Washington *Post*. During the war he served with Naval intelligence, attaining the rank of lieutenant commander. Starting as a *Fortune* writer, he became associate managing editor in 1951, managing editor two years later, and in 1959 editorial director, second in command to Luce, at a salary that eventually exceeded $100,000. With his wife, Dorothy Shannon from Erie, Pennsylvania, a daughter, and two sons, he lived in an eighteenth-century harbor-front house at Sands Point, Long Island.

Over coffee in River House Luce mentioned diffidently that he had a "rather personal" matter to discuss. Would Donovan care to undertake "not right away, in a few years or so," the functions of editor-in-chief? Donovan said he was flattered, but considered the post excellently served by its present incumbent. At the end of the evening, with no firm commitments made, Luce summarized their talk. "Well, it is left, then," he said, "that you are complimented by my suggestion, and will at least think about it, and I am complimented by your suggestion that the present editor-in-chief is good at his job."

A massive reorganization of Time Inc. was completed by 1964. Donovan mounted the throne and Luce assumed the more or less honorary title of Editorial Chairman. The reshuffling brought no pronounced changes of policy. As Luce put it, "Donovan, of course, will make the final decisions, but he will consult the Senate. I wouldn't have picked him if he hadn't been simpatico." He had abdicated authority, but he never abdicated his influence. When in New York, he occupied his old office, close to the seat of major decisions, and none were reached in opposition to his wishes. All apart from his direct participation, the impact of his personality, imposing the need to judge, take sides, and simplify truth, continued to be felt subliminally.

~ *thirty-six* ~

During the month of February, 1967, Luce looked fitter and less ready for retirement than when he transferred the reins of Time Inc. power three years earlier. Tanned by the Phoenix sun, so lean and trim that the outlines of his shoulder blades showed sharply through his jacket, he was in constant activity. On the first of the month he gave a talk at the Santa Barbara branch of the University of California. He accepted many such engagements as a kind of intellectual self-discipline. "They force me to re-think through an issue," he said. He sometimes spent weeks preparing a speech and he had taught himself to deliver it without any of the fumblings and ellipses that often ob-scured his informal conversation. The theme of at least a dozen speeches had been "the rule of law." Thus, in 1964, to the Southwestern Legal Foundation in Dallas, "I am convinced that the idea of justice and law is more universal, more readily understood, than is the concept of political liberty. As we proceed, we will be able to show how justice must make room for liberty and how liberty lives only by and through the law. 'Give us that order which without liberty is a snare and give us that liberty which without order is a delusion.' Those words state the terms of the great conversation of mankind." *Time*'s newest section, The Law, reflected this preoccupation of Luce's late years.

At Santa Barbara he reverted to a lifelong concern— *East and West—Basic Differences.* "The East," he said, "is in a highly unstable condition . . . seeking to become modern, that is, to become something radically different from what it has been. It is this painful quest for modernity which makes it the duty of the West to offer the best that it knows and has—not only in technology, but, more importantly to offer whatever we think we know of the universal goods of liberty and law . . . it is perhaps only in a serious confrontation with the East that the West can rediscover, even recreate, a knowledge of itself. There is one other thing. In trying to explain itself to the East, the men of the West will not only rediscover the meaning of the West, they will also discover with more precision what, in the year 1967, is most lacking in the West— whatever that deficiency may be. Thus, they—and we— will end up learning from the East—learning not what isn't there, but learning how our own assumptions need to be corrected and expanded in order that we may more surely make our way towards the goals of universal truth and concord. The future of mankind depends on the response of the East to the West. And that depends on whether the West knows what it has to say. . . . In our high office of citizens of the United States, we are called to be, every one of us, political philosophers. And my plea today is that each of us has a duty, of some urgency, to encounter the Orient—to encounter it in its thought and feeling as well as in the existential facts of the moment. To the degree that we attend to this task, we will receive the rich reward of a deeper understanding of what America stands for. We will know better what is meant by liberty under law. We will be proud of our inheritance. We will be eager to learn more—to correct, to deepen and to enlarge the meaning of our inheritance for our children and for all mankind."

For his part of the encounter Luce had requested a visa to Red China through its London legation, but as of 1967, not even an acknowledgment was forthcoming. "I think Chiang Kai-shek would have apoplexy if he knew," Karnow said to a colleague when he heard rumors of his former employer's intention. "I was tempted to tell Chiang when I last interviewed him, but I figured he should enjoy his twilight years in peace."

Back in Phoenix, after his Santa Barbara speech, Luce resumed work on a book, the first he had ever attempted, summing up his political, economic, and journalistic philosophy, and his concept of America's place "under God." He had written about six chapters, which he would let nobody see, not even his wife. All he told her was, "I've got a book." He was also busy as chairman of a drive to raise fifty million dollars for "capital needs of the United Presbyterian Church of the U.S.A." In the three years since he undertook the task, canvassing droves of wealthy fellow Presbyterians, the goal had been passed. A million dollars was jointly contributed by the chairman and the Henry Luce Foundation.

Toward mid-February Luce flew east to attend the monthly meeting of the Time Inc. board of directors. The corporation was luxuriating as never before. During the year just ended *Life*'s weekly circulation had climbed to 7,500,000 (500,000 above 1964)—the biggest of all magazines, and carried twice as much advertising as any other, yielding a revenue of $170,000,000. *Time*, with a circulation of 3,500,000 (600,000 more than 1964), was second only to *Life* in advertising revenue—$86,000,000. All together the four magazines (*Architectural Forum* had been discontinued and *House & Home* sold), together with the international editions of *Time* and *Life*, provided 65 per cent of the corporation's total revenues. The book division, doubling its 1964 sales to $16,000,000, accounted for 12 per cent. The rest flowed from real estate, industrial holdings, and broadcasting. The corporation now owned four radio and five television stations. It had also formed jointly with the General Electric Co. the General Learning Corp. for the merchandising of educational materials, systems, and services. With Time Inc. shares selling at around one hundred dollars, their combined market value was close to $690,000,000. In the ten years past, the organization that Luce and Hadden founded on a shoestring of $86,000 had doubled its revenue to $503,000,000 and tripled its net profit to $37,300,000.

During his stay Luce turned up at editorial conferences, his pockets stuffed with news clippings and notes for story ideas. Excited to learn that a forthcoming *Time* Essay, a comparatively new feature, would examine "The Mind of China," he sent for the writer, Hughes, and Grunwald, now an assistant managing editor in charge of the feature. "How can you do it in two pages?" Luce said. "Too big. Too complex. Can't be done." Pacing his office, brows bristling, chain-smoking, he spouted comments at machine-gun speed. "People think the Chinese are impassive. Go to any village market. Full of life, color. Waving their arms. There's a great book. Got it at home. Father Ricci [he pronounced it "Ritchie"], Jesuit missionary. Village life in the eighteenth century. Read it. Contradictions. China's full of contradictions. Impossible in two pages. . . . Well, very interesting. Hope you can do it. Sure like to see it." As they were leaving, he shook his head. "Here we've been talking an hour and a half [Luce, that is; neither Hughes nor Grunwald had managed to say much] and we haven't even mentioned 'face.' . . . Two pages. . . ." On the twentieth he gave a luncheon in Time Inc.'s private dining room for Prince Bernhard of the Netherlands. Before the prince was even seated Luce said, gesturing toward an array of editors, "I think some of us want to ask you a few questions." "I'd like something to eat first," replied Bernhard. "You can eat while we frame our questions," said Luce, and he turned to the first editor. Between soup and coffee they covered considerable ground in European politics and aviation, at which the prince was a skilled amateur.

Luce returned to Phoenix in time to accompany Mrs. Luce to San Francisco where, on the twenty-fourth, a Friday, she was to address the Commonwealth Club of

America, a forum of the city's most influential citizens who convened for a luncheon once a month. At her insistence he edited the speech, a scathing critique entitled "The U.N.—Services Unrendered," rewriting the end to make it more constructive. They arrived Thursday to be greeted at the airport by a young member of the local *Time* bureau, Judson Gooding. The drive to the Fairmont Hotel brought forth Luce's customary geyser of questions. He was fascinated by the city's projected automated rapid transit system, the new forty-five-story, aluminum-sheathed Wells Fargo Bank building, the new Alcoa building. As they passed Alcoa, with its shiny, packaged look, Gooding ventured a small joke. "How are they going to get it out of the box?" The joke eluded Luce.

In the Luces' hotel suite all was suddenly flap and flurry. Luce had left his briefcase, containing Mrs. Luce's speech, on the reception desk. Gooding retrieved it. Then Mrs. Luce discovered that her maid had neglected to pack the dress she had chosen for her Commonwealth Club appearance. "I'll go out and buy you a dress," Luce offered. "You just don't buy dresses that way," she said. Presently, she was on the phone to Otto Fuerbringer with a complicated series of pre-Kennedy recollections which she believed might be relevant to the recent arrest in New Orleans of an alleged conspirator in the President's assassination. When she finished (*Time* never managed to nail the story down), Luce took the receiver. "This is your favorite crime reporter," he said. "I suppose you're carrying a Chicago story next week." It would be the 2296th issue since Vol. I, No. I. "Chicago?" Fuerbringer echoed. "You don't know?" said Luce, gleeful as aways when he thought he knew something the editors didn't. "They've just had their thousandth gang killing. And how do I know that?" "Why, Harry, I assume you know everything." "The Chicago bureau told me a while back when I was there that they'd just counted their nine hundred and ninety-seventh gang killing. I told them not to bother me until it was a thousand. Well, they wired me before I left Phoenix. Wasn't that nice?" Not to be outdone, Fuerbringer said, "Oh, I thought you were calling about that breach of promise suit in Phoenix, man named Brown. He says he gave the woman a hundred shares of Time Inc. stock and the papers hint that most of his money was in Time Inc." "Brown . . . Brown. Yes, it seems to me I remember a man by that name from the early days. Friend of Hadden's."

In the afternoon Gooding and his French wife, Françoise, took the Luces to the M. H. de Young Museum where Luce wanted to view its newly acquired collection of Orientalia. Mrs. Luce, who preferred Western art, wandered apart with Mrs. Gooding, while the curator showed the men scroll paintings from northern China. "I have something like those," said Luce, who owned a small collection of Chinese art, and he began firing educated questions. One of the rarest treasures of the museum's acquisition, a four-foot-high clay camel of the nineteenth century, was not yet on display so the curator unlocked the storeroom. "How much do you want to see?" he asked. Luce's answer epitomized a whole vast area of his life: "I want to see all I can."

On the way back to the hotel, his curiosity still unappeased, he insisted they detour through the city's hippy-infested Haight-Ashbury section. "What are their goals? What are their motives?" he pressed Gooding, as they nosed slowly through streets full of long-haired, bearded youths wearing outlandish garb, and Gooding tried to describe their drug-centered way of life. A car backing hastily out of a side street brushed a small boy and kept going. Luce ordered his driver to stop and see if the boy was hurt. He wasn't.

For the evening he had asked Gooding by phone several days before to arrange a little dinner party of "interesting people." Gooding invited, with their wives, Wallace Sterling, president of Stanford University; Ransom Cook, a Wells Fargo executive; and Haydn Williams, president of the Asia Foundation; retained a private room in the wine cellar of Ernie's, perhaps San Francisco's most elegant restaurant; and ordered a Lucullan five-course dinner, accompanied by two choice French wines and one American (out of deference to Luce's patriotism).

Luce was in top form, alert, buoyant, genial. After two Scotch-and-sodas, he took his place at one end of the table and plunged into a discussion of education with Wallace Sterling, paying scant attention to the food and wine. Now and then his voice would boom above the general conversation, "May I say something?" . . . At her end of the table Mrs. Luce entertained with humorous theatrical reminiscences. Toward eleven o'clock the party disbanded in a glow of conviviality.

Next day around noon the Commonwealth Club assembled, some seven hundred strong, at the Palace Hotel. The Luces were no strangers to the forum. The year before Luce had spoken there on Asia and in 1941 both husband and wife had spoken on China. It had always been Luce's way, whenever the limelight centered on his wife, to efface himself. This was her day, and at sight of reporters and news photographers he tried to keep out of range. There was a moment of pleasant nostalgia for Luce when a man in his late seventies came up to him, Dr. Edgar E. Robinson, professor emeritus of history at Stanford. He had been Luce's history teacher at Yale.

Mrs. Luce delivered her U.N. polemic after the luncheon. During the question period following a listener asked, "To what extent does the U.N. charter supersede the Constitution?" "We were discussing that at breakfast," Mrs. Luce replied. "The Senate vote ratifying American participation in the U.N. and committing the U. S. to supporting it was . . ." The figure escaped her and she looked to her husband. "Ninety-two to two," said Luce.

While she recorded a radio interview, he walked with Gooding to the *Time* office where the rest of the staff joined them. "Well, what's on your minds?" Luce shot at them. Nobody could think of a meaningful answer. "How are the prospects for the coming year?" he asked an advertising salesman. Excellent, he was assured. A correspondent remarked that the London bureau chief had done a fine job of reporting during the Soviet premier's recent visit to England. Luce made no comment. The bureau chief was his son, Henry III. He picked up Mrs. Luce at the hotel and they caught a late afternoon plane back to Phoenix.

Saturday morning, when she read the local newspaper accounts of her speech, she told Luce, "I sweated over that speech for three weeks and all they quoted was your upbeat ending."

Luce wrote Gooding a letter, "You really did take good care of us. I hasten to send you thanks." He then wrote a memorandum to Hedley Donovan, Otto Fuerbringer, Thomas Griffith *et al*, the last they would ever receive from him, "The enclosed clipping, a week or so old, tells me that Wayne Hays, Democrat, Ohio, says that the people of his state are overwhelmingly against sanctions against Rhodesia. I must say that the more this seemingly minor matter is called to my attention the more dubious I become about U.S. policy and action in this case. . . ." And shouldn't they give thought to it?

Saturday afternoon Luce played nine holes of golf, riding the course in a golf cart with his favorite caddy, Andy. Some friends dropped in for cocktails later and they all went on to a dinner party at the Arizona Biltmore Hotel given by a Phoenix oil millionaire, Donald Harrington. During the postprandial merriment a pianist played the Yale Whiffenpoof song and Luce sang, "We are poor little sheep who have lost their way, baa, baa, baa. . . ." Reluctantly, he let Mrs. Luce drag him away before midnight. They omitted their usual reading hour. He was too tired.

While breakfasting at 9:30 Sunday morning, Luce suddenly excused himself. He came back a few minutes later, ashen-faced. "I lost my breakfast," he said. "I have a headache," and he went to his bedroom to lie down. She canceled a golf date he had made with a neighbor, and while he rested she painted in her studio. Toward midmorning he drifted in, complaining of fatigue. She led him back to bed and took his temperature. It was 102. She called Dr. Caldwell. By the time he arrived Luce was bleeding from the nose and coughing up bloody sputum. His pulse and blood pressure proved normal, however, and the doctor decided to let him rest for the moment at home.

When Dr. Caldwell came Monday morning and found no improvement, he ordered an ambulance from St. Joseph's Hospital. Grumbling, insisting that he wasn't that sick, Luce brushed aside his wife's attempt to support him, and walked to the ambulance, carrying his shoes in his hands. She packed the books he had been reading, a detective story, a theological work, his Bible, and followed close behind the ambulance in their chauffeur-driven car. Every so often he would sit up and wave at her through the ambulance window. When he got to his hospital room, he admitted, "I'm tired." Mrs. Luce sat by him through the day, awaiting the results of a series of tests. To distract her, some friends, Dr. Lowell Davis and his wife, in-laws of California's Governor Ronald Reagan, brought her to their house for dinner. But she was too uneasy. She went home soon after and phoned Luce at the hospital. "I'm going to watch Perry Mason," he told her. "So am I," she said. "Do you want me to come over?" "No, everything is going to be all right."

He slept fitfully and kept getting out of bed, ignoring his nurse's protests, to pace the floor. At about 3 A.M. he went into the bathroom. A moment later the nurse heard him cry, "Oh, Jesus!" then a heavy thud. He was unconscious when she reached him. She summoned a resuscitation team who applied shock treatment and heart massage. . . .

Mrs. Luce's bedside phone rang. It was the Mother Superior of St. Joseph's. "You'd better come," she said. Dr. Caldwell met her in the corridor. "Harry is dead." The cause was a coronary occlusion.

When the wire services flashed the news of Luce's death, the first person to reach his widow by phone was President Johnson. "All Washington is sad," he said. "He was one of the greats." She heard next from Luce's Jesuit friend, Father John Courtney Murray (to whom he once said, "I'm a Jesuit of journalism—a persuader"). She told Father Murray, "I don't know where Harry wished to be buried. We had no real discussion about it. In some way it will be made known. In any event we can't be separated."

At Our Lady of Mepkin, by the entrance to a garden white with camellias, stood a huge, old, twisted live oak. Beneath the branches two marble headstones marked the graves of Mrs. Luce's mother and her daughter Anne, with a space between reserved for herself. Five years before she had told Luce, "I am the lady foundress [the Trappists' title for her] and you are the founder and I intend to be buried there. Where do you want to be buried?" and he had answered lightly, "I'd be happy to be buried there too, providing a Presbyterian reads the service." He never referred to the matter again.

Not until this day of his death, when his son Henry arrived in Phoenix from London, did she learn that he had left instructions for his burial at Mepkin. "I would have been happier if I'd known," she told a friend in the weeks ahead, "but maybe he couldn't make such concessions." Nor did she know until his will was read that he had bequeathed her 180,000 shares of Time Inc. stock.

A company plane flew Luce's body to Charleston, South Carolina, whence the Trappists removed it to Mepkin. In New York's Madison Avenue Presbyterian Church, meanwhile, where Luce had worshiped for forty-three years, the Reverend David H. C. Read held a memorial service. The date was March 3, the forty-fourth anniversary of *Time*'s first issue. About eight hundred people thronged the church, among them governors and senators, financial and industrial leaders, publishers, educators, writers, and scientists, while twelve hundred employees gathered in the reception lounge and in the eighth floor auditorium of the Time & Life Building, to which the service was relayed over a private broadcast hookup.

The same day the Luce family went to Mepkin for the burial rites. A Presbyterian minister presided, the Trappists staying tactfully in the background. Before she left Mrs. Luce conferred with the Trappist abbot, Father Anthony, about a headstone. Smiling serenely, he told her, "When you had that great marble cross made for us, Clare, there was some left over. We have it for Harry. But you will be with us too. Why not the one marble for both of you?" The idea pleased her and she suggested as a decorative motif an abstraction of the old live oak tree.

There were some who felt that a fitting epitaph for Henry Robinson Luce would be a stanza from the John Bunyan hymn with which the Reverend Read concluded his eulogy:

Who would true valor see,
Let him come hither;
One here will constant be,
Come wind, come weather;
There's no discouragement
Shall make him once relent
His first avowed intent
        To be a pilgrim.

Whoso beset him round
With dismal stories,
Do but themselves confound;
His strength the more is,
No lion can him fright,
But he will have a right
        To be a pilgrim.

Hobgoblin nor foul fiend
Can daunt his spirit;
He knows he at the end
Shall life inherit.
Then fancies fly away,
He'll fear not what men say;
He'll labour night and day
        To be a pilgrim.

BIBLIOGRAPHY

From its archives Time Inc. furnished invaluable documentation without imposing any restrictions. This included interoffice memoranda, Luce letters and speeches, details of corporate structure and finance, historical data.

In addition, I drew upon the following books and articles:

Bagdikian, Ben H. "The Newsmagazines," Providence *Journal* and *Bulletin*, October 5–17, 1958.
Barzini, Luigi. "Ambassador Luce, as Italians See Her," *Harper's*, July, 1955.
Busch, Noel F. *Briton Hadden*. New York: Farrar, Straus & Co., 1949.
Chambers, Whittaker. *Witness*. New York: Random House, 1952.
Cook, Fred J. "The Ultras," *The Nation*, June 30, 1962.

Davis, Alvin. A ten-part series on Luce and Time Inc., *New York Post*, December 24, 1956–January 6, 1957.

Garside, B. A. *One Increasing Purpose*. New York: Fleming H. Revell Co., 1948.

Gibbs, Wolcott. "Time . . . Fortune . . . Life . . . Luce," *The New Yorker*, November 28, 1936.

Gwirtzman, Milton S. "What TIME Is It?", *The New Republic*, January 16, 1956.

Hatch, Alden. *Ambassador Extraordinary*. New York: Henry Holt & Co., 1952.

Harriman, Margaret Case. "The Candor Kid," *The New Yorker*, January 4–11, 1941.

Keyes, Quentin. "Fortune," *The Magazine of the Future* (London), May, 1948.

Luce, Clare Boothe. "The 'Real' Reason." *McCall's*, February–April, 1946.

——— "Without Portfolio, *McCall's*, February, 1960.

——— "The Lady *Is* for Burning," *The National Review*, November 5, 1963.

Luce, Henry R. "This Great Moment," *Life*, October 21, 1940.

——— "The American Century," *Life*, February 17, 1941.

——— "China to the Mountains," *Life*, June 30, 1941.

——— "Moral Law in a Reeling World," *The Christian Century*, May, 1950.

——— "Holmes Was Wrong," *Fortune*, January, 1951.

Matthews, T. S. *Name and Address*. New York: Simon & Schuster, 1962.

"The One-Sided Press," *Ammunition*, December, 1956.

"Recollections of Henry R. Luce," *Fortune*, April, 1967.

Rovere, Richard H. "The American Establishment," *Esquire*, May, 1962.

Sterling, Claire, and Ascoli, Max. "The Lady of the Villa Taverna," *The Reporter*, February 23, 1956.

Stewart, Kenneth. A three-part series on Luce and Time Inc. *The Newspaper PM*, August 27–September 10, 1944.

"Time: The Weekly Fiction Magazine," *Fact*, January–February, 1964.

"Washington 1962," *Columbia Journalism Review*, Spring, 1962.

Wilson, Edmund. "Thoughts on Being Bibliographed," *Princeton University Library Chronicle*, February, 1944.

J2

L96245K

Redwood Library and Athenaeum
NEWPORT, R. I.

Selections from the Rules

New fiction is issued for 7 days, new non-fiction for 14 days, and other books for 28 days with the privilege of renewal.

Books overdue are subject to a fine of 2 cents a day.

All injuries to books and all losses shall be made good to the satisfaction of the Librarian.

5 volumes may be taken at a time and only 5 on 1 share or subscription.

LIBRARY BUREAU CAT. NO. 1166.3